Who
do you think
you are?

*For Jeff and Ann —
with memories of
your boyhood and girlhood,
Love, Wally*

Who do you think you are?

REMEMBERING AGES THREE TO EIGHTEEN

Wallace Kennedy

Wallace Kennedy

YTTERLI PRESS
Saint Paul
2006

*deep appreciation to
Sylvia Ruud for thorough
edit and creative design*

Copyright © 2006 by Wallace Kennedy
All rights reserved.

ISBN 0-9771069-4-2

Published by Ytterli Press
2211 Buford Avenue, Saint Paul, Minnesota 55108

To contact the author: joywall@mninter.net
or write to Ytterli Press at the above address.

Library of Congress Catalog Card Number applied for.

Printed in the United States of America

Book design by Sylvia Ruud

for daughters Ellen and Katherine, and for son John
and
—for their amazing children

with fullest gratitude to
—sister, Olivia, always invincible
and
—Joyce, dearest and best

WHO DO YOU THINK YOU ARE?

FOREWORD	ix
CHAPTER 1 *Who Do You Think You Are?*	1
CHAPTER 2 I guess I must be *A Farm Boy*	5
CHAPTER 3 How I truly became *A Farm Boy*	10
CHAPTER 4 Will I now be *A Transient*?	18
CHAPTER 5 Is there such a thing as *A Traveling Boy*?	31
CHAPTER 6 Here in the South, am I just *A Stranger*?	40
CHAPTER 7 Could I learn to be a *City Boy*?	56
CHAPTER 8 Will I like being a *Garden Farm Boy*?	64
CHAPTER 9 Now I'm going to be a real *Cando Kid*	79
CHAPTER 10 Would I have to become *A Church Member*?	93

CHAPTER 11
> How did I get to be *A Bad Kid*? 104

CHAPTER 12
> Could I become *Trustworthy*? 116

CHAPTER 13
> Can a teen still be *A Good Kid*? 129

CHAPTER 14
> When did I become *An Adolescent*? 140

CHAPTER 15
> Can I become *A Really Good Son*? 148

CHAPTER 16
> Who says I'm *A Damn Yankee*? 156

CHAPTER 17
> Now I want to prove I'm truly *A Grateful Son* 165

CHAPTER 18
> When will I know I'm *The Real Me*? 172

CHAPTER 19
> Will I ever feel sure about *Who I Think I Am*? 186

EPILOGUE 201

FOREWORD

I began writing these boyhood memories when I was already seventy-five years old, but the memories came easily, in spite of their age. Why our earliest years have such a strong hold on memory is a question I won't try to answer. I only concede that for me, those years are as clear as yesterday and have left an indelible print.

Choosing to begin with my third birthday, I sketch an exchange with my mother that introduces an occurrence of mother's love. All through the next fifteen years, I show how the love and influence of my mother, my father, and my sister shaped my attitudes and choices.

Kids who grew up during the time I recall, 1931 to 1946, had a life of remarkable freedom and safety. People during the depression and war years shared a trust about children and young people that was just there. It didn't need to be stated or analyzed. I don't think kids were better loved then, but the whole culture in those years must have believed that kids were able to grow up without a lot of adult involvement. This childhood independence gave kids responsibility for their own actions.

It wasn't that a kid grew up in those years without worrying about life and about himself. I felt a continuous wonder, even perplexity, about what kind of person I could claim to be. And so the dominant theme of this memoir is a boy's search for identity, a search strongly affected by hard times in mid-America.

—Wallace Kennedy

Who
do you think
you are?

"What happens is not separable from what people think happens."
—John Lukacs, *At the End of an Age*

CHAPTER 1

Who Do You Think You Are?

I'm not sure when the question first became important to me. Maybe it began on my third birthday, May 5, 1931. I was pushing a little cast-iron tractor across a bare, coarse-grained, dark wood floor, a few feet from Mama's sewing machine.

A sudden, little-boy question lifted me from pushing my toy tractor to take hold of Mama's soft, round upper arm. Why does the whir and chuckle of the sewing machine start and stop with the seesaw of Mama's foot on that iron grill? Whatever I asked, Mama seemed to know I wanted her to show me how the machine worked. She pointed out its working parts. She showed me I could make the foot treadle go with my hands. She let me work the machine as she sewed, telling me when to start and stop. I felt proud that my hands had worked the machine. In thanks, I pressed my cheek against Mama's soft upper arm.

Mama lifted me to her broad lap and stroked the back of my head. I remember just what she said. "Do you know you are three years old today? Three years ago, this very day, you were born. Over at Zion, in Aunt Hattie's house." Her tone of voice told me, listen. Mama is telling you something you'll want to remember.

Mama rubbed the dent in my forehead. "This is your birthmark, from Doctor MacDonald's forceps. When he started to take you with those forceps, I was scared to death, because I lost my first baby when he was born, and I was desperate not to lose you." When Mama took her hand away, I rubbed the dent with my finger.

"When Doc got you, you were almost blue. So he held you by your heels and spanked your bottom. He had to, to make you start breathing. You started to cry, and Doc said, 'Good loud voice. Maybe a preacher some day.' I thought, No. A doctor. He'll be a doctor. And we'll call him Wallace, after my brother Wallace.

"Doc MacDonald tied up your navel. But I think he pulled the cord out too far when he was in a hurry to get you to breathe. Your navel never did look like he done it right. It sticks out too much."

I lifted my shirt and looked at my belly button, a funny wrinkle with a black thread curling through it.

"Mustn't pick at it," Mama said, and I pulled my hand back quick. "Your daddy was so proud to get his boy. He does so love his boy."

Mama had started me thinking, Who am I, anyhow? I felt I needed to get out and run. I nuzzled the cool back of Mama's upper arm with my face and then headed outdoors. I raced around the garden fence and down the drive between the garden and the granary. The part of the garden towards the barn was Mama's kitchen garden. A row of box elders separated Mama's garden from Aunt Delia's flower garden.

Aunt Dee was carrying water from a rain barrel at the corner of Grandpa's house to water her flowers. I followed her. "Earliest spring in years. Some of my garden is already in bloom." She poured water from the sprinkling can on a row of tall pink and yellow flowers.

"Come here. Smell my snapdragons. Stick your nose down there."

I bent over one of the flowers. Aunt Dee spread the mouth of a bloom and with her other hand pressed my nose against the yawning mouth of the dragon. "Now, I'll let him snap off your nose." I jerked my head back, striking Aunt Dee's fat stomach. She squeezed me against her stomach and pressed her cheek against my head. "I scared you, didn't I?" She shook with laughter, but her laugh didn't have much sound.

I climbed up on the big black boulder near the garden gate. It was tall, and I scooted myself up to its very top. Aunt Dee watered her other flowers.

"I'm three years old today. I was born over at Aunt Hattie's. The doctor spanked me. He had to."

That's what I remember of my third birthday. It wasn't the earliest day I remember. Several weeks before, I had gone to watch Daddy plow the big garden plot down by the barnyard. I plopped down on an anthill and was covered with red ants biting me. I ran to the house, bawling. Mama emptied a whole box of baking soda in the tub of rainwater on the porch and soaked me in it to rub away the sting of the ants.

Even earlier, one of the first warm days of spring, I found Daddy's hammer and a sack of shingle nails on the porch. I began to pound the nails into the porch. Mama brought me two big potatoes. "Here now, you pound these potatoes full of nails. Then we'll pull out the nails and put them back in Daddy's nail bag."

That was the porch of the little house where we lived. Aunt Dee kept house for Grandpa and Grandma in the big, eleven-room house. Grandpa had built it himself, long before I was born. I remember Mama told me about the two houses on the farm. She told me our house had once been a schoolhouse. Grandpa moved it from his Johnson quarter and built rooms in it. "Do you know what you said the day we moved in here? You said, 'This is my house, and Mama and Daddy and Sister live with me.'"

The way Mama said that was kind of like a song. One day I'd heard Daddy tell Uncle Charlie that Mama had the sweet voice of a Texan. It didn't sound like other women's voices. It was softer and went up and down, like a song. Mama's laugh went up and down, too, and seemed to come from her whole body, and her dark blue eyes laughed, too.

Aunt Dee laughed with hardly any voice. Kind of like a dog panting. Maybe she didn't laugh out loud because she had to take care of Grandma, who was always sick and stayed in bed most of the time.

Grandma always called me Baby, so I never liked to go near her. I knew for sure I was no baby. But one day when Aunt Dee was in the parlor reading a book, Grandma whispered loud to me, "Come here, Baby. You go bring me the bowl of crabapple pickles from the kitchen table." I did, and Aunt Dee bawled me out. She said crabapple pickles would make Grandma sicker, and I should never give Grandma anything sweet.

Aunt Dee was taller than Mama, with wispy, sandy hair and light blue eyes. Mama's hair was shiny black and her eyes were dark blue. Aunt Dee seemed to like telling other people what they should do. She wasn't really bossy, but she seemed to think she should be in charge.

One day when I had to stay with Aunt Dee because Mama went to help a neighbor woman have her baby, Aunt Dee said, "Come with me. I'll show you how to shut off the Delco engine." We went to the room off the kitchen where the cream separator stood. Aunt Dee lifted the big, brown trapdoor, letting up cool air that smelled of lignite coal and musty decay and oily smoke. I followed Aunt Dee, letting myself down backwards to the first step and from there one step at a time, holding one hand along the stone wall into the cellar. My hand kept catching spiderwebs.

There was a chugging noise in the cellar, which was quite dark until Aunt Dee turned on a hanging light above an engine taller than me. "This is what makes the electricity for our lights. It's our Delco engine." The oily smoke and loud chugging were scary as Aunt Dee pulled me close to the engine. "Here, you can stand on this battery box and turn it off." She balanced my step up on the box. "You see this lever?" She touched a short, rubber-tipped lever. "All you have to do," as she held my hand on the rubber tip, "is push this lever down." The lever tingled in my fingers. She helped me push it down. The motor popped, chugged several times and came to a halt. I felt kind of proud that I had made it quiet.

"Now I'll show you how to start it again." Aunt Dee held my fingers under the rubber tip of the lever. "Now pull it up and hold it up there. No! Tight!" I had jerked my hand back when the lever caused a shot of sparks. Again she took my hand, and I grasped the rubber tip and lifted it tight into place. I jumped with the sparks again, but held tight. The motor buzzed, turned and caught and roared, running fast.

"All right!" Aunt Dee backed away, "Now you can shut it off again." I pushed the lever down cautiously and the motor died to silence. I jumped off the battery box, proud. "There. You showed you're a good mechanic."

Upstairs, Aunt Dee opened a geography book to a map of the U.S. and told me I was an American. She pointed out North Dakota on the map, telling me I was a North Dakotan. Then she gave me a pencil and the cardboard cover of a big boot box. She said I should draw a map of the U.S. by looking at the map in the geography book. When I was finished, Aunt Dee said, "You're a good drawer."

I knew for sure I was not the baby Grandma called me. But Aunt Dee said I was a mechanic, and an American, and a North Dakotan, and a good drawer. How could I be all those things at the same time? It sure made me wonder who I really was.

CHAPTER 2

I guess I must be *A Farm Boy*

It must have been Grandpa who started me thinking I was a farm boy. Sometimes he'd take me on an evening walk around the farm. He'd point out each farm building and tell me how it helped a farmer do his work. He'd tell me, "Farming is a good life." Sometimes he'd say, "You're a farm boy, you know."

On those walks with Grandpa, he'd let me talk, too. Not like at his dinner table. Grandpa had a rule that only grownups could talk at meals. If a kid broke that rule, he'd get thumped on his temple. Grandpa's finger, cocked by his thumb, would hit your head so hard, he'd almost knock you out.

Daddy had other relatives besides Grandpa and Grandma and Aunt Delia, but they all lived in town, in Cando. They were Aunt Hattie with her husband Uncle Charlie, and five Kensinger cousins. They were Russell, David, Veora, Jimmy, and Vesper. Daddy's brother, Uncle Jesse, and his wife, Aunt Ella Mae, had just one daughter, Rosamond, who was my oldest cousin. I thought they must be kind of rich, because Mama told me they owned their own home. Uncle Jesse was a well driller with a big shop out behind his house. It had a sign painted in big black letters, **J. E. Kennedy – Well Drilling and Well Supplies.** That sign seemed to make Uncle Jesse important.

Daddy told me one day he was already fifty years old when I was born. "Old enough to be your grandpa," he said. But he didn't look at all like a grandpa and he was strong and able to do all the farm work. Except one time when he strained his back putting horseshoes on Alex. Daddy asked me to make his back feel better by walking along his backbone barefoot. I liked the way Daddy helped me know I was a farm boy by taking me along to haul hay or straw. He'd let me hold the reins, and had me tramp down the load so it was spread evenly. He had me put oats in the manger feed boxes at milk time, too.

Mama helped me be a farm boy, too, by asking me to work with her in the garden. She showed me how to plant all the different seeds, and how to recognize weeds and pull them up. I helped her feed chickens and gather the eggs, too, and I carried in kindling wood for the stoves and carried out the ashes.

Only one time did Sister and I make Daddy get mad at us. He and Mama were milking. Sister and I were waiting for a cup of fresh warm milk, just outside the barn as the sun was setting. Sister called out, "See, oh see the beautiful sky." She began to make up a song about the sky, singing loud. Daddy came out of the barn mad. "Stop that yelling and singing. You made Star kick over the bucket." He'd stepped up close to Sister and lifted his arm to hit her on her seat. I rushed to him, grabbing his shirt. "Don't you hit my sister!" brought for me a bunch of whacks on my butt. It was the only spanking I remember from Daddy.

One day, though, at dinnertime, as Daddy was washing up, I heard Mama and Daddy argue about spanking me. I really liked horses, so I'd joined the horses as they gathered at the water tank, pushing each other for a place to drink. I was right in there among them, but they didn't push or step on me. Mama blamed Daddy for not keeping me out of danger. Daddy said he hadn't seen me among the horses. Mama said he should have been watching out for me.

"Well, just tell him, if he goes in among the horses again, he'll get a licking," said Daddy. Mama argued, "No. I won't tell him that. He'll do what we say without being threatened."

Our family always stayed right at home except on special occasions. When I was four, late afternoon on Christmas Eve, Mama put bricks in the oven to heat. When it started to get dark, Mama bundled up Sister and me in the warmest winter clothes we had. Mama and Daddy dressed for the cold, too. Mama wrapped the hot bricks in a blanket and Daddy led us to the grain wagon he had set on sleigh runners. Mama had Sister and me sit on the blanket that wrapped the hot bricks and pulled a heavy quilt over herself and us. Daddy, in his sheepskin overcoat, drove us away.

It seemed to take a long time to reach the Duffys' farm. But when we got there, Dad and Plenny Duffy put our team in the barn and Mama and us kids went inside to stand near a blazing hot Round Oak stove and drink cups of hot cocoa. After we warmed up, we went into the parlor where there was a big Christmas tree. It was decorated with bright colored balls, and strands of popcorn and cranberries, and burning candles.

Fern Duffy, who was in high school, had a shiny trumpet. We sat to listen to her play "Hark the Herald Angels Sing." Then Fern called us all to the piano to join her in singing carols. Everybody sang well, in harmony some of the time, and I thought it was really special.

We had a big supper with a baked ham that Plenny Duffy said had been in his smokehouse for fourteen months, and all kinds of other tasty food. After supper, Mrs. Duffy gave Sister and me presents from under the tree. Sister's present was a girl doll with fancy clothes and my present was a gold-colored toy trumpet. Its sound disappointed me, though. Instead of sounding like Fern's trumpet, it only honked one sound.

We stayed all night at Duffys', and Sister slept with Fern. I slept with Mama and Daddy. Next morning we got presents again from under the tree, hand-knit wool mittens. At breakfast, Mrs. Duffy said, "Christmas just isn't real if there aren't any children to get presents." When we left the Duffys' farm, Mama said, "The Duffys know how to be good Christians." I was sure she was right about that.

We spent most of Christmas day at Grandpa's house, with Aunt Hattie's and Uncle Jesse's family out from town to join us. I got more presents. The one I liked best was a toy hayrack my cousins Russell and David made for me. It was painted yellow and had slings in it to hoist its hay. I played farm boy with that hayrack for days. Another present I liked was a riddle book from Mama. I've never forgotten one riddle in that book: *"What children in Germany take pleasure in making, children in America take pleasure in breaking."* The answer to the riddle was Toys, but the answer bothered me. I remembered how, pushing around my toy roadster, I had smashed down its roof. But I didn't remember getting any pleasure out of breaking my toy car.

Sister and I always knew who gave us our Christmas presents. We were not told any of our presents came from Santa Claus. I was glad Mama and Daddy never told us the fibs about Santa Claus. And Sister and I never begged for presents because we knew our family had no money to spare.

Because Aunt Dee asked Sister and me to go with her to the Zion Church of the Brethren, I learned some good lessons from my Sunday school teacher, Mrs. Burkhart. Ruby Burkhart had a sweet gentle voice with her students. She always tried to give us a lesson with a rule to remember. One of those rules was, "Give first to God, next to others. Give to yourself last." She said the golden rule was "Do unto others as you would have them do unto you." In another lesson with pictures of guns and soldiers, the rule Mrs. Burkhart gave us was, "If our side makes its army and weapons bigger, the other side must do that, too. Then both sides will use what they have and go to war." She told us that the Church of the Brethren believes war is murder, and its men and boys should never join the army. I thought that was a good rule.

Aunt Dee found Dad's velvet suit in Grandma's cedar chest and decided I should have my picture taken wearing it.

When Mama took me to help her in the garden, she told me about her life in Texas before she married Daddy. So I learned a lot about her family, even though Texas was far away. And what Mama told seemed like stories.

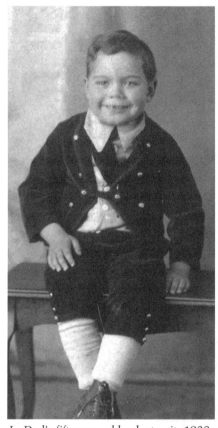

In Dad's fifty-year-old velvet suit, 1932

Mama said her father's name was Henry Lindsay, but her mother's name was Mary Craven. How both families got to Texas was like a story. The Cravens had come with Sam Houston from Tennessee, and were a very proud family. Her mother had been promised to marry Sam Goodnight, who was from another proud Texas family. An uncle in Colorado sent Mary a wedding ring made of gold from his Colorado mine. But just before the wedding Sam Goodnight was shot by cattle rustlers. They mistook him for his brother because he was riding his brother's horse. So her mother never wore that ring when she married my grandpa Lindsay, but passed it on to Mama, who kept it in a little jewelry case.

Mama said the Cravens were not happy about her mother's marriage to her father. Henry Lindsay owned no land, but tried to make his living writing dime novels. Mary's parents bought the new couple a farm near Weatherford, where Mama was born. She said her dad never learned to be a good farmer, because when he was a boy his daddy was killed as a Confederate soldier during the Civil War. Just his mother and three little brothers were left on their Kentucky farm. Mama said, "Yankee bluecoats" took all their horses and killed all but one of their cows. After their mother died, Henry and his three Lindsay brothers moved to Texas.

Mama had one older brother, George, and two younger brothers, Wallace and Jay. But Jay died when he was four. When Mama was twelve, her mother died, and as with Jay, the doctor couldn't tell the cause. So Mama had to quit school and become the housekeeper for her father and two brothers. Of all the sad stories in Mama's family, it seemed the saddest to Mama was about her brother Wallace. She cried as she told me how good and smart he was. "He did so well in school, professors at Keene Academy took him on to become a doctor. But a cholera epidemic broke out and Wallace was helping take care of the sick when he took cholera and died, at only twenty." That story made me cry, too. I felt bad that Mama's life had been so full of sorrow.

I learned that the sorrow didn't let up. Mama took upon herself to become a nurse and was working at the Fyke and Rohr clinic in Weatherford. She met a soldier at Fort Worth named Jim Foster, and they planned to get married. But Jim Foster died in the World War flu epidemic. Mama said, "If I'd have married Jim Foster I'd be living on a beautiful fruit farm in Michigan now." It seemed Mama was telling me she would have been happier on a fruit farm in Michigan. But if she'd married Jim Foster, would I be a Michigan farm boy named Wallace Foster, or would I be anybody at all? All Mama's stories, but that one especially, made me think a lot about who I was, and who I wanted to be.

Mama had so wanted to be a nurse. She went to the Loma Linda Sanitarium in California for nurses' training, but before she got "capped as a registered nurse," her dad developed eye cataracts and injured himself in a fall, so she had to return to the farm to take care of him. It seemed so unfair that one sad event after another kept Mama from being who she wanted to be.

CHAPTER 3

How I truly became *A Farm Boy*

After I'd just turned five, Dad made me prove I was a farm boy. He came home with a brown and white collie pup, the cutest pup you could ever see. He put the pup in my arms and told me, "He's yours, Bud. Take care of him and teach him to fetch the cows the way Queen could."

Queen was a black and white collie that Dad loved and trained to be one smart dog. One day when rain had stopped the threshing, I was in the barn with Dad and all the harvest hands waiting out the rain. When Dad said, "It's milk time, Queen. Better go get the cows," the men all laughed. One guy said, "Boss, you think that dog knows what you said?" And Dad answered, "Just watch." Queen went to the pasture and brought up the milk cows, putting them in their proper stalls. All but one. Dad pointed to the empty stall and said, "Queen, where's Star? Better go get Star." Star was with the heifers and steers, still down in the pasture. Queen sorted out Star and brought her to the empty stall. That evening I saw that the guy who asked if Queen understood was helping Dad with the milking.

But early April that year, Queen was helping Dad separate lambs from their mother ewes when Billy, the sheep buck, slammed Queen into a doorpost, breaking a couple of her ribs and puncturing a lung. Queen died late that night as Dad held her head in his lap. Dad cried. I cried, too, because I think I loved Queen almost as much as Dad did. So when Dad put that collie pup in my arms, I knew I'd been given a real farm job.

I named him King, and right away began training him to be like Queen. Each evening I'd carry King to the pasture and set him down behind the milk cows. I'd run at the cows, making barking sounds, and King would run at them, too, yapping at them. I knew the cows weren't afraid of a dog that wasn't as tall as my knee, but they knew it was milk time and they took King for their signal to go get milked.

I'd heard some people say cows are awfully stupid, but I didn't think so. I admired the way they used their tails to swat flies off their backs, and the way they could wriggle their hides fast to chase off the flies. And they seemed to know what was expected of them.

By late summer, King could bring the cows to the barn all by himself. And King quickly became my best friend. He'd wiggle and bark when he greeted me. I'd snuggle him, and he'd lick my face. I talked to King a lot and sang songs to him, too.

But that summer on July 4, something terrible happened. Our neighbors the Kuhlbergs invited the Stong family and our family to celebrate the fourth with them. King had come from a litter at the Kuhlberg farm, so I took King with me. I took him to the barn to let him visit his littermates still there. He looked at them in their boarded pen, and they jumped at the boards and barked at King, but he didn't bark back.

After the huge July Fourth dinner, I had to poop. So I headed to the outhouse, a two-seater, and took King along. When I sat down, King jumped up to be beside me and dropped through the open hole. I rushed my poop and dashed to the house for Mama, who was helping Mrs. Kuhlberg with dishes. Mrs. Kuhlberg didn't think King down the toilet hole was any problem. She said, "Oh, there are still more pups out in the barn. You can have another one."

That terrified me. I ran to find Dad gabbing with the other men in the shade of the barn. Dad found a length of rope and a grain measure in the barn and led me by the hand back to the outhouse. I held open the door to let in light while Dad dropped the bucket down by King. King was smart. He crawled into the bucket and got a bath in the horse tank to top off his rescue.

King and I became the best of playmates. We played hide-and-seek in the tall weeds along the edge of the barnyard. I'd say, "King, stay," then go deep into the weeds to hide before calling "Wah, wah, wah, wah, King." That meant, come find me. When he'd find me, King would wiggle all over and give a little yip. Then I'd say, "You go hide, King." He'd run into the weeds and wait for me to find him.

By rescuing King, Dad had shown me I could really count on him, and I felt I wanted to be just like him when I grew up. Not long after, Dad showed me again a reason to want to be like him. Owen Stong asked to borrow a team for haying, and Dad lent Owen his best team.

Dad had told me about that team. Jim was Percheron, and Morgan black with a white diamond on his forehead. Alex was a big gray Belgian. Dad said, "They can outwork any team in the Zion community." The day Dad loaned his best team, he had to patch the roof of the grain storage shed on the Johnson quarter. Working up on the roof gave Dad a view of Owen in his hay field.

When Owen brought Dad's team back home, he was riding Jim, still in harness. Dad grabbed Jim's bridle to halt the team. I heard Dad say, "What do you mean, whipping my horses?"

Owen slid off Jim to face Dad, looking mad. "I didn't whip your horses."

Dad said, "Don't tell me. I was fixing the roof of the grain shed on the Johnson quarter and saw you."

"You calling me a liar?" Owen showed clenched fists, and they started fighting, at first with fists, circling around to get in a good punch. Then Owen, who was much younger than Dad, threw Dad to the ground and began choking him. I went looking for a rock or stick to hit Owen, but Mama had heard the shouting and came to stop the fight. "You men stop your fighting, right now!" Owen got off Dad and began his walk home without a word.

Mama said, "Now look what you've done, Noah. Now we won't have neighbors that are close friends." I'd often seen Mama and Ethel Stong laugh and talk together. But blaming Dad seemed unfair. Dad had shown he believed animals should never be abused. I thought that was worth fighting for, even if it meant losing a neighbor's friendship.

One night that November, we woke up from a loud pounding on our door. I heard Owen's voice. "Noah. Ethel's got to have Hadie right away. Doc MacDonald is with another woman, and Ethel's about to have the baby. Now!" Mama got dressed and went with Owen. Just after daylight, Owen drove up in his Chevy and asked Dad and me to come to breakfast. We saw the new baby boy nursing Ethel and saw Mama looking happy. The two oldest Stong girls had fixed pancakes and sausage for breakfast. I thought our breakfast was sort of an apology to Dad. Like Mama, I felt being good friends with neighbors made life better.

By this time, I felt really good about being a farm boy. I liked any work Dad and Mama gave me. And I liked being around farm animals. When new colts and calves and lambs were born, I felt close to the new babies and their mothers. The new ones grew big and strong so fast. I could see the ways they were like us people. I felt sorry for the calves when they were being taken from their mothers and they and their mothers called to each other. I felt proud when I helped the calves learn to drink from a bucket by letting them suck my milky fingers and then lowered their mouths to the milk.

But I learned that animals, just like people, might be mean, too. The spring I turned five, two colts were born. One was a filly we named Betty. The other was a feisty stallion we named Bill, that Dad said he'd never geld. Every day I went to the barn or barnyard to watch them; they were so peppy and pretty. One early winter morning Dad came right back to the house when he went to do chores. His voice was broken as he told us that Bet, the filly, was dead. I went to the barn with Dad. One of Bet's eyes and the bones around it had been smashed back into her skull. Her mouth was torn and bloody and ribs on one side were sticking out through her hide. Dad's hand shook as he gripped my shoulder. "I should have known they were getting too big to both be in the same box stall." But it was hard to believe Bill would kill Bet. The sad strangeness of Bill's meanness haunted me for days.

Sister knew so much meanness from her schoolmates she had to change schools. During first through third grade, Sister went to Prairie Rose one-room school. Some days she'd come home crying and tell me about other students being mean to her. Sister rode horseback to school, but had to count on some older boy to saddle her horse for her ride home. One day the boy who saddled her horse didn't cinch the saddle tight. Out on the highway, the saddle slipped, and Sister was hanging upside down on a runaway horse. She was saved when Amy Converse drove by and one of her sons stopped Sister's horse. That night Mama decided that Sister had to leave Prairie Rose and go to Cando School. So Sister lived with the Kensinger family during part of her fourth grade year.

The terrible drought of 1933 gave me a chance to think about wanting to be something different from a farm boy. Dad told us crop failure meant he had to sell some of his milk herd, which he'd worked so hard to build up, if we were to get through the winter. An ad in the *Cando Record* said a man from Arkansas would buy cattle for good homes where pastures and hay hadn't suffered drought. Dad said he'd feel better selling some of his cows to someone who'd save them from the slaughterhouse. That cattle buyer caught my imagination.

He and his wife came in a pickup with a handmade sleeping hut in back. The way he looked really caught my eye. His tight blue jeans were tucked into cowboy boots, and his cowboy shirt clung to his skin. On his head was a greasy black cowboy hat. In his shirt pocket was a green pack of Lucky Strikes, not a bag of Bull Durham and papers, like farmer smokers carried. The cowboy had a lariat, and the evening they arrived he showed me he could lasso me as I ran from him. He could twirl that lariat above his head and down in front of his feet.

His pretty, red-haired wife asked if I liked cowboy songs. She played a guitar and sang this song:

> *We have no use for the women. A true one can never be found.*
> *They'll use a man for his money, when it's gone, they'll turn him down.*
> *They're all alike at the bottom, selfish and grasping for all.*
> *They'll stand by a man when he's winning,*
> *But laugh in his face when he falls.*

I especially liked the chorus about "little doggies," not knowing that doggies are calves without mothers, not dogs like King. The chorus was just

> *Roll on, roll on, roll on little doggies, roll on, roll on,*
> *Roll on, roll on, roll on little doggies, roll on.*

I learned the song right away and kept singing it after the cattle buyer and his wife left. When Sister came home for a weekend, I sang the song for her. She didn't like it. She said, "That's a horrid song. What does that mean, 'We have no use for the women'? What about Mama? What about me? Do you think we're selfish and grasping for all?" Sister made me ashamed of the song, so after that I only sang the chorus to King, who seemed to like it. I had thought I wanted to be a cowboy, and asked Mama to make me some chaps from an old sheep-skin coat and give me a straw hat to wear like a cowboy hat. But when Sister shamed the cowboy song, she made me wonder if there might be something mean and nasty about cowboys.

Sister liked her school in town, and Mama took Aunt Hattie meat and eggs for her room and board. So everything went well until Sister came down with double pneumonia in February.

Mama rushed into town to be Sister's nurse. Mama kept hot mustard plasters on Sister's chest day and night for more than a week. Dad and I were worried sick that Sister might not live. But the doctor told everyone that Mama's mustard plasters saved Sister's life, and she came back home on the farm to finish getting well.

I felt so happy to have Sister back home, I brought her dandelion blooms. While she was getting well, Sister got me ready for school. She made flash cards on cardboard using black crayon. She put phonics sounds on one set of the cards and simple addition and subtraction on another set. Sister had long before taught me to sing the alphabet and to name the numbers and letters on my toy blocks, so she felt I was ready to learn to read and work arithmetic. She was a very good teacher. By my sixth birthday I was reading books that Mama had brought home when Prairie Rose School had changed readers.

Now I could enjoy the funnies in the *Grand Forks Herald* Aunt Delia got every day from the mailbox. I liked *Dick Tracy* because he fought bad guys. When he was shooting out gangsters in an abandoned factory full of big machinery, I played that Grandpa's grain elevator with its engines and machinery was the old factory. Dad made me a wood pistol and rifle to play crime fighter until *Dick Tracy* ended that story.

So I went back to being a farm boy again. I knew being Dick Tracy was just make believe, but I liked the power I felt playing him fighting imaginary bad guys.

In 1934, the drought was even worse than the year before. Hay dried up before it was tall enough to mow. No rain came with the summer winds, only dust from topsoil. Dust seeped through windows, covering curtains, beds, and floors. Banks of dust piled up at fences like dark gray snowdrifts. Dried Russian thistles, taller than me, clung to fence lines in drifts. As if the drought wasn't bad enough, grasshoppers came in clouds that could make a shadow on the ground below them. The County Agent gave farmers grasshopper poison, but hoppers had already chewed the scrubby grain down to nothing but stems. Mama said the hoppers were like in the Bible, a sign of starvation and doom.

What made the drought worse were loud arguments between Dad and Grandpa about how to carry on farming. And their arguments spread to Mama and Aunt Dee. So many quarrels made me think all the grown-ups were mad at each other.

I could tell we were really hard up when Mama said Dad should go to the county courthouse for kids' clothes given away at the welfare office. I went with Dad and was given a heavy black wool sweater and a pair of ugly high-top shoes. The woman giving out the clothes suggested a shoe size too big. I protested that they didn't fit, but Dad took the woman's advice. I agreed with Dad when he said to the woman, "It's a terrible time when a man can't even buy clothes for his children."

Mama and Dad found a way out of their miseries when Sister went back to the doctor for a checkup. Dr. Olafson said Olive's pneumonia had left her with rheumatic fever and a heart leakage. He said she'd not likely live many more years if she stayed in North Dakota, but needed a warmer climate. Dad talked about two of his Troyer cousins who'd bought orange and grapefruit groves in Florida. Dad wrote to one of his cousins and he wrote back that there could be work in fruit groves and that there was still land to buy in Florida for fruit farms. Dad said he'd sell out his share of the farm and we'd go to Florida. Mama looked happier than she had in a long time.

School was about to start and I was ready for school. Neighbor Owen said I could ride his Shetland pony to Prairie Rose School, and off I went on the first day. The teacher was a daughter of close neighbors and knew Olive had been teaching me. That first day she handed me flash cards for first grade reading and addition and asked me to hold them up for the other three first graders to learn.

On the playground, though, even before school started, I felt unwelcome. Three brothers surrounded me and asked, "What's your dad's name?" When I said, "Noah," they all three laughed and began to mock, "Noah's ark, Noah's ark, Noah's ark."

I felt I should ask what their Dad's name was. The oldest brother said, "Chas Dix."

I said I'd never heard the name Chasdicks before, and the oldest brother said, "We're the Dix brothers. Our dad's first name is Chas."

I had seen my uncle Charlie write C-h-a-s for his first name, so I asked, "Maybe his first name is Charles?"

The oldest boy said, "You dummy. You don't know nothing." He gave my shoulders a push and I tumbled to the ground, tipping over the second boy on his knees behind me. Those three brothers bullied me through the several weeks I was at Prairie Rose School. They made me as convinced as Mama and Sister were that what was called "the good old one-room school" was a place where kids could easily get away with being mean bullies. Not a good place for someone who just wanted to be a farm boy.

CHAPTER 4

Will I now be *A Transient?*

By the first week in October, Dad had bought new tires and a new battery for his 1929 dark blue Dodge sedan and had tuned up its engine. Then one day he drove into the yard pulling a house trailer. Dad called it a trailerhouse. It was one room on four wheels. We went through a door at the back by climbing hinged stairs that folded down from beneath the floor. There was a small window at the front and a window in the door to let in light. There was linoleum on the floor, but otherwise the trailer was bare.

Mama furnished it with things held back from the auction we had scheduled. A bed was at the front of the trailer. A foldout couch sat along one wall, and Mama's chest of drawers stood beside the couch. On the opposite wall was our kitchen table with four chairs tucked under it. Near the table was a short cabinet to hold cookware and dishes. A washbasin made it also our washstand. Dad cleaned up a two-burner kerosene stove that could be set on the washstand for cooking.

Sister and I spent some time in the house trailer, talking about living in it on our trip. I could tell Sister was as unsure about the trip as I was.

The day of the auction came. Everything from our house except what we'd travel with was out in the yard between the house and the barn, even jars of vegetables Mama had put up. On the second Friday in October, the auctioneer began selling household goods. When the auctioneer moved out to the barnyard, I heard Mama tell Aunt Hattie that nothing was selling at as good a price as she'd hoped.

The auctioneer started the bidding on tools and farm machinery. Those things went quickly, but I could see from Dad's face that he was disappointed with the bids.

When Dad saw me in the crowd he motioned me to come to him.

He told me to have King ready for sale when the farm animals came up for sale. I said, "Dad, I have to take King with me."

But Dad said, "We can't keep King cooped up in the trailerhouse every day. He'd go crazy. He's a farm dog, used to running around, doing his job on a farm. You bring King to me as soon as the horses get sold."

I took King with me down to my swing, where Sister and cousin Vesper were. I told them Dad had said King must be auctioned off, and began sobbing. Sister tried to comfort me, saying what Dad had said about what was fair to King. But all I could think was how unfair it was for me to give up King. That feeling of separation was horrible. I petted and hugged King until my sobbing ceased, then took King back with me to wait for the auctioneer to finish selling the horses.

I watched Dad's best team, Jim and Alex, get sold with their sets of harness to a farmer I had never seen before. Dad motioned me to come, and King and I went to his side. Stepping close to the auctioneer, Dad said in a loud voice, "Listen! My boy has a collie here that that he trained to bring up cows from the pasture all by himself. This is the best farm dog you could ever buy. Who will start the bidding at five dollars?"

The auctioneer began chanting, "Five, do I have five dollars for this special farm dog?" He kept repeating his chant until finally someone bid three dollars. Then the bid went to three-fifty, then four, four-fifty, and finally reached five. No one would carry the bid beyond five dollars. The auctioneer pointed to the same man who had bought Jim and Alex. Dad said I could keep King with me until the auction was over.

King and I went back to the swing and I told Sister and Vesper about the sale. They both said five dollars is a lot of money. But King was priceless to me, and I couldn't see why they didn't understand that.

When I went back to watch the last of the cattle get auctioned off, I stayed beside Dad until the man who bought King came over to us. He held out his hand to me and said, "I'm Ralph Girard. I bought your dog, son."

I took his hand weakly and said, "His name is King."

"Is King as good as your dad said?"

"He's the best dog in the world."

Girard took a five-dollar bill from a clip and handed it to me. "Well,

I want you to know he'll have a good home. I have a boy in Rolette High School and a girl in third grade, and they'll take good care of him."

"You bought Jim and Alex, didn't you?"

"The big gray Belgian and the black Percheron with a diamond forehead? Yup."

"So he'll still have friends from home, too."

Dad patted me on the head and asked Girard, "You want to put a rope on King and tie him up in the truck box?"

"No. He could get hurt with those two big horses. He can ride in the cab with me." So I hugged King and led him over to the cab of Girard's truck where Dad lifted King up on the seat.

I gave King one last look and ran away, wanting to be alone. I was more full of sorrow than I'd ever been before.

That night after the auction, Mama and Dad and Sister and I had our first sleep in the house trailer. Ever since her pneumonia, Sister had been sleeping with Mama. So they slept in the bed and Dad and I slept on the pullout couch. We all woke up to the sound of rain on the roof and felt a wind that made the house trailer sway.

Next morning, we said our goodbyes in Grandma's bedroom. I felt I had to do what Sister did, so I kissed Grandma and Aunt Delia and gave Grandpa kind of a hug. Mama choked up and cried during the goodbyes. Dad said, "Well, Pa, don't know when we'll ever see each other again."

As we drove away, Sister and I waved to Aunt Dee as she stood outside the house waving at us.

I was full of mixed feelings. Never seeing Grandpa and Aunt Dee again made me feel kind of empty. Leaving the place I'd learned to be a farm boy made me feel even emptier. At the same time, looking ahead at the road made me tingle. I was sure we were headed for a real adventure.

Dad drove us to Cando and parked the house trailer in front of Aunt Hattie's home. Then he went to the bank to pick up the rest of the money from the banker who had clerked the auction. While Dad was downtown, Mama walked with Sister and me the short distance to Uncle Jesse's to say goodbye. Aunt Ella Mae had wrapped going away presents for us kids. I got a pair of little binoculars and Olive got a book of paper dolls. Dad met us there in Aunt Ella's kitchen, and we all went

Ready to leave for Florida, October 1934

out to Uncle Jesse's well shop to say our goodbyes. Uncle Jesse unsnapped his leather coin purse and gave Sister and me each a nickel. He said, "When you get all hot and thirsty down south, you can stop and buy a coke."

Aunt Hattie had fixed a big dinner for us. Cousin Russell took a photo of us and then we said goodbye to all the Kensingers and finally we were on the road to Florida. I tried out the binoculars Aunt Ella Mae gave me. They brought things a little closer, but it was easier to look out the car window with my own eyes. I grew impatient with Sister because she took up most of the back seat with her paper dolls and their clothes changes. I told her, "Paper dolls look pretty dumb, especially those Shirley Temple paper dolls Aunt Ella Mae gave you."

"You're a boy, and wouldn't understand," Sister said. "Just mind your own business."

It was almost dark before we got to Jamestown. Dad said there was a tourist park where we could eat supper and spend the night. But at the tourist park there were big Caterpillar machines to redo the place, so the tourist park was temporarily closed. Dad drove downtown and parked alongside a hotel. He got us a room, and after we ate the last of the sandwiches Aunt Hattie had sent with us, I went to bed on a little sofa. The hotel man brought Sister a rollaway bed. We all had a better sleep the next night in the tourist park at Aberdeen, South Dakota.

The Russian thistles along fence lines in South Dakota looked even thicker than back at Grandpa's, and crops looked just as raided by grasshoppers. Dad had to stop twice in towns to wipe the smashed hoppers off the windshield so he could see the road. We spent our third night at a park in Woolsey, but it wasn't really a tourist park. The town constable came not long after we parked there, and after he and Dad talked, he said it was all right for us to stay.

Next morning Dad wanted to get an early start, so he let Sister and me stay in bed while he and Mama started the drive. We stopped in a little town off the highway for breakfast in a café, where they fixed us good pancakes and bacon and eggs. I could tell Mama liked the jolly woman who waited on us.

We continued heading south on Highway 281. A little before noon I heard a sudden snap, then a scraping sound. Out the back window I saw the house trailer lurch into the ditch and fall over. We all went back to see that the house trailer had broken open on one side. We could see inside that nothing was broken, not even the oval framed mirror Mama had hung on the wall. It was leaning face out against the couch. Mama was awfully upset about having left Sister and me in the house trailer to sleep until breakfast. She said, "If this had happened before breakfast, you children might have been killed." But I didn't think so, because none of the furniture got smashed.

We drove without the house trailer to Plankenton. Dad found a garage where they said they'd haul the house trailer to their garage and try to repair it. They said it might take two or three days. Dad asked if he could help work on it, and they said he could.

So Dad got us a room in the Plankenton Hotel. The hotel had chairs on the front porch and the balcony above the porch had chairs, too. It was a good-looking old hotel with a lobby that had soft chairs and sofas, and there were tables and writing desks, too. It was much nicer than the hotel in Jamestown.

The white-haired woman who ran the hotel told Mama she could use their washing machine, and she told Mama that for help in the kitchen she'd take money off our hotel bill. So, in a way, the breakdown with the house trailer gave our family some comfort. Next day when Mama went to work in the kitchen, Sister sat at one of the writing desks and wrote postcards to Aunt Dee and Aunt Hattie and Aunt Ella Mae, telling them about our accident. The postcards with a picture of the hotel were right there, free for anyone to use.

I found a daily paper from Sioux Falls on a table, and sat in one of the big soft chairs to read the funnies. There was story on the front page about the Civilian Conservation Corps or CCC. Reading it made me think I'd like to join the CCC someday. I thought they must have fun making places better for people. That kind of work would be maybe more fun than farming, even.

When Sister finished writing her cards we went to the post office. Sister spent part of the nickel Uncle Jesse gave her on stamps for the cards. With the other two cents she bought each of us a sucker at the drug store. We kept exploring Plankenton and found a park with seesaws and swings. Sister met a girl about her age and those two talked and laughed like old friends.

Saturday night there was a dance at the hotel, with a band. Mama and Dad went but they only sat in a booth and watched. Sister and I watched from the little balcony on the second floor until Sister said it was time we went to bed. Sister claimed that Aunt Delia and Aunt Hattie said dancing was sinful. I said, "Ah, it looks like fun." Some of those couples just ripped around in circles so fast, I thought they'd get dizzy. And I liked when the music stopped, and the dancers hooted and clapped their hands and laughed.

The men at the garage didn't work on Sundays, but they let Dad work on the house trailer in the garage until he had it all fixed. After lunch Dad let me go along to help load up. Dad showed me the house trailer had a new shaft and a hitch for the car so the trailer could be connected. Monday morning Dad pulled over in front of the hotel, and we loaded up and started out. Dad said he'd been told if we went through Sioux Falls we'd have a better road. So Dad drove into the sun that morning, and at evening we stayed in a tourist park near the south edge of Sioux Falls. It was good to eat Mama's cooking again, even though the hotel restaurant did let us choose what to eat.

By Tuesday, we were headed south on Highway 75, and a day later crossed the Missouri River into Iowa. I thought it was queer that South Dakota had a Sioux Falls and Iowa had a Sioux City. Dad said those names were from the Indians, who once had their own nations, such as the Sioux, and Cherokee and lots of other names. Mama added that for more than a hundred years after white people came it wasn't even the United States. Sister said she'd learned about the colonies and the Revolutionary War, and I said, "Hey, I want to learn about everything. Wish I could get back to school."

Mama said, "Just read all the signs and watch for everything along the way. You can learn a lot from travel as your school for now."

I thought about that and about how long I'd be in travel school. I did some counting in my head as I studied the road map of the U.S. and took a guess. "It might take us about forty more days to get to Tampa, Florida."

Mama said, "Oh dear!" and Dad said, "If we're lucky."

It was as if Dad had a hunch we might have more trouble to slow us down. The day after we drove into Nebraska, the Dodge began to make squeals and grinding sounds. Dad said, "Oh, oh. Sounds like maybe brake drums are shot, or maybe the wheel bearings." He stepped on the brakes and we could feel the house trailer push us. "Well it ain't the brake drums." We drove on with the sound getting louder and came into the biggest town I'd ever seen, with signs that said Omaha.

I could tell from Dad's face he was worried about the noise the car was making.

He pulled off Highway 75 and drove into a vacant lot across the alley from a long, two-storied brown house with lots of windows. Dad went to the office in that house. He came back to say, "The guy says there are plans to build on this lot, but it's all right to stay here a couple days. He says we can use the toilet next to his office daytimes." I knew we wouldn't be allowed to just pee alongside the car here in the city.

Dad unhitched the house trailer and jacked up a front wheel of the Dodge as I watched. When he pulled off the wheel, Dad said, "Yup. Wheel bearing's shot. Probably all four wheels." He started up the street, pushing the wheel he had taken off.

Late afternoon a bunch of boys bigger than me came to the lot and started to play football. Shoot, I didn't know it was football, because I'd never seen a ball shaped like the one they used. I went over where they were playing and watched them make two lines and smash into each other, while a couple of guys behind one line tried to run toward the end of the lot. One guy called the others on his side to make a circle. He usually got the ball first. He looked at me and said, "Hey, kid. You wanna play football?"

"Just let me watch for awhile." All the other guys laughed, but the leader nodded and said, "Okay." I watched until Sister came to say it was time for supper.

"Hey," the leader guy yelled. "What's your name?" I told him and he told me, "Come on over and join us tomorrow, Wallace. Maybe you'll want to play by then."

It felt good he called me by my name and said I could play with them. It was the first time I had ever been asked to play with other guys.

Mama had made an omelet with bacon, a favorite family supper. When she sat down, Mama shook her head. "I just used the last of our eggs from the farm." Dad told Mama where there was a grocery store and said he'd found a place to fix the wheel bearings, but it would take some time.

Next day Sister and I went with Mama to a grocery called Piggly Wiggly that was bigger than a barn and had aisles with shelves stacked with all kinds of food. We picked out what we needed and took it in a basket to a counter where Mama paid for it.

On the way to the store and back, we went by the biggest and prettiest church I'd ever seen. When we got back to the house trailer, Sister asked Mama if she and I could take a walk, and I guessed right that she wanted to go back and look at that big stone church.

We stood out front of that church amazed. A number of steps led up to three closed doors. Between the middle door and the two others were round pillars that supported a sort of porch roof as wide as the steps. Above that roof were three windows with pretty colored glass, each window framed with blocks of stone and a little peaked roof at the top. Above the three windows was a bigger round window of even prettier glass. Above that was a kind of balcony where a statue of a robed woman stood. On the peak of the roof above the statue was a stone cross and at the edges of the entire front were big pillars, each with a statue on top.

I started up the steps and called back, "Come on, Sister. Let's run up these steps."

A woman in a long brown dress and wide white hat had come to where Sister stood. She reached her hand out to Sister and said, "Good morning. I'm Sister Mary Joseph."

I heard Sister say, "My name is Olive Kennedy. My brother is up there on the steps."

I came down the steps toward them and the woman took a step toward me. "Tell me, brother of Olive, what's your name?"

I told her, and then, I don't know why, added, "Mama named me Wallace after her brother that died taking care of people with cholera." As soon as I said that I felt really dumb.

"And I'm Sister Mary Joseph, happy to meet both of you. Would you like to see Saint Cecelia's?" I nodded my head and Sister asked if Saint Cecelia was the name of the church.

"This is the Cathedral of Saint Cecelia. You must not be from this neighborhood. How do you happen to be here?"

I guess I wanted to say something to show I wasn't dumb after all. So before Sister answered, I said, "We're on our way to Florida. We have a house trailer Dad parked in a lot up the street, 'cause he has to fix the wheel bearings on our Dodge. We were on a farm outside Cando."

"North Dakota," Sister said. "Cando is a little town in North Dakota."

Sister Mary Joseph smiled and nodded, and then looked at me. "And what grade are you in, Wallace?"

I smiled this time before I said, "I barely started first grade at Prairie Rose, but Sister taught me to read last spring when she was getting rested up from double pneumonia."

"And you call Olive 'Sister.' When I heard you say, 'Come on, Sister, let's run up these steps,' I thought maybe you were inviting me to race with you." She laughed.

I laughed, too, but wondered if she really thought that.

"Maybe, while I'm showing you Saint Cecelia's, you'll call Olive by her name, so I'll know you aren't talking to me." She laughed again and pushed my cowlick up off my forehead. "Come, young Kennedys. I imagine you've never seen a cathedral before. And I'm guessing that you haven't been raised Catholic, either. Am I right?"

I shook my head no, and Sister, that is, Olive, said, "No, we went sometimes to Aunt Delia's Church of the Brethren."

Sister Mary Joseph nodded and took Olive by the hand. She pointed to the statue above the round window. "See there above the rose window? That's a likeness of Saint Cecelia. Do either of you like music? Saint Cecelia is the patron saint of music. She was a very early saint who was martyred in Rome with many other early Christians."

Inside the cathedral, the colored glass windows were like big paintings, but even prettier with the light shining through them. At the very front was a rounded arch and set back into the arch was a life-sized statue of Jesus on the cross. It looked very real. We walked along with Sister Mary Joseph as she kept telling us what everything in the cathedral meant as she named it. She seemed smarter than anyone I'd ever heard talk before, and it seemed almost magic the way things would appear as we moved through the cathedral. Sometimes she bowed and crossed her chest, and twice she knelt to pray as she held a string of beads from her pocket.

She showed us great pipes at the front of the cathedral that she said were organ pipes and said we would be thrilled at the sound of the organ. She took us into one of the small spaces she called Saint someone's chapel, where candles were burning. She told us we could light a candle for someone we loved, and Olive lit a candle for Mama. When Sister Mary Joseph led us back out the front door, she said, "I hope you felt some of the sacredness of Saint Cecelia's. And I hope you will want to come back again. Maybe bring your mother and father for mass Sunday."

Well. To have been taken through that cathedral would have been amazing, but it never really happened. I wish it had. The front of the cathedral had impressed me so much that over the years I have imagined what it would have been like to be taken on a tour by a Sister Mary Joseph. It's a made-up memory, included here because I believe memory at its best is one way to explore life's meanings. It seems right to insert it here because I could already see that our travel was going to be full of meaning.

Sister and I did walk back that day to look at the big church. We just stood on the sidewalk and talked about how pretty it was and wondered about how it was built. When we told Mama about going back to look at the big church, she told us it was a Catholic church and that there are priests and nuns in the Catholic Church who never get married because they think of themselves as being married to God and the church. I couldn't see how anyone with a job on earth could be married to God if God is in heaven like people say. And I sure couldn't see how anyone could be married to a church.

When the guys came back to play football, I got to play with them because the kid who seemed to be a leader waved for me to come on over. He told me some of the rules and said I should play in the line and do what the other guys there did. Our side kicked the ball, so I ran to drag down the guy who caught the football. I'd watched enough to know that much. On the third down for the other side, I did get to the guy carrying the ball and helped drag him down. Guys on our side said, "Good going, new kid."

I liked it better when the other side had the ball, because when our side had it, those guys came storming at us, and we were supposed to stop them without using our hands. That was hard. I was sure it'd be really fun to run with the football myself, but figured I was too new to be given that job.

The guys talked about going to the Armistice Day parade Saturday, so at supper I asked Dad and Mama if we could watch the parade. Mama said she'd like to take us to watch it, but Dad said he'd be putting the wheels back on the Dodge and cleaning the spark plugs and changing the oil.

In the Omaha paper Dad bought, Olive found an ad for movies and another ad about a beauty parlor where permanent waves for girls were marked down to a dollar. Olive said there was a Shirley Temple movie on Howard Street and told us she'd love to have a permanent for curls like Shirley Temple's. Next day we went first to the beauty parlor. A woman put Olive under a machine that had dozens of wires with little clamps. When she put the roll of hair into a clamp, she dabbed it with a brush dipped into a jar of dark sticky looking stuff. After she filled a couple dozen clamps, the woman turned on the machine. It made a roaring sound. You could almost see the force of its hot air that blew over Olive's head.

Watching Olive get that permanent made me so happy not to be a girl. Getting a permanent seemed like an awful torture. It took almost an hour before it was over. Finally the woman let Olive out from under the machine. The woman rolled the curls to make them bigger, flicking them around with a comb. Olive's hair began to look all frizzy. I wondered what Mama and Olive would think, because to me, the permanent had been a frightful mistake. But Olive looked happy when the woman held a mirror behind her to see both behind and in front. Mama smiled at Olive when she joined us, telling her she looked nice. So I guess if you weren't a boy, the permanent didn't look like a mistake.

Soldiers carrying flags led off the Armistice Day parade. Next came an army band, which was followed by brown trucks with big guns on them. Then came some open cars, one with the mayor's name on it. Another had a sign that said "Miss Omaha." She stood and waved to everyone. A second band had a drum that said Creighton University. Men marching behind a banner that said American Legion were in the parade, too. People cheered at everything that went by.

On the way to the movie, Mama said, "It's all too sad, thinking about so many men who lost their lives. Not just the ones who fought for us, but those who died from the flu, too, like my friend Jim Foster." I hadn't heard his name for a long time, but I remembered Mama had showed me his picture with a horn under his arm. I asked Mama if Jim Foster was in the army band. She told us he was the company bugler. Mama wiped her eyes with a handkerchief.

A couple blocks up Howard Street was the movie house, and Mama bought us tickets to see Shirley Temple. The movie was *Little Miss Marker* and was about a man who couldn't stop losing his money betting on horse races until Shirley Temple got him to stop gambling. The man was pretty funny some of the time, and Shirley Temple could sure sing and tap dance. But I felt glad to be a boy, so I didn't have to try to look like someone in the movies.

Back at the vacant lot, Jimmy, the guy who acted like the leader in football, was watching Dad put the wheels back on the Dodge. When I came up, he said, "If you want, you can come over to our place and look at my pictures of Nebraska football."

We went up the stairs of the long brown house to a long hall on the second floor.

I asked Jimmy if he had any brothers or sisters and he said, "Nah, but I used to have a dog 'til we moved here. They won't let us have a dog in these apartments."

I told Jimmy about King and how smart King was. Jimmy snickered when I told about King and me playing hide-and-seek in tall weeds. "You're just spoofing me, aren't you? I don't believe any dog could play hide'n'seek. Did you really live on a farm once, or are you making that up, too? Mom said she thinks your family must be transients."

That was the first time anyone told me they didn't believe what I'd said. That hurt my feelings. I know I sort of whined when I said, "We did, too, live on a farm. It was Grandpa's farm, and Grandpa built the big farmhouse himself, and the barn, too. We lived in a littler house, but Dad and Grandpa farmed together. And we're not transients either. But I have to go now."

I didn't get to see any pictures of Nebraska football, and walking down the apartment hall, I was almost crying.

At supper, I asked Dad and Mama what transients are. "Are they some kind of church?"

Dad laughed and said, "Nope. Transients aren't any kind of religion. They don't have any say about who they are."

Mama didn't seem to think my question was funny. "Transients are folks who don't have any real home, so they move from place to place."

"Well, are we transients then? Until we get to Florida?"

I thought about that and about what Mama and Dad both said, and I couldn't be sure. I thought as long as we live in a house trailer, maybe we are transients to other people, like Jimmy's mother. It didn't sound like a transient was a good thing to be, though. So I felt I'd rather take Dad's word that we're travelers. Next morning, we left Omaha and were traveling.

CHAPTER 5

Is there such a thing as *A Traveling Boy*?

Dad said we were going to stop and visit some of his relatives in Kansas. Mama asked if that would take us out of our way, and Dad said, "A little, but it'll be worth it." Dad handed me the road map of Kansas that he got from a gas station. "Look for Baldwin City and Ottawa." I found them on the map and told Dad what roads would take us through Topeka and on to Baldwin City and Ottawa.

Dad pulled to the side of the road and looked at the map. "You're getting to be a real map reader. Good for you." Map reader sounded like a better thing to be than transient.

It took us two days to drive through Nebraska and almost another day to get to Topeka, Kansas. Topeka had a nice tourist park and looked almost as big as Omaha. Next day, Dad drove us by the state capitol. It was a bigger building than St. Cecelia's, but not as pretty. I had already found a special place in my heart for that Omaha cathedral.

As Dad drove down through Kansas he told us his Aunt Jenny had married a Chris Lantz, and they had a son named Joe who owned a café in Baldwin City. Dad stopped to fill the car with gas and learned how to find his cousin's restaurant. He parked around the corner from the restaurant and said, "Come on. I want Joe to meet the whole family."

Ideal Café was what the sign said. It was pretty big with a row of stools along the counter, a row of booths along the wall across from the counter, and tables and chairs in between.

Dad led us to a table with four chairs. When a waitress came with a pitcher of water, Dad asked, "Is the manager on the premises?"

The waitress said, "What should I tell him this is about?" Dad said, "Tell him its about his cousin Noah Kennedy." The waitress went to the back of the restaurant and right away a tall, slim man came to our table.

"Cousin Noah. Tell me what you're doing here in Baldwin City." Dad introduced Mama and Olive and me and explained about our traveling to Florida. He told Joe we'd go first to Arkansas, because we wanted to show Olive the farm where she was born. That's why we were traveling straight south instead of through Indiana, Kentucky, Tennessee, and Georgia.

Joe Lantz said we should have some dessert before following him to his home for supper. He said he'd like us to see his yard and garden while it was still daylight. The waitress told us the kinds of cake or pie we could have. I chose apple pie and the waitress asked if I wanted it à la mode. When I looked puzzled she explained that was pie with ice cream. It sure was good and I told myself if I ever have pie in a restaurant again, I'll always order it à la mode. After our desserts Joe asked Olive and me if we'd like to ride in his new Ford V-8. It was dark blue and smelled brand-new. I was disappointed Joe had to drive slow for Dad to follow, because I was sure his Ford V-8 had lots of zip.

Baldwin City isn't really a city, so we soon got to Joe's home. He drove his car up on a driveway in front of his garage. The house looked pretty fancy with an entry that had brick planters on each side of the cement steps and a nice roof over the front door. Joe's wife opened the door and told us her name was Evelyn before she asked Olive and me our names. Mama and Dad were right behind us. Evelyn shook Mama's hand with both of hers, something I'd never seen before.

Joe said if we weren't too tired, he'd like to walk us around his backyard and garden. Mama said she'd be happy to help fix dinner, but Evelyn told Mama to go along to see Joe's garden. We walked across a short space of grass through a gate in a low stone wall. What a garden! Flowers all laid out in beds surrounded by shrubs. But there were also plaster statues on little hills and cliffs. There were big birds like owls and hawks mounted on branches of deadwood. And there was a coyote and a wildcat and a fox, too, all looking ready to spring at you. The wildcat was hiding behind a bush. The fox was at the edge of a cave, and the coyote was on top of a hill.

I thought the garden was amazing and Mama seemed to really admire it. She looked at Joe all the time as he talked about his garden and wanted to know the names of all the plants. Dad maybe thought the statues were silly, the way he grinned at them. Olive seemed to lose interest. She asked if she could go into the house and did. Dad and I stopped awhile at a pool with a stone waterfall and big goldfish swimming around like they were lazy. I didn't know goldfish could get so big.

Evelyn fixed us a big dinner with Swiss steak, she called it, that had a tomato gravy. She had mashed potatoes, and peas and carrots mixed together, but they must have been cooked separately, because the peas weren't at all mushy. There were pear slices in lemon jello with whipped cream for dessert. It was dark by the time we finished dinner, and Dad said we'd better go find a place to park the house trailer. But Evelyn said, "Just leave it where it is. You'll spend the night here with us. We have two extra bedrooms and one has twin beds where the kiddies can sleep."

We went into the living room where Joe turned on a table lamp with a shade that looked like a forest fire when the lamp was turned on. Joe said the shade had liquid chemicals in it that grew active when warmed by the bulb. I watched the forest fire leap up around the trees while Joe and Dad talked about relatives and other things.

At breakfast next morning, Joe sat for just a cup of coffee. He said he had to get down to the restaurant to check in the deliveries. First, though, he told Dad how to get to another cousin's on a farm towards Ottawa. Evelyn fixed us scrambled eggs and bacon and toast from an electric toaster. She gave Olive and me orange juice and ice-cold milk. Joe and Evelyn sure were good to us.

We drove to Ray Lantz's farm north of Ottawa and got a big welcome there, too. He said Joe had phoned him that morning, telling him to expect us. Ray Lantz had a big farm that looked like it had never been hit by drought or by the depression. Ray's wife, Ruth, showed us where we'd be sleeping. Mama and Dad and Olive were all taken upstairs. Ray showed me I'd sleep in a bunk bed in what he called the boys' dorm, downstairs off the kitchen.

I went with Dad and Ray Lantz to look over the farm. His barn was almost as big as Grandpa's. He had a big pigpen and both a chicken and a turkey house. He had two machine sheds, one holding two tractors. Outside that shed was parked a big grain separator. Ray told us he kept only one work team since he had two tractors. He said he kept two riding horses for the boys. Next Ray took us to his pear orchard, where pears were ripe. He handed me a pear and put another pear in his over-

Who Do You Think You Are?   33

alls pocket. Then we went to his apple orchard. Dad said he'd like to have an apple, and Ray told him to just reach up and take one.

Ruth Lantz rang a bell by the back porch and we went in for noon dinner. I decided that Dad had some well-to-do cousins in Kansas, because Ray told Dad he should be sure to visit his other cousin, Ray's sister, in Ottawa. Her husband, Len Garrison, owned the Buick garage, Ray said, and he was sure we'd like to see their big home. Ruth Lantz said, "Since tomorrow is Friday, why don't the Kennedys stay here until Sunday, when Len won't be at work. I'll call Alice and tell her the Kennedys will stop for Sunday dinner with them. And tomorrow, Olive and Wallace can go to school with the boys." I could tell Ruth Lantz was someone who liked to plan for everybody.

Late afternoon, along came the two Lantz boys. One was about Olive's age, named Warren. The other was two years older, named Melvin. They both seemed big for their ages, and talked loud. The boys asked their dad if they could show me their pet coon before they went after the cows. Ray said they should give the coon a clean dish of water and feed him the pear Ray had put in his overalls pocket. I wasn't sure what a pet coon was. I'd heard Mama say something wouldn't happen in a coon's age.

Turned out the pet was really a raccoon. Warren said his name was Ricky. Melvin reached into the cage real quick for the water dish. Warren held out the pear for Ricky to take when Melvin put the water dish back in the cage. Then the best thing happened. Ricky put his paws in the water dish and rubbed off both paws before eating the pear. He picked up the pear with both front paws and turned the pear with his paws as he ate it. I said, "He eats with his paws like he has hands."

Warren said, "You should see him eat chicken wings. He likes 'em best cooked."

I asked if I could pet Ricky. Melvin said, "Not unless you want a bloody hand. He ain't really tame yet." When I asked how long it'd take to tame him, Melvin told me his dad said the coon would never be really tame, but might finally get used to his cage. I asked how they caught Ricky and learned Ricky had got into the turkey house but was caught by throwing a washtub over him. Warren said, "Dad put him in this cage we use for turkey toms when we geld 'em. Turkey hens don't like a raft of toms. They all want to get screwed by the same tom, so we keep one big healthy tom and castrate all the others."

I said, "It's the same with chickens and sheep and pigs. Cows and mares, too."

The Lantz brothers said together, "Yeah. You a farm boy, too?" I started to tell them all about Grandpa's farm as we went down in the pasture with their collie, Buster, to bring up the milk cows. I told them about how King and Queen both could be sent to the pasture to get the cows all by themselves.

They both laughed and said, "Yeah. Tell us another."

I told them my dad would tell them I was telling the truth. When we put the five milk cows in their stalls, I said, "I know how to milk, too."

Melvin said, "Okay, you milk the Guernsey. She don't spook easy."

I thought the Lantz brothers were kind of rude, and two things they did after supper showed me I was right. The first was after we four kids played kitten ball 'til it got dark. Melvin and Warren headed into the house while Olive asked me to wait for her as she went to the biffy. When we came around the corner of the house, Olive was leading the way. The Lantz boys with sheets over themselves jumped out in front of Olive and yelled, "Boo!" Olive jumped like she'd been shot, and screamed and started to cry. I put my arm around her and could feel she was trembling. The Lantz boys pulled off their sheets laughing, and Warren said, "We sure scared her, hunh?"

I was mad. I said, "That was a mean thing to do. My sister has heart trouble. Last winter she almost died from double pneumonia. You guys just now probably made her heart trouble worse."

They laughed again, and Melvin said, "That another story like your dogs bringing up the cows by themselves?"

After we'd gone to bed in the boys' dorm they showed bad manners again. There were two sets of bunk beds. I was on the lower bunk of one set. The Lantz brothers were in the other set. I was about to fall asleep when Warren leaned down from his top bunk. "Hey, Wallace, you playing with your dong?" I'd never heard the word dong before, but I guessed he meant my peter, which is what Mama always called it. I told them I didn't do that. They both laughed and Warren said, "That another one of your stories?"

I wanted to go to sleep, but Melvin asked me if I'd ever heard the story of the farmer's daughter and the traveling man. When I said no, he told a story about a traveling man staying all night on a farm. He was put to bed with the farmer's daughter, but a table board was set between the two of them. Next morning when the traveling man straddled the yard fence to go, the farmer's daughter said, "How can you climb over that fence when you couldn't even climb over a table board last night?"

The Lantz boys laughed long and hard, but I didn't know just why. I felt like I was in kind of a dangerous place with those Lantz brothers.

But Melvin and Warren were friendly the next day when Olive and I walked to school with them. Melvin had Olive walk with him because she would be sitting in his row at school. I walked along with Warren.

Their one-room school wasn't as big as Prairie Rose School, and it didn't have nearly as much playground stuff. But there were more students. I counted fourteen, six boys and eight girls. All six boys were in grades five and up and sat in bigger desks. The one girl in fifth grade laid claim to Olive right away.

Mrs. Humboldt, the teacher, was friendly. She had the biggest boy lead the pledge of allegiance and then went to the piano to play and lead the kids in "My Country, 'Tis of Thee." I could hear Olive's voice clear over all the other voices. When the song was over, Mrs. Humboldt said, "I see we have two guests today, and I heard a very pretty voice that belongs to this one. Will you tell us your name, young lady?"

Olive told her name and said she was a fifth grader. She then told them my name and that I was in first grade.

Mrs. Humboldt said, "We welcome you both as our visitors." She chuckled and added, "You should know that you must be relatives to all but four of the students here. Ten of our students are first or third cousins."

That was about the most interesting thing I learned at that school. I read aloud when it was reading time for first graders, and Mrs. Humboldt told me I was a good reader. There was no morning recess, but at noon, after we ate our sack lunches, Melvin and a boy named Fritz did "hands up" on a bat to see who chose first for kitten ball. Fritz chose Olive for his side. Melvin chose me and said I should play right field. I didn't get up to bat until afternoon recess. I hit the ball, but it went right back to the pitcher, and I got thrown out.

We left the Lantz farm Sunday to find that Ottawa was less than a half hour from Lantz's farm. With Ray's directions, Dad drove right to the Garrisons' home. They had a big house of brick and stucco and shingle siding in a big, well-kept yard. All the homes nearby looked as if they belonged to rich folks, too. A big-bellied man in suit vest and white shirt and tie beckoned us into his driveway when we drove up. I figured he must not know how hard it is to back up a house trailer. But Dad drove in onto the driveway as the man signaled.

A woman in a shiny blue dress came down the front steps and gave Dad kind of a half hug, calling him Cousin Noah. She gave Mama sort of a hug, too. She said, "Harriet, I'm Noah's cousin Alice." She introduced the big-bellied man as her husband Len. When she looked at me, I said, "My name is Wallace, and this is my sister Olive."

Ethel Garrison said, "Well come right in the house and meet our two girls." We went up the porch, then through an open front door with a fancy glass window into a hallway next to an open stairway. All the wood everywhere was sparkling dark brown and the stair steps, not covered with anything, sparkled, too. There was piano music coming from behind the two girls in plaid skirts and white blouses. They sat on the sofa and both wore kneesocks and patent leather shoes. They stood up at the same time.

Ethel Garrison introduced Mama first, then Dad, then Olive, and finally me. She called the girls Beth and Lorraine. The girls smiled, but didn't say anything. Olive went to Beth, who looked a bit older than Olive, and said, "That's beautiful piano music. Do you have a Victrola?"

Beth nodded, "Behind the sofa. We're playing a piano concerto. Our piano teacher loaned us this record and said we should listen to it every day before our lessons next Thursday."

Lorraine came over to me and said, "Your name is Wallace? You must be in second grade. I'm in third grade." She held out her hand, so I shook her hand and told her I was only in first grade, but added that I can read.

Ethel Garrison asked Dad and Mama to sit in the armchairs. She said, "Girls, you take care of your cousins. Maybe they'd like a Coca-Cola. Len, why don't you bring us grown-ups some iced tea?" I'd never heard a man told to bring people something, but Len Garrison said, "Righto," and went through the dining room and through a door that swung both in and out. I'd thought Joe Lantz had a fancy home, but the Garrison house was lots fancier.

Beth said to Olive, "Come upstairs. I'll show you my room."

Lorraine said, "Would you rather see my room or our backyard? We have a swing back there." She had a low-pitched, husky voice, not much louder than a whisper as she stood close to me.

I said, "Let's see the swing."

In a flash Lorraine turned and was out the front door, saying, "Come on then, Wallace."

I remembered her mother had mentioned Coca-Cola, but I guessed that had to wait awhile, and followed Lorraine as fast as I could without running.

"Should I push you, or do you want to push me?" Lorraine asked at the swing. It hung from a limb of a tall tree that had spiky brown leaves on branches that were more even and balanced than I'd ever seen on a tree. I stood admiring the tree before Lorraine said, "Well, which?"

"Oh, I'll push you," I told her.

She sat on the swing in such a way that the back of her skirt hung behind the swing board and the front of her skirt dropped to just above her knees. She backed up in the swing a few steps and said, "Push me high, Wallace. Real high." I gave her lower back a strong push, so that she began to swing in a good arc, but she said, "Higher, Wallace." So I gave a stronger push. "Run under me." So I did. She pumped the swing on her way back and pointed her shiny black shoes on the way forward. "Run under me again, from the front."

I put my hands on the swing seat on each side of Lorraine and ran under the swing as fast as I could, pushing with all my might. I went back behind her to wait for further commands. "Okay. Just let me die down." When the swing got lower, Lorraine jumped off, falling to her knees. I ran to her to be sure she wasn't hurt. She reached for my hand and lifted herself up, putting her face close to mine. Her husky voice said, "Your turn, now, Wallace."

She gave me a good swing, too, and finally I got that Coca-Cola. She poured the bottle into a glass with ice that she chipped from the block in the icebox. She cut two slices of yellow cheese for each of us, saying, "Here. This is what goes good with Coke. Come out on the back porch."

We sat in big white wicker armchairs facing each other to drink our Cokes. Each of us talked about ourselves, and Lorraine smiled as she listened. I'd never met a girl that seemed so neat as Lorraine did.

Sunday dinner was mid-afternoon, and when we finished the meal, Len Garrison said, "You'll find Ottawa's tourist park as good as any, I'm sure. I'm on the park board. We try to do our best in every way." As we were leaving, Len guided Dad's backing the house trailer out of the driveway, making sure Dad didn't back on the grass of his freshly mowed lawn.

Once we were away from their house, Dad said, "Thinks he's a high muckety-muck, doesn't he? Thinks we're not good enough to spend the night in his home."

Mama said, "I never felt at ease there, either. But I wouldn't want to be Ethel, married to him."

Olive seemed to dislike the visit, too. She said, "Beth acted like she was much more important than I am. But I'm not sure where we would have slept in their house. I only saw the three bedrooms and a kind of reading room upstairs. And I don't think Beth would want to share her bed with me."

Even though it seemed silly, Olive's mention of Beth and Beth's bed made me wonder where I'd sleep, and that made me think about Melvin's story of the traveling man. I knew I'd remember Lorraine for a long time. But I didn't tell the family I'd had a great time at the Garrisons. I'd just keep Lorraine my secret.

Traveling had made me feel I was big enough to have my own opinions about what we saw and did. But some of my feelings were so new they made me feel good, but kind of scared, too.

CHAPTER 6

Here in the South, am I just *A Stranger*?

Next day Dad drove to Clinton, Missouri. We were no longer in big-farm country. All the way from North Dakota to Kansas, the land had been flat and mostly farm fields. But in Missouri, we passed by little farms with small farm buildings usually surrounded by trees. At Clinton, the tourist park was close to a lake.

Dad bought a fish line, with some sinkers and a bobber and some hooks and bait. He wound the fish line around a short stick. With a worm on the hook, Dad threw the line out quite a ways from shore and caught a sunfish. Dad put another worm on the hook and let me throw out the line. No fish came near the hook for me. When Dad took over again, he caught another sunfish. So we had fried fish for supper. Just a taste for each of us, but it sure was good.

We drove on next day to Stockton State Park by Stockton Lake. I was surprised how cold it turned, because now we were obviously down south. Of course, it was the day before Thanksgiving, so back in North Dakota we'd likely have had a big snow, and it would be a lot colder. Dad parked not far from where people had set up tents. The park had a smelly shack with toilets and sinks with mud and toilet paper on the floor.

Mama told us she'd met Mrs. Jamison, who had asked Mama to bring our supper over to their spot and we'd put our food together for a Thanksgiving dinner. So Mama baked biscuits in the little oven on top of the kerosene stove and opened her last jar of canned chicken to make a gravy dish for topping off the biscuits. Mama heated a jar of her green beans, and we carried the whole batch over to where the Jamison family was camped. By then it was dark, but they had a good fire going in a pit close to a park table. They told us their family was from southern Illinois. There were two Jamison kids, Ginny, who said she was ten, and Pete, who was eight.

Mrs. Jamison had fixed what she called a fish boil. It was a soup with carrots, onions, potatoes, and pieces of fish. I told Mrs. Jamison I liked the fish boil, and Mrs. Jamison praised Mama's biscuits and gravy.

After we had finished that unusual Thanksgiving supper, Mrs. Jamison told her husband to get the flashlight, so we could look at Pete. I thought that was a strange thing to say, but when the flashlight was shined on Pete, we saw that the back of Pete's hands and his face skin looked kind of like fish scales. Then the flashlight was shifted to Ginny, and she had the same kind of skin. Mrs. Jamison said, "Both kids, poor souls, have what they call alligator skin. A nurse at the public clinic in East St. Louis says it's a kind of eczema. She said they don't know what causes it, but girls and women don't often get it." Ginny told us, "At first it was like a bunch of boils that oozed a kind of water, but they dried up and turned into these fish scales." I felt so sorry for her and Pete.

Back at the house trailer, Olive asked Mama if she'd ever seen anyone with skin like Pete's and Ginny's. Mama said, "No, but there was a tent at the county fair one year back in Cando with a sign, 'See the boy with Alligator skin.' Maybe that boy had the same kind of eczema, and they'd put him in that freak show."

I asked Mama what a freak show was, and she said, "It's a kind of sham, really. Folks that run freak shows find people suffering from something strange and call those people freaks because they don't look quite like the rest of us. The nasty thing is, those people have some kind of sickness that nobody tries to help."

At least Pete and Ginny hadn't been put in a freak show.

Dad said he wanted to bypass Springfield, so he drove us west of it. Winding our way south through Missouri, we had to climb hills that were so steep the Dodge sometimes could barely pull the house trailer. Dad said these hills were part of the Ozark Mountains. Going downhill, Dad had to drive in low gear and, even then, often step on the brakes, because the house trailer was pushing us. After we passed by Silver Dollar City, we came to a gas station at the top of a long flat space. Dad pulled in. A sign on a shingle-covered building said, "Ginger with Eats, Phil with Gas," which was pretty funny, I thought.

Dad asked the big kid who came to fill our gas tank where he could find Phil. When he came back to the car, Dad told us we'd stay here while he fixed the brakes and maybe put new rings in the engine. I tried to picture where the Dodge engine would wear rings, because I didn't know yet about pistons.

After Dad moved the house trailer to a place to sit parked, Olive and I took a walk to look around. We found a well-worn path across the road that ran along the edge of the woods. We took off on that path and saw that those woods were on the edge of a bluff. We walked to the edge to see that it dropped down into thicker woods. We looked down on the tops of those trees and Olive exclaimed about their beauty. I felt excited about the high drop-off.

Next day, while Dad worked on the Dodge, Mama took Olive and me down to a cave Mama'd been told we should visit. It was called Marvel Cave. It opened into a big, well-lit room where Mama bought us kids tickets for a nickel each and bought one for a dime for herself. We waited with other folks for a man to give us a cave tour. He led us down a dimly lit path along a slow-running stream. The guide said fish in that stream had eyes that couldn't see, because for so many generations they had lived in the dark. As we got deeper into the cave, the guide pointed out hanging gray spears he called stalactites and bigger spikes from the ground he called stalagmites. Marvel Cave was the strangest place I'd ever seen.

Most everything in southern Missouri seemed strange to me. Even Ginger with her orange hair, who ran the diner. Ginger talked with a kind of singsong voice, using words I didn't always know. But she was nice to Olive and me. She made a milkshake in a big metal can on an electric mixer and poured it into two glasses for us. When Mama reached in her purse to pay for it, Ginger said, "Aw, jist let it be ma treat, a-rat? Yew folks air gonna need avery cent yew got, if yew avah git to Florida." Her way of talking was the strangest I'd ever heard.

It took Dad three days to put on brake linings and new piston rings. I watched some of the time, and Dad explained how piston rings hold the oil in place to smooth the work of the pistons. Dad said it was safe now to drive down into Arkansas, but fixing the Dodge had cost a bundle. I soon learned that the Ozark Mountains are in Missouri and Arkansas both. We were headed towards Morrilton in Arkansas, and most of the drive was through hilly woods in the Ozarks.

On the way to Morrilton, Mama and Dad talked about when Olive was born. Dad said, "The night before Sister was born, I wanted to get the doctor there on time, but my car had a flat tire, and I didn't think I had time to fix it. So I went out on the road and flagged down the first car that came along. I told him our need, and said, 'You got to get me to Doc Campbell,' and he did. I don't remember that man's name, but he told me he was sure I was a robber when I stopped him."

Mama had lots to say, too. She said she was scared she might lose another baby and wanted the doctor right away. She said she'd done everything she knew to make sure it would be a good birth. "Right after Noah left for the doctor, Lucy Tresvant came to borrow sugar for a cake she was going to make. My, but I was happy to see her! I gave her the sugar and asked her to send her mother over as fast as she could get here. Mamie Tresvant came quickly and she was a great help and comfort. You'll meet the Tresvants when we get there."

Dad said he had to promise the doctor he'd sell one of the cows right away to pay for his work. "But he was a pretty good doctor, wasn't he, Mother?

"Oh yes. He was all right. He smelled bad of cigar smoke. But he washed up before, and he didn't use forceps, the way Doc MacDonald did on Wallace."

Dad said, "And just before sunup, we had ourselves the prettiest baby girl you ever saw." It was fun to hear Mama and Dad both tell that story about the night Olive was born.

The next morning we drove up a tree-lined lane to a big, two-story house with a wide front porch. As we neared the house, we heard loud barking, some coming from towards the barn, and some from in the house. A stocky gray-haired man came toward us from around the house. Dad went to meet him. We heard him say he was Sidney Rove. Mr. Rove invited us all into the house and led us up the porch steps to the front door calling out, "Mrs. Rove, come meet these folks used to live here."

Four yapping little dogs came scooting at us, two with puckered noses. We were told their names, but I didn't even want to remember them. After knowing collies, those four little dogs seemed miserable.

Mrs. Rove, who looked kind of like a witch with loose black hair and a long, sharp nose, showed us around the house. I liked the way the house was built. Downstairs was a big living room, dining room, and kitchen, all with stone fireplaces. Mr. Rove's funny-smelling bedroom off the living room had a stone fireplace, too. Mrs. Rove told us we should stay with them that night in two of the upstairs bedrooms. She said the third bedroom upstairs was hers, but she said she shared her bed with the two of the dogs. She told Olive she could have one of her dogs to sleep with, but the fox terrier and bulldog slept with Mr. Rove. Sleeping with little dogs made her seem even more like a witch.

Mrs. Rove gave us soup and cornbread for lunch. Mr. Rove told us the eight dogs fenced in near the barn were for protection from nigger thieves. He said us kids should stay away from the fence, because those dogs could get pretty mean. He said he fed all his stock up for market, except two cows he milked. "Mainly for the dogs, but we keep the cream for butter and cookin'."

After Mr. Rove showed us his wild barking dogs and the barn, Dad told him we wanted to walk over the hill and visit the Tresvants. Mr. Rove's face went kind of sour, but he said, "Y'all do what you want."

We walked from the Roves' backyard through a small grove and across a pasture up a hill to a cornfield. Two times we had to straddle barbed-wire fences. I said to Dad, "Fields here sure are small," and he said fields in Arkansas are never as big as fields in North Dakota.

After crossing the cornfield, we came to a small house set on short cuts of tree trunks. The house was unpainted and had weathered to a dark gray. The one window facing us had closed wood shutters. We walked around the house where the two windows had no glass, only plain curtains. The doorway had a hanging quilt instead of a door. A split tree trunk was the step in front of the doorway.

Mama called out, "Mamie, you have visitors," and right away a smiling dark woman pushed the door quilt aside and said, "Lord almighty! Hadie! I knew it was your voice. After all these years, I still knew it. Come in. Come in! Just look at that baby girl, half grown. And a little brother, too."

We stepped up into the house, which was all one room except for a corner where pulled-aside quilts marked off space for a bed and clothes hanging on pegs. On the wall at that side of the house was a ladder to an attic opening through the plain board ceiling. At the other side of the room were shelves and a cupboard and a round cookstove near a stone fireplace. There was a table with four cane-bottom chairs and four empty apple boxes standing on end. Standing by two of the apple boxes were two big barefoot girls in faded blue dresses.

Mama said, "Effie and Sally! You're both young women! Effie, I knew you when you were six and Sally was almost four." The young women grinned and nodded to Mama, then looked at Olive and me. Mama introduced us.

Dad asked, "Mamie, where can I find Joe?"

"Just up on that west slope, hoeing cotton, Mr. Kennedy."

Dad took my arm and I ran alongside him as he walked fast into rows of thick green stalks with leaves that were curled shut. Way up one row was a man with his back to us, hoeing around the stalks. Dad called out, "Joe, I'm here to see you." The man in bib overalls and gray shirt and a floppy felt hat turned, shading his eyes with his hand. Then, with a big toothy grin, he ran towards Dad with his arms open. Dad ran into his arms, and they hugged each other, laughing.

It was the first time I'd ever seen Dad hug any grown man. Dad said, "Joe, this is my boy, Wallace." Mr. Tresvant shook my hand with a firm squeeze. "Wallace. My, what a fine little fella you look to be. You grow up to be like your daddy, and you'll be a real gentleman."

Dad asked Joe where he might find another hoe to help with the cotton and Joe said, "Wallace, I bet you can run back down to the house twice as fast as I can. You oughta find a hoe leanin' on the web fence of the kitchen garden. Will you bring it back here for your daddy?"

I ran down, found the hoe, and ran it back to Dad. A hound had showed up, and Joe said his name was FDR, because he got him as a pup the day Roosevelt was elected president. I patted my legs and FDR came to be petted. I hadn't touched any of the dogs back at Rove's place, but it felt good to pet a good dog again. I found a broken piece of hoe handle at the edge of the field for FDR and me to play fetch while Dad and Joe hoed and talked.

At the end of the rows, Joe said, "Come on in the house and we'll see what we might find to wet our whistles." Sure enough, on the table were eight cloth napkins beside glasses of cold tea next to saucers of ginger cookies. The Tresvants sat on four apple boxes set on end, giving us the cane-bottom chairs. Mamie said thanks for our visit and for the food and good weather. Joe and the girls said "Amen" at each break in Mamie's prayer.

When the Tresvant girls finished their cookies and tea, Effie said, "Excuse us, please." And they left the table, taking their dishes. Sally, the tall one, came back for an apple box that she took to the front of one of the cupboards. She stepped up on the box to take from a cupboard shelf a bag of Bull Durham and cigarette papers. Effie carried an apple box to set in front of the fireplace and Sally joined her with the other box. Seated there, they both rolled cigarettes. Sally stretched out her bare foot into the fireplace where she picked up with her toes a stick still glowing with embers at the other end. She brought the stick back to her hand and lit both girls' cigarettes.

Boy, I thought. Not many people could do what Sally just did with her toes.

As they were smoking, the quilt in the doorway was pushed aside and a young dark woman stepped into the house. "Hello! Looks like company!" The young woman looked like a picture in a bright yellow flowered dress and yellow anklets in shiny black shoes. She said, "I'm Helen Robeson, the local schoolteacher."

Mama introduced our family, and Mamie Tresvant said, "These Kennedys were the best neighbors we ever had, but they been livin' way up north."

We learned that Miss Robeson taught students in a one-room school where she lived in a corner of the schoolroom. She said she made the rounds to homes of colored people in the neighborhood, sometimes eating dinner with them and always taking provisions to fix for the students' lunches. She spoke very well with a pretty voice.

After a while, Dad said we should get back to the Roves where we were expected for supper. Dad hugged Joe Tresvant again, and Mama hugged Mrs. Tresvant, saying she would try to get in touch with Lucy, their oldest daughter, in Little Rock. Joe Tresvant shook hands with me, and Effie and Sally both kissed me on the forehead and hugged Olive. Miss Robeson smiled her pretty smile at all of us. It felt like we were saying goodbye to some good friends.

For supper, Mrs. Rove had fixed cornbread and a dish of mixed vegetables all mashed together. The meat was stringy beef with stewed tomatoes. Nobody mentioned our visit to Tresvants, but I felt like saying it was unfair that the Tresvants had to live in a house with no glass windows and no real door.

While we were eating our dessert of rice pudding, Mrs. Rove said the silliest thing I'd ever heard. "Now you folks need to take seriously the offer I'm going to make. Why don't you leave these children with us? We'd pay you, of course, five hundred dollars for the two of them.

I know you could sure use the money. And think how much better off they would be living here."

Mama said, "Mrs. Rove, you might think that's funny, but I don't. Our children mean the world to me."

Mrs. Rove started to say more, but Dad pushed his chair back from the table and stood up. "We'll leave here, right now. We thank you for giving us dinner and inviting us to spend the night, but we're going to move on."

Mr. Rove just sat there, looking as if he didn't care what we did, but Mrs. Rove said, "Oh now, don't be offended. You can still spend the night with us."

Mama had stood up, too, so Olive and I got up from the table. Mama said, "Noah's right. We should go." It was easy to go, because we hadn't yet brought anything in from the house trailer.

Dad drove out of the Roves' yard saying, "We'll see if the Johnsons will let us park in their yard." A short drive from the Roves Dad turned in at a lane to a small white house. He said, "I'll just see if we're welcome."

An older man, sort of limping and carrying a pail of milk was coming from the barn and called out, "Hey there. What can I do for you?" Then quickly he said, "Noah Kennedy? My lord, you've come back."

From the back door a very slim woman with white hair and smiles came to Mama's side of the car. Mama said, "Mrs. Johnson. It's Hadie. And our two children, Olive and Wallace."

Mrs. Johnson led us into her kitchen. "My lands! Y'all just pull up to the table and I'll put on the tea kettle. Would you kiddies like milk with your cookies?" She gave oatmeal cookies and milk to Olive and me, and cookies and tea to the four grown-ups. Mama explained that we had stopped to see Olive's birthplace, but didn't want to stay with the Roves. Dad asked if we could park the house trailer and spend the night in their yard.

Mrs. Johnson said, "Well, as you know, we don't have a big place. But we have two couches in the parlor, and the children are sure welcome to sleep there."

I nodded and Olive looked at Mama, who said, "That'd be nice."

Next morning Mrs. Johnson made us a breakfast of scrambled eggs with grits, and sausage that she pushed out of a small cloth bag and shaped into patties. She made cocoa for Olive and me. She said to

Mama and Dad, "I want you to stay long enough to tell us all about your lives since you left here."

Across the road from the Johnsons was a thick growth of pine trees on a hill. I asked, "Could my sister and I explore around? It's so pretty here, especially that hill across the road."

Mr. Johnson said, "You have a good eye, young man. You kiddies can look around all you want. Just stay away from the Roves' place. He's got mean dogs over there."

While Mama and Dad talked with the Johnsons, Olive and I went across the road and through the trees to the top of the hill. We saw a train way down below and heard three long whistles and the chugging sound of the train engine. Olive broke into singing "Down in the Valley." I sang with her while we watched until the train was out of sight.

I suggested we go back across the road to the pasture where I could get a closer look at a mare and colt. We took our time because there were so many rocks we stopped to examine. When we got to the Johnson's pasture, I saw that the colt had long ears and a head shaped not really like any horse I'd ever seen. I remembered Dad once told me that mule colts are born to mares that are bred by donkey studs. I wanted a closer look at the mule colt, but as I walked closer, the mare pushed the colt with her head and chased it across the pasture on a run.

Olive wanted to take a closer look into the woods next to the pasture and led the way. We came to a clearing surrounded by tall leafy trees. In it was a cemetery with several gravestones and several little homemade wood crosses. We saw one gravestone with the name Betty Lou Bonner, 1912–1921. "Only nine years old," Olive said with a sad voice. The other stones marked older folks, all named Bonner. Olive said, "This is such a pretty graveyard." I nodded in agreement.

Back at the Johnsons' house, we were given cold grape nectar. I asked how she had made it so cold and Mrs. Johnson said, "Come on out back and I'll show you." She led Olive and me to a short stone wall with a wood roof and rigging for two pulleys with ropes dropping down into the black circle.

"You can pull on this rope," Mrs. Johnson said, pointing to a rope with a stretch of white paint on it. I pulled the rope using the pulley 'til a milk bucket came to the top. Mrs. Johnson set the bucket on the stone wall and said, "See. This is our icebox. Just feel." I felt the cold jar of butter and quart jar of milk. "Let it back down now, 'til you come to the white paint on the rope." And I did.

"Now use the other rope to bring up cold fresh water," Mrs. Johnson told us, and went back to the kitchen for her water pail. She emptied the pail in a hanging geranium basket and filled the water pail from the bucket I brought up from the well.

Back in the house we finished our grape nectar and learned we were going down the road to visit people named Balsh. We said goodbye to the Johnsons. In the car, Mama said she was sure Mrs. Balsh would welcome us for as long as we wanted. We drove past the Roves' place and down around a hill to a big place that looked like a calendar picture of a farm.

Mama was right about our welcome. When Mrs. Balsh finished hugging Mama she said, "I'll always thank the Lord for you, Hadie Kennedy. You saved our daughter Naomi when she almost died of pneumonia, even though you were expecting your baby. That was you, sweetie," looking at Olive. "Saved Naomi with hot mustard plasters she kept changing all day and all night long on the poor darling's chest."

Olive said, "Mama saved me, too, last winter when I had pneumonia."

Mrs. Balsh was a real talker. She told us Naomi was at university studying to be a nurse herself. "She must have been about your age, sweetie, when your mother was her nurse. And you were born in June. Tell me your name. I knew it once, but I forgot."

After Mama told our names and ages, Mrs. Balsh went to the kitchen and poured cold iced tea she had stored in her icebox. She brought us what she called scones, too. They tasted kind of like cookies, but were bigger and were sort of like crusty cake.

Mrs. Balsh nodded when Dad said, "Sure looks like you've made the place prosper."

She was off talking again, telling us they were dairy farmers now, and that the two boys' delivery carts covered Morrilton. She added that Hugh had a truck for hauling cream twice a week into Little Rock. "That's where he's gone now."

Dad asked if the boys still lived at home, and Mrs. Balsh said, "Oh yes. They're too tied into making this dairy business grow to take to looking for sweethearts. They should be back around two or so, and

Hugh should get back with the cream truck about four. Then, Noah, you can see how thirty cows get milked in less than a couple of hours."

She asked Dad to go down to the chicken yard and catch her two young roosters for supper. Then she took Mom and Olive with her to their root cellar to pick out food to go with fried chicken.

I went along with Dad, eager to help catch a couple roosters. As we headed for the chicken yard, Dad told me it was hard to believe how well off the Balsh family had become in a little more than ten years. I could tell by his voice he wondered if he and Mama should have stayed in Arkansas.

We found a chicken hook hanging at the gate to the chicken yard and saw a number of young roosters flocked together in one corner of the big fenced-in yard. I knew from experience that chickens run less from a kid like me than they do from a man. So I asked Dad if I could use the chicken hook first.

Dad laughed and handed it to me, saying, "Go get 'em." I held the hook on my shoulder as I walked slowly to where the young roosters were pecking up grain from the ground. My first try hooked a leg and as I held on, Dad took the rooster off the hook. He handed him to me, not needing to explain that he could handle the second rooster better if he hooked it himself. He needed two tries, though, because the roosters were skittish after the first one was caught.

When we closed the gate behind us, Dad said, "Guess I'll have to wring their necks." There was no hatchet or chopping block we could see. I watched as Dad used a quick twist of his hand to drop the chicken. The head came off in Dad's hand. He took the other rooster from me and said, "Let that one quit flopping before you pick him up. You don't want to bloody your clothes."

When the Balsh sons came home, they knew Dad right away. Dad and I helped them unload their wire baskets of empty milk bottles, then watched as the brothers drove the thirty cows into the barn and hitched them into their stalls. They gave each cow a measure of ground feed and attached milking machines to the first five cows. Milking machines took about fifteen minutes for each cow, so then in a little more than an hour and a half, all thirty cows were turned back to pasture. The milking machines were emptied into a big cream separator and the separated milk and cream cans were set in a tank surrounded by a larger tank of water that had chunks of ice in it.

But chores were far from finished. They used a big bottle washer with hoses attached for washing the milking machines before they ran the bottles through for a scalding wash. Everything was electric, except the heating for the water. Bob and Roy Balsh showed us a furnace boiler that stood in a small brick building outside the barn. Dad shook his head and said, "What a great, up-to-date system."

Hugh Balsh drove up in a truck wth a big closed box. We helped him unload about twenty cream cans that we took to the washing shed where Hugh hosed them out with hot water. He seemed happy to see Dad and told me I was a good-looking kid.

At supper, Hugh Balsh told Dad it was a shame he had sold out and moved, because dairy farming had given the Balshes a good life. Mrs. Balsh added that the Roves, who now had our place, were no neighbors at all. She said, "No one around has anything to do with them." We stayed all night at the Balsh dairy farm, which was, for sure, the nicest farm I'd ever seen. It made me wonder what our family life would have been if Mama and Dad hadn't sold the farm where Olive was born. And it made me think about how hard it must be for grown-ups to decide where they will live in an effort to make life better. Thinking about that just added to my feeling that I was a stranger. I was a long way from where I'd lived the first five years of my life.

The next day, when we drove into Little Rock, it seemed like such a big city, I felt even more like a stranger. Dad found us a hotel right on the street above the Arkansas River. He found a lot that charged two dollars a week to park the house trailer. And the next morning Dad set out to find work, saying we were in bad need of cash.

After Mama took Olive and me to a little eat shop for breakfast, she said Olive and I could explore the neighborhood if we'd be careful. Across the street from the hotel was a courthouse. We walked into it and looked up at its big dome. Down the street a ways we looked at the outside of the Old Statehouse, which was a museum that cost money to enter. Olive said she wanted to go back inside with Mama, but I wanted to explore some more. Further up the street I came to city hall. Inside was a big police station where I met a policeman who asked me if he could help me find what I was looking for. I told him my name and where I'd come from, and that our family was headed to Florida. He took me into the police offices where he introduced me to a policeman he called the captain, and then other policemen, too. They were all nice and friendly. Back at the hotel, I told about the friendly policemen I'd met. Mama said she guessed being friendly with policemen was all right.

Next day, Mama took Olive and me to where our house trailer was parked in the pay lot. We went into the trailer and Mama lit up the kerosene stove and made coffee to go with the half-dozen cookies she had bought in a little bakeshop on the way there. With the loaf of bread she'd also bought, Mama made peanut butter sandwiches using peanut butter from our cupboard.

Mama told us the oldest Tresvant daughter, Lucy, worked just a block or so from the pay lot, and she was going to join us for lunch. Lucy Tresvant was a pretty, well-dressed young woman who seemed really happy to have lunch with us. She said, "It's so good you have this house trailer for us to meet. You know I wouldn't be allowed to eat with you at a café or even go to your hotel room." That sure seemed strange to me, because Lucy Tresvant was an elevator operator in one of the insurance company buildings nearby. She said she was happy to have a good job. Like all her folks back near Morrilton, she was really nice. She told Mama that there was a dime store nearby where Mama could by a kit to make flowers Olive and I could sell. We stopped at the dime store and Mama did buy a kit. Back in the hotel room, Mama started making roses out of crepe paper and wire.

When Dad came back to the hotel room he said he hadn't yet found any work, but he'd found a place where we could get free suppers. I knew if we had to eat free somewhere, we must be really poor. We walked several blocks past city hall to what must once have been a store. There we stood in line with other families, taking trays for people to give us plates of food. Olive and I each got a little bottle of milk to go with our chicken on rice with carrots. We were told we could have as many slices of white bread as we'd eat. At the end of the line a man punched four holes in a card Dad had.

Dad told us he got the card at the Transient Bureau, and had signed up there for any job they could find for him. He said he'd signed up for a furnished apartment, too, because the Transient Bureau would only pay for one week at the hotel.

I said, "So we really are transients, aren't we?" Mama wiped tears from her eyes and said, "You children might as well know we're as poor as church mice." That sounded funny to me, so I laughed, but Olive said, "That's not something to laugh about."

For the next two days, while Dad went looking for work, Olive and I went out on the street at noontime and tried to sell the crepe paper roses Mama had made. Mama said we should ask for a quarter a bunch. Only one lady stopped to look at the roses we were trying to sell. She said she couldn't give us a quarter for a bunch, but she'd give us fifteen cents. I told the lady, "Mama said to get a quarter for a bunch," but Olive said we would take the fifteen cents, since we weren't selling any flowers anyway. When Dad came back that evening, he shook his head and said he still hadn't found any work.

Next day I met a kid tossing a football up and catching it in the hotel hallway. He had long straight black hair and told me his name was David Boston. He was two years older than me and said he was part Cherokee. He and his folks were transients from Oklahoma. David asked if I'd play catch with his football, and he could really pass the ball with a spin. But a hotel cleaning woman told us we had to stop playing catch in the hall, so David took his ball to his family's hotel room and I met his mother.

David asked if I'd ever been down where junked cars are piled next to the river, so we went to ask Mama if I could go see them. Mama said I could if we'd be careful, so we went down where dozens of worn-out cars were parked close together on the riverbank. We had fun exploring those cars. There were lots of makes I'd never seen before close-up. David asked if I'd have any firecrackers to shoot off on Christmas, and I told him I'd never heard of firecrackers for any time except Fourth of July.

But he made me wonder what kind of Christmas we'd have in Little Rock. Back in our hotel room Mama told me that going through our trunk she'd found the five-dollar bill I'd been paid for King. She said it was up to me, but maybe I'd like to use some of that bill for Olive and me to buy each other Christmas presents. I said sure, but Mama should decide what to do with the rest of the five dollars. Olive and I went with Mama to Woolworth's and Mama said Olive and I could pick out our own presents as long as they didn't cost more than fifty cents. Olive chose some fancy hair clips and a Big Little Book. I found a police set that had a badge, a billy club, a whistle, and a pair of handcuffs that cost only forty-nine cents.

Who Do You Think You Are?

Mama said we could have our presents to use right away before Christmas, so I put on my badge, and put the whistle on a string around my neck. I hooked my billy club and handcuffs to my belt and went over to the city hall police offices to show the police I looked like them.

Christmas Eve it seemed strange to hear firecrackers being shot off in the street outside the hotel. Mama had learned that the Salvation Army would serve Christmas dinner to transients, so that's where we went Christmas Day. They gave Olive and me each a sack of candy and nuts.

Two evenings after Christmas, after supper Dad went to the transient office, and Mama and Olive and I started back to the hotel. The night was heavy with fog, and walking back was like being in thick, dark clouds. At the signal light at the courthouse across from the hotel, I saw the signal light was green and ran across the street, calling to Olive to come, too.

I saw Olive start just as the light turned yellow and then I heard a screech of brakes and a thud, and my heart seemed to jump right to my throat. I could see Olive crumpled in front of a taxicab. I ran to where she lay on the concrete with the taxi driver bending over her. Traffic was backed up from both directions, and there were police there right away. A policeman said he'd called for an ambulance and began questioning the cab driver. Another policeman asked Mama if the girl was her granddaughter. Mama set him straight.

When the ambulance came and they put Olive inside, Mama got in to be with Olive. She gave me a key and told me to go to the hotel room and wait for Dad. Just as the ambulance pulled away, Dad came, and one of the policemen and I told Dad what had happened. The policeman said he'd take Dad and me to county hospital, so Dad and I got a ride in a police car.

We found Mama in the emergency waiting room. She told us doctors were stitching up the wounds in Olive's head and that Olive was still unconscious. What seemed a long time later, Olive was brought by on a steel table on wheels. We could see her head all wound tight with bandage. Mama walked with the nurses pushing the table and Dad and I followed. Odors in the hospital were strong and strange. Up on the ward Mama talked with a doctor and nurse. Mama told Dad and me the doctor said she could stay and be Olive's special nurse. Dad and I took a taxi back to the hotel, and when Dad told the cab driver about the accident, the cabbie told us there'd be no charge for our trip.

Next day Dad drove us to the hospital, but stopped first to see the flat on 316 Spring Street that the Transient Bureau had assigned us. It was a big old two-story brown house with a black iron fence at the front of the yard. Steps led up to its front door. Dad said we'd come back and move in, but parked a couple of blocks up Spring Street where a man stood at a pushcart with hot coals under a kettle. Dad bought us two hot tamales for a nickel each and told me this was a real Mexican treat. My tamale was wrapped in dry cornhusks that I had to pull away to eat the ground meat packed in cooked corn meal. It tasted really good.

Right where Dad parked was a sports store and in the window was a toy pistol in a sheepskin cowboy holster. Dad said he could tell I wanted it, and bought it for me.

At county hospital Olive was still unconscious, sixteen hours after the accident. We told Mama about the furnished apartment on Spring Street and she said we should go right back to the hotel and get our things and move in. I was eager to shoot my cap pistol and pretend to be a cowboy. We loaded everything into the Dodge and left the hotel for 316 Spring Street.

We'd come such a long way through places that were strange and so different from Grandpa's farm in North Dakota. Some of the people we'd met made me feel they weren't much like our family. And Olive getting hit by a taxicab seemed like a strange nightmare. I thought if I could pretend to be a cowboy I wouldn't feel completely like a stranger.

CHAPTER 7

Could I learn to be a *City Boy*?

At 316 Spring Street we met Mrs. Colby who was in charge of the house. She explained that she looked after the tenement for the owner, Mr. Thurston, and took care of the old man who was partly crippled and spent most of his time in bed. She showed us our two-room flat on first floor, then showed us the bathroom up on second floor that we'd have to share with all the other renters. Our flat opened to a small room that held a couch and three wood chairs. It was separated from a dinky kitchen by a counter with two stools. There was a small bedroom with a bed, a two-drawer dresser, and a rocking chair.

Dad told me he'd learned that men were being hired to build a golf course and that he was driving out there to see if they'd hire him. He said he'd be back with some groceries before suppertime and told me to have a good time with my cowboy pistol. When it turned dark I was worried because Dad wasn't back yet. I sat in our flat with the ceiling light on, feeling hungry and about to cry. When there was a knock on the door, my heart began pounding. I thought it must be a policeman to tell me something terrible had happened to Dad. But I opened the door to a boy a head taller than me.

He said, "Hi kid. I'm Robert. We're just down the hall. My mom says you're welcome to come play with my brothers and me." I was sure glad to go with him. He took me to a bigger flat than ours. One of his brothers was called B.O. for Bertram Oliver, he said. The other told me he was Z.T. for Zacharias Thomas. B.O. said he was in third grade and Z.T. said he was a first grader. Robert was in fourth grade.

"Now you come over and meet me, too." The woman sitting up in bed smoking said. She looked quite a bit younger than Mama with light yellow hair that hung down to her shoulders with some curl at the tips. Nearer her bed I could see she had dark blue eyes. There was a book turned open upside down on the bed. Her nightgown had a fancy collar with open front that showed the tops of her breasts. I thought she was pretty, but I didn't like the way her fingers were yellow from cigarette smoke.

"Now, tell me your name, young fella." I said my name. "And what part of up north did you come from? I know you're a northerner, not just because Mrs. Colby told me, but I can tell by your accent." I felt like saying, you folks are the ones with an accent. "Mrs. Colby told me your daddy went lookin' for a job and left you alone next door, so that's why I sent Robert boy to rescue you." She spoke with a breathy, low-pitched voice, sort of letting the words leak out of her mouth. She took my hand and said, "Now Wallace, you just make yourself at home with my sons, the Harkinson brothers."

I saw B.O. was putting a train track together and asked if I could help. He told me to finish it up, and he'd bring over the engine and cars. I asked Z.T. if he was going to help, too, but he said, "No sir. That's B.O.'s train. I got a tennis ball if you wanna play catch."

I figured that the Harkinson brothers each had their own toys and you had to be asked to play with them. B.O. brought over the box with the train so we set the cars and engine on the track all hooked together. B.O. said, "Salvation Army lady told me the train wouldn't run without a transformer, but I can push it around the track."

Robert was busy in the kitchen. He'd set bowls on the table with spoons beside them, and was setting glasses of water at five places. I could smell something cooking on the stove. Robert said, "Soup's ready." B.O. and Z.T. went to the table and stood behind their chairs. Robert said, "Come on to the table, Wallace. You can sit over here by me." Mrs. Harkinson took her seat at the head of the table, and after she sat down, her sons did, too, so I did.

"Robert, you can put the loaf of bread and the apple butter on, too."

Robert said, "Yes ma'am, I wasn't sure." He brought a loaf of white bread and a jar of apple butter to the table.

"You've done very well, Robert. Now, we must ask the Lord to bless our food. And tonight, because we have a guest, we must use our best manners." I saw Z.T. and B.O. grin when Mrs. Harkinson mentioned manners. I was happy for her short blessing. It was just, "God is great, God is good, let us thank him for our food. Amen."

As we ate the canned tomato soup, Mrs. Harkinson opened the bread wrapper and passed the loaf of white bread to Robert. She took the lid off the apple butter and passed that to Robert, too. Robert said, "Thank you Ma'am," as he took a slice of bread and a spoonful of apple butter. When he passed them on to me, I said, "Thank you Robert," and put a slice of bread by my soup. Doing as Robert had, I put a spoonful of apple butter on the bread and passed them on to B.O. He thanked me and passed things on to Z.T. who thanked his brother.

Taking slow spoons of soup, Mrs. Harkinson began the story about herself. "I was the only Lawrence daughter of a respected Louisiana family," she said. "I met soldier boy Rob Harkinson in 1918 when I was sixteen, just finishing high school. My parents didn't think a soldier boy from Tennessee was good enough for me, but I was crazy for him, so we eloped. My mother never forgave me for cheatin' her out of a big church wedding. Would you believe that? As it turned out, I might have had an easier life if I'd have listened to my mother. But then, I wouldn't have my dear Harkinson boys, would I?"

"Our dad," B.O. said, "is in the Vet's hospital."

Mrs. Harkinson asked me to tell about my family, so I said in as few words as I could that I'd been a farm boy in North Dakota 'til Dad and Mama decided to move to Florida. I explained that Mama was at county hospital with Olive, because my sister had been hit by a taxi, and that we had traveled here with a house trailer. After each part of my story Mrs. Harkinson would say, "Do tell," "Oh, my," or "Dear Lord, what a pity, what a pity."

When Dad came back to 316 Spring Street he came down the hall and met the Harkinsons. The brothers told me they'd see me tomorrow. I was happy as could be to have found some friends. And the Harkinson brothers were just the friends I needed. They had a coaster wagon we'd scoot down the sidewalk in. They took me to alleys behind tall office buildings to climb into big wooden boxes. In the alley boxes we found paper clips and rubber bands and women's hair pins and finger nail files and stuff like that. We took what we found back to Mrs. Harkinson. The brothers took me to a building where the *Little Rock Democrat* could be bought to sell on the street. For a dime we could buy five papers and then sell them for three cents each. Some people would give us a nickel and say keep the change. If we earned ten cents, we could go next day to a Tom Mix show at a nearby movie house. I was sure Tom Mix was the best cowboy in the world, and I took it to heart when he said, "Real cowboys never cry."

Though she didn't seem sick, Mrs. Harkinson spent a lot of time in bed. One evening when I was in their flat, a young man came to visit her. He sat by her bed, looking at the tops of her breasts, and told her she was beautiful. Mrs. Harkinson asked him to sing some of the new songs. After he'd sing a song, they'd sing it together. One song I remember was "The Man on the Flying Trapeze." One day, after that guy came back again, B.O. told me, "If I was his age, I'd beat him up and throw him out of here."

Olive had been put on a ward with other kids, and one day that ward had a fright. Mama saw that two kids showed signs of meningitis, and told the doctors. They quarantined the ward and found that one kid did have meningitis, but was treated early and got okay. Nurses told Dad that Mama might have prevented a meningitis outbreak.

After being in county hospital more than a week, Olive had all her stitches taken out and came to 316 Spring Street to get well. When the Harkinson brothers met her, Robert said we'd give the stuff we found in alley boxes to Sally Goodin, which is what he called Olive. I'd heard Mrs. Harkinson sing, "Oh I had a piece of pie and I had a dish of puddin', but I gave it all away just to see Sally Goodin." I thought maybe Sally Goodin was some kind of movie star like Shirley Temple that people bought tickets to see.

One day the Harkinson brothers took me to a place where the old signboards with colored bulbs spelling out the name of a building had been stacked. Neon lights had replaced the old sign-boards, so the Harkinson brothers and I unscrewed some of the colored light bulbs to have fancy lights in our flats.

In the yard behind 316 Spring Street were two one-room unpainted shacks that were lived in by a black family. In one of the shacks was a young woman named Betsy. She showed Mama the scars on her back and legs made by a leather whip, and told Mama she'd been beaten at a jail called the Tucker Farm. Betsy's parents lived in the other shack. Her mother took care of Betsy's father, who could never get out of bed because he was paralyzed from being beaten so badly by police.

Fred, Mrs. Colby's fifteen-year-old son, told us how old Mister Thurston, who owned 316 Spring Street, got crippled. Fred had hit him on the head with a hammer when Thurston was drunk and tried to hurt Mrs. Colby. Fred said, "The judge said Mom has to take care of

Thurston for as long as he lives, 'cause I smashed him. But we get free rent."

I could see that in Little Rock, if you weren't white or didn't own property, the laws weren't very fair. But I thought it kind of amazing that there were two old men living on that property who had been crippled by getting beat over the head.

Mama went to Peabody Elementary to enroll Olive and me. On our first day of school we walked the seven or eight blocks with the Harkinson brothers. They warned us that the playground was divided into four parts, keeping boys and girls apart and keeping the first through third graders apart from the fourth through sixth graders. No one was allowed to cross the sidewalks into another zone.

Z.T. led me to our playground area. Right away, I heard a shout, "New kid, new kid." Three boys grabbed me and threw me to the ground. Two held me down while the third one turned my pockets inside out and took the two nickels Mama had given me for lunch and for a tablet. Z.T. told me to tell the kids who were sidewalk monitors I had to get some lunch money from my sister.

A monitor led me across the girls' area for grades one through three and called a monitor of girls grades four through six, so Olive could meet me on the sidewalk. Olive gave me a nickel for lunch and told me to tell the teacher I'd bring a nickel for a tablet next day.

When the bell rang, Z.T. showed me where to line up to be marched into school. Z.T. was in a different line because I was to go to the beginner's first grade class. My teacher was a gray-haired woman named Mrs. Snodgrass. She had us pledge the flag, repeating phrases after her. Then she set up a boxed record player and spun a record of kids singing "Arkansas I Salute Thee." When the song was over she played it again, telling us to sing along so we could learn the state song. After that she spent a long time taking roll and asking if anyone knew the students who hadn't answered present.

Next, she took a box of colored sticks from a shelf and walked around to choose a student helper. She put the box in a girl's hand and told her to give each student a bunch of sticks wrapped by a rubber band. Mrs. Snodgrass told us to sort the sticks by color and be ready to show that we knew the colors of each set. It took me about a minute to sort the sticks, but it took Mrs. Snodgrass about half an hour to go from desk to desk to see if we'd sorted the sticks right.

When that was done she read aloud what was on a page she gave each of us to take home. The page named with prices the three books we were to buy. They were a reader, an arithmetic workbook, and a spelling notebook. I read the paper before Mrs. Snodgrass read it to us. She told us our parents should be able to read the names and prices of the three books, but to remind our parents that the cost of all three was two dollars.

By then, she said it was time for her coffee break and marched us, boys in one line, girls in another, to a little room with chairs where two sixth grade girls were put in charge of us. The big girls had a good time making kids who whispered stand at the blackboard with their noses in a chalked circle that gave the kids a chalky nose.

After we were marched back to the classroom, Mrs. Snodgrass had another student pass out the colored sticks again and told us to pick up one stick at a time and hold it up, repeating after her the count of the stick until we reached fifteen. After the chosen girl gathered up our sticks again, Mrs. Snodgrass told us to look at the border of letters above the blackboard and repeat after her each letter after she read it. She had us say each letter a second time as she pointed to it with her long stick. Then she said it was time for lunch and marched us in two lines to the cafeteria. I paid a nickel for a plate of pork and beans with a piece of cornbread and a bottle of milk. After lunch, there was no more learning than before lunch, but at least it was shorter. At three, we were let out.

I knew I had learned much more traveling than I'd ever learn at Peabody School.

But I learned a lot that day after school. When Z.T. told B.O. and Robert about my being jumped as a new kid, Robert said, "We'll teach you to be a street fighter, so that'll never happen again." I was too much bigger than Z.T., so I was matched with B.O. Robert gave orders as B.O. showed me how to punch with my elbow held out level. He showed me how to throw the other guy to the ground and squat on him. He showed me how to use my elbows and feet to break loose if grabbed from behind and how to use my hands and knees to get free if held from in front. With practice I felt I maybe could be a street fighter. I didn't think I could ever match B.O., because he was one tough kid. But being taught something about how to fight gave me a different feeling about myself. I felt I could stand up to bullies and fight back without being scared.

A couple weeks later, Mrs. Harkinson asked Dad if he'd drive the three brothers on Sunday to visit their dad at the veterans' hospital. Mama talked Mrs. Harkinson into going along, and I went too. The hospital grounds were like a big park, but the hospital inside was kind of run-down, and all the men there looked unhappy.

Mr. Harkinson met us in the room for visitors. He was tall and slim and good-looking, and winked at us when he smiled. The boys told him about the things they'd been teaching me. Then Dad took the Harkinson brothers and me out on the grounds to leave Mrs. Harkinson alone with her husband.

On the way back to town, Mrs. Harkinson sat wiping away her tears as she looked out the car window. Once home, B.O. said to me, "We never shoulda gone there. Our dad's a drunk, you know. That's why he's in the vet's hospital."

In a couple weeks, though, Rob Harkinson was out of the vet's hospital. He came home just when our family was packing to leave Little Rock for Fort Smith. The taxi company had paid Dad some money because their cab hit Olive. Dad called the same real estate man that years ago sold him and Mama the farm near Morrilton to tell him we wanted a farm near Fort Smith.

Rob Harkinson wanted to look for work in Fort Smith. He told Dad he was afraid he'd start drinking again if he went back to work at the 555 Garage in Little Rock, because that's where his old drinking buddies worked.

I almost had to cry when I said goodbye to Robert and B.O. and Z.T. They'd been the first pals I'd ever had, and they taught me how to be a city boy. I'd come to see that living in a city has as many surprises as living on a farm has.

When we stopped for gas, Rob Harkinson talked Dad into letting two women hitchhikers ride with us. One sat in the middle of the front seat, and the other one sat on Rob Harkinson's lap. The one in the middle pulled a bottle of whiskey out of her purse and took a swig, then handed the whiskey to the other woman. She took a swig and handed it to Rob Harkinson. He drank some and handed it to Dad.

Mama shook Dad's shoulder. "Noah, you're driving. Don't you drink that whiskey!"

The woman on Rob Harkinson's lap said, "Oh, hell. One little drink ain't gonna hurt none."

Mama said, "Noah, pull over, right now. I don't want these women riding with our children. You two, get out. Right now!"

Dad said, "Better do what the lady says." As the nasty women left the car, one of them said, "Bitch. Henpecking bitch."

We drove on to Fort Smith in an almost silent car until Dad pulled into a parking lot for the house trailer. When Rob Harkinson got out with his satchel, he said, "I wish you all good luck, and thank you for the ride. I hope I can find work."

Dad said, "I hope I can find work, too, and good luck to you."

Mama didn't tell him goodbye, but I did. I hoped he'd find work so that the Harkinson brothers and I might see each other again. They had shown me how much was expected of a real city boy. I didn't think I'd yet quite made it, but I thought if I had kept being a friend of the Harkinson brothers, some day I'd become a real city boy.

CHAPTER 8

Will I like being a *Garden Farm Boy*?

After Dad parked our house trailer, he drove to a real estate office. He came back to our car with a man he introduced as Mr. Webb. Mr. Webb gave Dad a card with his home address and said he'd call Mrs. Webb to tell her we'd be their guests until we could move to the farm Dad had arranged to buy. When Mr. Webb went back to his office, Dad told us he'd given Mr. Webb one hundred and fifty of the two hundred dollars the taxi company paid for hitting Olive. Dad said he'd made earnest payment on a mortgage for a garden farm.

Mr. Webb's home was in a neighborhood that looked well-off. Dad went to the door and Mrs. Webb came out to our car, showing she was friendly like her husband. She led us upstairs to a bedroom with one bed. She said she had two canvas army cots in the garage for Olive and me to set up in the hallway. Back down in her kitchen, Mrs. Webb gave Olive and me cocoa and Mama and Dad coffee with a plate of store-bought cookies. She said she hoped we liked chicken-noodle soup, because that was what she was fixing for supper.

Dad set up the army cots for Olive and me before the Webb girls came home from school. Amy was in sixth grade and it seemed like her freckles got brighter when she was told that we were to stay in their home. Lorie, a third grader, just ran her hand through her dark hair and shrugged her shoulders. Amy asked her mother, "How long they gonna stay? You know my birthday party is Friday."

Mrs. Webb said, "Mr. Webb didn't say how long the Kennedys will be our guests, but if they are here Friday, Olive can go to your party, too. There won't be any boys at the party, Wallace, so maybe you'll be satisfied with just a piece of cake?" I answered, "Yes, Ma'am," because I'd learned from the Harkinson brothers how kids should talk to grown-ups.

We were still at the Webbs' until Saturday, so Olive went to Amy's birthday party.

Olive said Amy told the girls at the party that Olive was from a northern family that were old friends of her father.

Saturday, pulling our house trailer, we followed Mr. Webb a few miles south of Fort Smith before turning on a dirt road just before a little store. There were two homes each side of the road before a railroad crossing. After the tracks came a big old farmhouse and barn on the Fort Smith side and two more houses and a small farm on the south side. When we stopped, Mr. Webb said, "Here's as pretty a six-acre farm as you could find anywhere, and it's your farm, folks."

The front porch had two front doors, one that opened straight into the front room and the other into a hallway. Down the hall were three bedrooms and behind the living room was a small dining room and behind that the kitchen. There was a back door off the kitchen and a back door from the hallway. A wide-spread flowering tree that Mama said was a mulberry tree stood in the front yard. To the west was a wire fence that ran south past a little barn to fence in a little field that seemed waiting to be planted. Below the field was grass and Mill Creek.

Mr. Webb said to Dad he'd mail the bill of sale and mortgage deed just as soon as he got the mortgage registered. He and Dad shook hands and we never saw Grover H. Webb again.

But having a new farm was so exciting, we never thought about Mr. Webb for a while. We brought everything from the house trailer into the house and then Dad went to the little store on the corner and came back with groceries. He told us the couple that ran the corner store were friendly and promised we could have credit after we'd lived there a month. They told him the school was only a mile farther south down the highway.

Next day we went to Mill Creek School. Miss Lawson, who taught fifth grade, was head teacher. After she met us, she pointed out a desk for Olive and gave Dad some papers to fill out. She led Mama and me down to the first grade room and introduced me to my teacher, Miss Bailey. Miss Bailey asked about where I'd been in school and said she'd put me with the starting group of first graders, at a table with four other kids. Another table nearby had four kids around it, and on the window side of the room about a dozen kids sat in desks. After Mama left, Miss Bailey told the other students my name and gave me a worksheet for addition before she went over to teach the kids at the desks.

I hurried through the addition worksheet so I could listen to Miss Bailey lead the students at desks in a lesson about the State of Arkansas. She asked what was the capital of the state, and of course I knew it was Little Rock. I wished I could be part of that lesson and tell my classmates that I'd visited the state capitol and I'd seen the Old State House and the federal courthouse and Little Rock City Hall. But I wasn't with the students Miss Bailey was teaching.

At midmorning recess, a kid named Richie said, "Hey, Walrus, or whatever your name is, you wanna fight?" Before I could answer, Richie grabbed me around the chest and put his foot behind mine to trip me. But using lessons from the Harkinson brothers, I brought up my fists to push his arms away, and tackled him to the ground. I squatted on him, pinning down his shoulders, and asked "Enough?" Richie said, "Yeah," giving up.

Right away, a heavyset, red-haired kid came to me, "At noon, kid, you get me. Ol' Richie always tries to prove he's the toughest guy in first grade, but I already cleaned his clock. So now, you gotta fight me." I began to see being toughest was a mark of importance there at Mill Creek School.

After recess, our beginner's section of first grade had our reading lesson. Miss Bailey had us say phonics sounds on flash cards. Then she told us to turn to a page in our readers and asked who could tell the name of the lesson. I waited to see if another kid would raise his hand. No one did, so I raised mine and said the name of the lesson.

"That's right. Now who can read the first sentence of our lesson?" Again, I was the only one who put up his hand, and again I was called on. I read the first sentence and looked at Miss Bailey to see if she wanted me to go on. She nodded, so I read the two pages of that lesson. Miss Bailey gave me a smile and said, "Let's see who else can read today's lesson." Two kids kind of stumbled through the lesson and one girl read it fast, making me think she knew how to read.

That girl, whose name was Rose, raised her hand and told Miss Bailey she'd like to teach us some songs. None of the kids laughed, and Miss Bailey said, "All right, Rose." Her first song was "The Eensy Teensy Spider," which some of us knew and sang after she sang it. But the second song she sang, "There Was an Old Woman Lived under the Hill," must have been strange to all of us. Miss Bailey told Rose she could teach that song to us some other day.

At lunch in the school basement, I looked for Olive, because I had no lunch money. Richie, the kid I'd fought at recess, was right behind me, so I asked him how much lunch cost. He said, "Oh, it's free now. My brother said we're gonna have to pay for it starting next month, though."

I sat with Richie to eat pork and beans with chunks of wieners. We had a bottle of milk, too, and as much white bread as we wanted. No butter, though.

Richie asked me if I was going to fight Billy Cecil, and I said, "I guess I'm supposed to."

"You can back out, but then you'll be called chicken."

I told Richie I'd fight, because I wasn't chicken. So after lunch I went with Richie to look for Billy Cecil. When Billy Cecil saw me, he strutted up and asked if I was ready to fight. I said yeah, and he squared off at me, showing he wanted to fist fight. When Billy Cecil swung at me, I struck his fist away and hit him on the cheek with my right, then pounded his belly with both fists. As he doubled over, I brought both fists together up under his chin, jerking his head back. He started to cry, so I said, "Enough?" Billy Cecil nodded, sobbing. I put my arm around his shoulder and told him I didn't mean to hurt him much, but he was the one who started boxing.

Between sobs he said, "I know. I shoulda rassled you." He stopped crying, and squeezed his lips tight. "Tomorrow we'll fight again, only rassle. Okay?" I told him, sure, if that's what he wanted. And the next day I beat him in a kind of wrestling fight.

A kid named Mick Green told me I had to fight him next, even though he was in second grade. After I licked Mick Green, kids told me I'd have to fight the toughest kid in second grade, Dallas Blaylock. So Friday of that week at lunchtime I fought a kid who reminded me of B.O. Harkinson. He was tougher than any of those I'd already fought, but at the end of lunch hour, neither of us had said "Enough."

Next Monday, when I went into our classroom, a girl who sat with the other kids in desks came to me and said, "My brother is gonna beat you so bad!" Then she walked away. I asked a kid at our table who she was and he said, "Mary Blaylock. She's as smart as she is pretty."

Monday, at noon, when Dallas and I fought again, neither of us would say "Enough." Dallas said, "I'll fight you again, right after school."

That afternoon our whole first grade was taken to the stage of the gym. Miss Bailey told us we were going to have rhythm band with the district music teacher, Miss Carrol, to lead us. When Miss Bailey called our names, we went up to get an instrument. There were triangles to be struck with a little steel rod, hollowed sticks to clack together, bells to shake for jingles, and sticks called clog sticks with ridges to be rubbed together for crackles. There were little cymbals to be dinged together, and little whistles shaped like birds with water in their bellies that twittered when you blew them. Miss Carrol played the piano as she directed us, teaching us a song with words that told us when to use each rhythm band instrument. I was given both clog sticks and a bird, and thought the rhythm band was great fun, and it made me quit thinking about having to soon fight Dallas Blaylock again.

After school, as promised, Dallas and I fought. This time even a few girls joined the boys to watch us fight. I got in a good punch to Dallas's mouth that cut his lip, but a moment later, his fist slammed my nose, making it bleed. Two fifth grade boys came and grabbed Dallas and me to stop the fight. "You kids come with us into school. Miss Lawson is gonna fix you good."

The way Miss Lawson fixed us was to bawl us out and give us each a note to our parents. The note said if we fought again, on the school grounds or off, Miss Lawson would make us stay home. She said, "Now you two shake hands and say to each other, 'I'm sorry.'" We did, but it was more than a week before we talked to each other again.

On the way home that afternoon, Olive told me she knew about my fighting and being scolded by Miss Lawson. I showed her the note I was taking to Mama and Dad, and Olive said, "They will be so ashamed of you."

Billy Cecil Dillard was walking with us and said, "They shouldn't be ashamed a'tall. Wallace had to fight 'cause he's a new kid, and all the other kids have to know how tough he is."

Olive said, "That's just dumb. Nobody cares how tough anyone is if they never fight. Fighting is dumb."

Billy Cecil said, "That's not the way us fellas think about it."

I felt that Olive and Billy Cecil were both right. But I felt what Billy Cecil said was what I couldn't escape thinking. I wanted to feel proud of myself as a fighter among other guys.

Mama did scold me for fighting and causing Miss Lawson to send home a note, but Dad didn't scold me. At supper he told us a story about a time when he thought he had to stop a fight between two Donahue brothers. Dad said he was afraid they'd fight on until one of them was killed, so he hit them both on their heads with a doubletree.

Mama said, "You might have killed them both, hitting them with a doubletree."

Dad said, "Nah. They were both pure Irishmen." He laughed and poked me in the ribs.

Mama was eager to get our garden farming going, so Dad bought a Jenny mule and plowed and harrowed the cropland that stood between our yard and the grass along the creek. He bought a cow and some chickens, too, so it sort of seemed like we were farmers again. Garden farmers anyhow. I helped plant long rows of beans and peas and carrots and onions and potatoes, and I helped set out hundreds of strawberry plants. I especially looked forward to the strawberries.

After Miss Lawson stopped the fight between Dallas and me, I didn't have to fight anyone else at school, and I began to make a number of new friends. Herbert Minton, a fourth grader, said before school one day, "I saw you and your family at church in town last Saturday." Mama had been raised Seventh Day Adventist, so we had started going to that church in Fort Smith. Herbert said we should be friends, and that I'd like his brother Billy Bob, a second grader who would soon be back in school after breaking his leg.

A couple days later, Herbert told me he was inviting some of us to Billy Bob's birthday party after school next Friday, and that I should bring Billy Bob a present. When I told Mama about being invited to Billy Bob's party, she gave me half a dozen eggs and said I could trade them at the corner store for a present.

Kids at Mill Creek School had seasons for different kinds of play. Right then it was tops season with everyone playing spike tops, where all the players but one put their tops in a circle drawn in the dirt. The kid who was it would wind the string around his top to throw the spinning top at those set on the lines of a cross in the circle. If you'd knock one of the tops out of the circle, you'd get another chance, and the kid whose top was knocked out had to quit the game. I had traded a sandwich for a top to spin and was learning the game, so I traded the half-dozen eggs for a nice spike top to give to Billy Bob.

Mama wrapped and tagged the present for Billy Bob, and I took it with me Friday. I found Herbert before school and asked if I could walk with him to the party after school. But Herbert told me, "The party is off. Mama got called to the canning plant today. They're getting ready for the spinach run. But give me Billy Bob's present, and I'll take it to him." I felt so disappointed I wanted to tell Herbert I didn't have a present, so I could keep that spike top for myself. But I knew telling a lie would make me feel guilty, so I gave the present to Herbert.

One of my most interesting friends was Leroy Knight, a second grader who came to school every day barefoot, even when it was cold. He always wore bib overalls with a wide belt around his waist and a wide-brim, brown felt men's hat. Leroy and I got to be friends because in warm weather the school stopped serving lunch, and we'd eat our bag lunches on the playground. One day Leroy sat with me at lunchtime and said, "Would you give me the orange peels 'stead of throwing them in the trash?" I gave the peels to Leroy and was amazed to see him eat the peels with obvious pleasure.

I learned that Leroy lived west of Mill Creek, about a half mile from our house, up the hill towards Oklahoma. He said we should meet at the road that crossed the creek next Saturday morning and we could catch crawdads. Saturday Leroy pointed out crawdads along the creek bank. We caught about two dozen, dropping them in a pail Leroy brought. Leroy said his step-ma would cook the crawdads for us and give us some Johnnycake. Arkansas kids always called cornbread Johnnycake.

We walked through the woods by the creek to cross a field of potatoes. Up the hill we came to Leroy's unpainted house set on cement blocks, where we were greeted by three hounds. There was no glass in the windows, only open shutters, and instead of a door, there was hanging a braided rag rug. In the yard were two younger boys and in the house a baby girl in a cradle.

Leroy's stepmother was young and pretty, with long black hair that hung below her shoulders. She boiled some water and dropped the live crawdads in to cook. She said, "You boys eat first, then get back outside." She put a piece of cornbread on each of our plates, and after a couple minutes, put four crawdads on each plate. Leroy said, "The other crawdads are for my step-ma and little brothers." The crawdads were tasty, but they had scarcely any flesh once their shells were peeled off. After eating and a drink of cold water at the pump outside, Leroy and I went back to Mill Creek.

We saw a white-haired woman stringing a fish line across the creek as she waded in her dress in water up to her armpits. She asked us to hand her the short lines of baited hooks that lay on a rock at the side of the creek. We watched her tie those baited lines to the line crossing the creek. She told us it was her line, and she'd be back to take the fish off just before supper. She gave Leroy and me each a fishhook, some fish line, and the rest of the worms in a can of dirt. She told us there was a log that crossed the creek upstream where we should try our luck fishing.

We tried our luck, but didn't have any, so we decided to go back where the creek next to the road wasn't very deep, and hand-crawl in the creek. We left our clothes on the bank and were enjoying our pretend swimming until a car with two young couples pulled up and stopped. The man in the back seat said, "Hey, boys. Y'all come over to the car, and we'll give you each a nickel." The women in the car cackled laughs, so we knew these people wanted to make fools of us. We stayed in the water to hide our nakedness, and finally they gave up and drove away.

I kept running into what seemed like coarse rudeness. One day, walking home from school, a fifth grade kid called me over where he was playing. "Hey Yankee, I bet you fuck your sister."

I didn't know what fuck meant, but I was sure it was something bad, so I said, "Never." I asked Billy Cecil who was with me if he knew what fuck was.

He said, "My uncle told me it was like paddling a canoe upstream." I was sure that wasn't what the word meant to that fifth grade boy, so when Olive came home I asked her about the word.

"It's what parents do to have a baby. Mama told me last week she was afraid she was going to have another baby, but because we're so poor, she thought she'd have to do something to get rid of the baby before it's born."

I was dismayed. "Mama would never do that, would she?"

"Mama made me understand that women have to do that sometimes, if they're poor, and women can even die having a baby, especially when they're older, like Mama is. Mama told me she almost did something to get rid of you, before you were born, but she didn't, of course."

I felt shocked and went out under the mulberry tree to sit and think. The more I thought about Mama wanting to get rid of me, the worse it made me feel. I thought, if I'd never been born, Mama might want the baby she doesn't want now. I didn't know what I should do, but I started walking towards the highway. I thought, maybe I should catch a ride with someone, and just leave home, so I wouldn't be an expense to our family.

When I got as far as the railroad track, I decided to lie down right there, because I knew the train would be coming before too long. I lay down between the tracks with my head on one of the tracks, so the train would smash my head and kill me right away. I started to cry as I lay there, feeling so unloved and unwanted, I felt I should die.

But it wasn't long before Mama and Olive came where I was. Mama pulled me to my feet and whacked me across the butt a number of times. Then she burst into sobs and hugged me to her, telling me she loved me and would rather die than lose me. As we walked back toward home, she told Olive and me that she was not going to have a baby, that it was only that her period had been late. It had been a hard day for me. I had begun to feel confused and ignorant when that stupid kid called me Yankee and said that he bet I fucked my sister. Learning the meaning of the word seemed to steal away a lot of my self-assurance. By the time I got Mom's spanking, I was full of self-doubt, and even when she told me of her love and that she wasn't going to have a baby, I felt dumb and confused.

After we had put in our garden crops, Dad said he had to find a job in town. He came home happy, telling us he'd been hired by Fort Smith city to run a tractor and dredge to help make a golf course, just as he had in Little Rock. Mama said, "Poor people everywhere, but cities spend money to build golf courses for the rich." But we were all glad Dad had found work, because he'd bought furniture on time, and had to make monthly payments.

Some woman in an office in Fort Smith called Mama to ask if a boy and girl could be our foster kids for a month. One was a boy of fourteen named Roberto, but who wanted to be called Junior, and the girl was Rosetta, a twelve-year-old. I had to share my bedroom with Junior, but he slept on the couch from our house trailer. Rosetta slept with Olive.

Mama said the woman who called told her Junior and Rosetta didn't have to start school at Mill Creek, because Easter vacation would take up one week, and the foster kids would be back in Fort Smith schools as soon as their parents got out of jail. Junior spent a lot of time drawing pictures of women in their underwear, and he and Rosetta sang songs I'd never heard before. One was called *La Cucaracha*, and had Spanish words.

I was beginning to learn something at Mill Creek School. Miss Bailey had put me in the part of first grade that had desks. She often called on me, and made me feel part of that class. I was also learning new things from other kids. In March, top-spinning season had given way to stilt-walking season, then marble season.

But when kite-flying season started, a heavy rain came that lasted day and night for five days. Mill Creek flooded, and water rushed over our garden crops. When the rain stopped, our strawberry plants and the peas and beans had been washed away, so we had to plant new crops when the field dried out enough.

Although the water had left our field, Mill Creek was still about twice as high as it had been before the flood. With Junior and Rosetta, Olive and I went down to the creek to look at it. At the stretch of the creek where I'd been able to hand-crawl before it flooded, the water was deep enough for a real swimming hole. Junior stripped down to his underpants, and I followed him. Olive and Rosetta tucked their dresses into their underpants, and we all waded in.

The creek had a fast current, but Junior told us it was shallow enough to wade across. Olive lost her balance in the current and started to be swept downstream. Thank goodness, Junior could swim. He caught up with Olive and pulled her to the creek bank, coughing and shaking, but all right. We ended our creek exploration that day. In another week, Junior and Rosetta went back to their parents.

On my May 5 birthday, Mama told me I should go to meet Dad at the corner of the highway. By this time, Dad was working as suit cutter in a clothing factory located near the south end of Fort Smith, so he walked home from work each day. When I met him, Dad handed me a softball and a bat with my initials he'd carved into its bottom as he walked home. It had become softball season at Mill Creek School, so no birthday present could have made me happier. I was proud to take my bat and softball to school and ask other kids to play softball with me.

One day Olive brought one of her classmates home to play ball with us. Reba said she loved to play softball, but the next day at school, Reba told other students that Olive's talk and manners, that had made other kids think she was better off than most kids, was all phony. She said Olive's home was just plain and kind of run-down, which it was, of course.

That was a mean thing that Reba did, and it made Olive feel bad. Mom and Dad had raised Olive and me to never be mean, but to be generous to others, even if we were a hard-up family.

The end of our school year at Mill Creek turned out to be a kind of honor to our family. The last week of school an operetta called "Moonlight Town" was presented. Olive was the soloist who called Princess Glory down from her home on the moon to visit Moonlight Town. And I was part of the operetta, too, singing in a trio with two girls a song called, "I'm Forever Blowing Bubbles." And when Dad and Mama came to see the operetta, Miss Lawson and Miss Bailey both told them everyone at Mill Creek school was sorry to see Olive and me leave, because we'd been just the kind of students Mill Creek needed. The final honor to our family was that Mama won the lottery quilt that had a map of Mill Creek community stitched on it.

The reason we were leaving was that the sheriff brought a couple to our house saying that the mortgage papers sent to us by Grover H. Webb were a fraud, just like a couple of other deals Webb had made before he disappeared from Fort Smith. So Dad said we had no choice but to leave Mill Creek and Arkansas, and give up our home to the couple who had a genuine title to the place.

Dad sold all the vegetables that were ready for market, and he sold our Jenny mule and cow and the chickens. The furniture he'd bought on time was taken back to the store. We packed the house trailer with the belongings we had left and headed back to North Dakota, only to find that the Dodge needed a new clutch if it was to pull the house trailer. We found a tenement house in north Fort Smith for a few days while the clutch was replaced. Dad found some day labor unloading boxcars for a lumberyard. Two guys working with him, learning that Dad had a car, tried to convince him to be their driver for a bank robbery they were planning. Dad said he told them he had a family and wasn't about to risk himself for part of the robbery money.

In the tenement house was another Kennedy family with two daughters, each about the age of Olive and me. So we had playmates during the week we were there. Those Kennedy girls wanted to show us how to have fun in ways we knew wouldn't please our folks. So we turned down their invitations to sex play. But Olive did submit to Noreen giving her a fancy makeup and hairdo one day. And one day Clare showed me a good time visiting stables where horses that pulled milk delivery carts were kept.

Seeing those horses made me think that garden farming wasn't nearly as much fun as real farming in North Dakota. I didn't know if I'd ever like being a garden farm boy. When we were on our way again, I asked Dad if we'd go back to farming with Grandpa, and he said no, that he had no money to start farming and would find some other work where we'd live in Cando. As we crossed the border from Arkansas to Missouri, Dad said, "By God, we're finally out of this damned state. I'll never come back to Arkansas again."

Mama said, "Well, you don't have to curse about it."

But I felt I understood why Dad swore at Arkansas. Those Roves, the people who live now where Olive was born, were awful. The Tresvants were really nice, but showed if you weren't white in Arkansas you were even worse off than other poor folks. We'd come south for Olive's health, but as soon as we got here she was almost killed by a taxicab. Our hopes for being garden farmers had been ruined by Grover H. Webb, someone Dad had trusted. Dad said, "We know North Dakota is a better place to raise our kids." Olive said she was going to be happy to go back to Cando School, but I felt disappointed that I wouldn't be a farm boy again.

As we drove back towards North Dakota, I spent hours thinking about what I'd seen and learned in the year we'd been traveling and living in Arkansas. I looked at road maps, tracing our trip down and recalling all the people we'd met and places we'd visited. Maybe everyone else in the family was chasing memories, too, because it was a quiet trip, and not much happened. Dad bought a bamboo pole and the other stuff to fish with, and every time we stayed near a lake or river he caught us fish to eat. He tried to teach me how to fish, but not once did I ever catch a fish.

The place that seemed most fun to me was Swope Park in Kansas City, Missouri. It was the first time I'd ever visited a zoo, and I was amazed that chimpanzees acted so much like us people. And Swope Park had fireworks on July 4 that were really beautiful.

Iowa seemed to be the place Mama would most like to live. She said, "Look at how black the soil here is, just beautiful. These farms and small towns are so well kept. They make Iowa the prettiest state we've been through." I couldn't think Iowa was the prettiest state, but maybe Iowans took better care of things than most people did. I guessed Mama was probably sick and tired of the careless ways of folks in Arkansas, and that's why Iowa looked so good to her.

When we got to the southwestern part of Minnesota, I thought that was a beautiful place. Being all prairie, it looked quite a bit like North Dakota, but with more hills and trees and lakes. And the small towns, if not as well taken care of as Iowa's small towns, seemed to me to have more going on. What impressed me most was that the drought we had lived in when we left North Dakota a year before seemed to be missing there in Minnesota.

And the southeastern edge of North Dakota seemed drought-free, too. When we got near Fargo, Dad drove onto a road along a grove of trees that lined the Red River. A dark, curly-haired kid about fifteen or sixteen, I'd guess, ran alongside our car, pointing at Dad's bamboo fishing pole, yelling, "Gimme that fish hook, gimme that fish hook." We learned that he was a gypsy kid when we came to the gypsy camp that he ran into. As soon as Dad stopped, women and kids and a few gypsy men surrounded our car and trailer house. They all acted friendly and happy that we'd come. Dad talked with some of the men and drove on past the gypsy village for us to park and stay overnight.

Mama and Olive both had an old gypsy woman in a tent tell their fortunes by reading the palms of their hands. Girls about Olive's age decorated her with their own beads and bracelets. I was invited to pitch coins for keeps by some gypsy boys, but I begged off, saying that my dad told me I should never gamble. That made the gypsy kids hoot with laughter. Dad came back to the house trailer carrying a roast chicken that he said one of the gypsy men gave him. Dad said the men all seemed to drive new cars, but they didn't say where they got their money.

That night the gypsies had a big campfire and cooked what looked like a feast for the whole village. They kept the fire going and began playing music with violins, guitars, and accordions, and soon women and girls were dancing, and even some of the men and boys. I thought gypsies were about the happiest bunch of people I'd ever been around, and wondered why people everywhere don't have as much fun as gypsies do. Their party kept going way after we went to bed.

Next day we drove into the biggest farmyard I'd ever seen. It was the Thompson Farm, where harvest season was beginning, and Dad had learned that harvest hands were being hired. We were moved into one of the six furnished cottages for families of hired hands. We stayed on the Thompson farm for almost two weeks, and were treated very well. There was a grandson of owner Thompson named Howie, a couple years younger than me. He made me his playmate right away, and his mother asked Olive into the big family home to sing while she played sheet music on a grand piano. We were treated so well by the Thompsons, I began to think that even if they are rich, some people may still be good people.

When we left the Thompson farm early one morning, Dad's goal was to reach Cando by suppertime, and we did. Mama had written Aunt Hattie that we were coming and when Dad drove into the alley behind Aunt Hattie's, the whole Kensinger family gave us a loving welcome. My two oldest cousins, Russell and David, were already grown men, both home on vacation from Minneapolis where they were both in Bible colleges, studying to be ministers. They made me feel important by asking me lots of questions about where we'd been and what I'd done. They even asked me to sing "Arkansas, I Salute Thee" when I told them I'd learned the state song in school.

At supper we learned that the Pentecostal church that Aunt Hattie had helped start had grown much bigger. Russell and David said Pentecostal churches were growing fast all over the country, and that was one reason they were studying to be ministers. Veora had just graduated from high school and was working as "central," the night operator for the Cando telephone exchange. She was saving money to go to a Bible college, too. Cousin Jimmy had just entered high school and cousin Vesper would be a fifth grader.

Aunt Hattie told us that Uncle Jesse still had his well-drilling business, but, shaking her head, she said Uncle Jesse had opened a beer joint and pool hall on Main Street. We learned that our oldest cousin,

Rosamond, who had attended the University of North Dakota, was now in Washington, D.C., as a secretary in the Department of Agriculture, but was coming home soon for a visit.

Dad got work right away as a harvest hand in the crew of Willard Smelzer, a neighbor when Dad had been farming with Grandpa. Aunt Delia and Grandpa Kennedy welcomed us, too, and Aunt Dee was happy for Mama to help take care of Grandma, whose diabetes seemed worse. So Olive and I with Mama moved into the big home on Grandpa's farm for the several weeks until school would begin. I was happy to be back on Grandpa's farm again.

When cousin Rosamond came home, one day she brought her boyfriend, John Anderson, to meet everyone at Grandpa's farm. When she told us they were getting married and John would leave farming with his brother to live in Washington, D.C., Grandpa told them they were "plum crazy." But Rosamond said, "No, Grandpa, we're peach crazy."

The last two weeks before school began, Mama was hired to help cook for threshers on the Lichty-Maust farm. The weekend before school started, we moved to Cando, right downtown into a three-room apartment next to Pollack's Barber Shop. Dad got a job with the Public Works Administration, helping to put in Cando's first sewer system.

CHAPTER 9

Now I'm going to be a real *Cando Kid*

So, now I could start to be a real Cando kid. Being a new kid at Cando School didn't mean I had to fight anyone. The Cando kids were, if anything, bigger and tougher than kids in Arkansas, but didn't seem to have to prove it like the Arkansas kids did. My main challenge was to shed my southern accent if I was going to be a real Cando kid.

My second grade teacher, Miss Frost, put me at first in one of the slower reading groups, but after two days she moved me into the best reading group. I thought I might want to be friends with kids in this reading group. One was John MacDonald. I was sure he was son of the

Second Grade class of Cando School, 1936

doctor that had put the scar in my forehead. Others were Melby Miller whose dad was Superintendent Miller, and Llewellyn Tewksbury, whose name must have been hard to learn to spell, and Sammy Louis King, who lived only one block away from our apartment. Girls in that group included Betty Belzer, who acted like she was our class leader, and her friends seemed to be Joyce Martin and Jeannine Gleeson, and Phyllis Jean Burkhart and Elgie Jacobson.

Sammy Louis King lived closest to us, so he was the first classmate I played with. He had two older brothers who, like Sammy, were crazy about sports. In the vacant lot next to the Kings' house, they played football, and I joined them in games with five or six kids on each side.

In the schoolyard before school started, bigger boys played a game called free-for-all and let anybody join in. One guy would kick the ball into the bunch, and whoever got the ball would run towards the goal with everyone trying to tackle him. Then he'd throw the ball up in the air and somebody else would run until tackled. I really liked that game, because you had the chance to tackle lots of bigger guys. One day an eighth grader said I was a good tackler, and that made me feel good.

I saw right away that going to high school football games was part of being a real Cando kid. Cando Cubs was a good football team that fall, and might have gone undefeated if their best pass receiver, Warren Jacobson, hadn't broken his leg. I went to all the games on the field across the highway from the high school and soon learned the names of all the guys on the Cubs team. Jim Whalen was quarterback, and Frank Primeau was fullback, who carried the ball much of the time. That year, Frank, or "Poochie," as his friends called him, was named All State in football. I learned that Frank Primeau's dad had moved the family to Cando from the Turtle Mountain Indian Reservation so his kids could go to Cando School, and I thought that Frank's dad deserved some kind of trophy, too.

Our teacher Gladys Frost was friendly and pleasant, but strict about what kids did. One day she took a kid named Georgie Geary out to the sink in the hall and washed his mouth out with soap. Georgie had called another kid a son-of-a-bitch right in class. A couple days later, though, I felt sorry for Georgie. He had an accident during school and after school he had to hear kids chant, "Georgie wet his pants, Georgie wet his pants."

Miss Frost showed how friendly she could be to me one day. She let me show off by singing to the whole class two songs I'd learned in Arkansas. One was "Boola Boola," and another was "A Spanish Cavalier." When I went back to my seat after singing, Betty Belzer whispered to me, "I liked that song about the Spanish Cavalier because my grandma lives in Cavalier." When I learned that Cavalier was a town in northeastern North Dakota, I wondered why it took the name of a Spanish soldier.

Three things made my year in second grade seem special. The first was meeting Miss Jolliffe, the fourth grade teacher who was also school librarian. Miss Jolliffe always gave me a big smile when I checked out two books each week, and soon began suggesting books to read. Her help made library day my favorite day of the school week.

The second special thing was being in the all-school operetta, *The Old Lady Who Lived in a Shoe*. The lead character, of course, had many children in her shoe house. I was a twin to a third grade girl named Susanne Menness. Susanne and I were the same height and both had dark brown hair. Susanne had brown eyes that sparkled, and she had a lively way of talking that was full of laughter. Our costumes were green flannel pajamas because the only scenes we were in were when all the Old Lady's children lined up for a song before being put to bed. The stage set was a stack of bunks where Susanne and I bunked side by side. The director had us hug before climbing into bed, and hugging Susanne every day at operetta practice made me tingle.

The third special thing also involved Susanne. All students were given the California Achievement Tests, and several weeks after the tests, I was asked to go to Superintendent Miller's office. Susanne had been called there, too, and outside the door she laughed and said, "Do you think we'll get to be twins again?" Superintendent Miller had us sit together on a bench as he leaned against his desk. He said, "I called you two here because you both scored way beyond your grade levels on the achievement test, especially in vocabulary and reading comprehension. It's your scores in vocabulary that interest me most, because you both scored at the eighth grade level in that test. Can you give me some reason why you know the meanings of so many words?"

Susanne said, "Well, I live with my grandparents who have guests for dinner two or three times a week, and after dinner they sit and talk about all sorts of things. I think I learn a lot of words from being with them. I ask what a word means if I don't know it."

I told the superintendent about traveling to Arkansas the year before, and said that the trip gave me the chance to read lots of road signs and lots of newspapers. I told him I thought finding new words was fun. Superintendent Miller told us to keep up the good work and sent us back to our classrooms.

When winter brought snow, Dad bought me a sled at Sitz Hardware. After supper I'd run and drop onto the sled to slide up and down the street. There was little traffic, so the street was safely mine. One day at school, Joyce Martin asked if I'd like to go sledding with her. When I met her in front of her home she introduced me to Ramona Holien, a third grader and her neighbor. Sledding with Joyce and Ramona made me feel special. But I think I made a mistake in inviting them for cocoa in our apartment one evening, because after that, they didn't seem to want to go sledding with me. Anyhow, I learned that the best place to go sledding was creamery hill near the water tower. On Saturdays I'd go there with lots of other kids and we'd make snow jumps on the tracks downhill to make sliding down the hill scary.

When spring came, we didn't have seasons of play like at Mill Creek School, but we did play marbles, in games of chase and games of pot. We played for keeps, of course, and I learned to hold my own and won some pretty shooters. Cando Drug had a whole shelf built to hold marbles and going there to buy one or two at a time was a treat, even if Mrs. Martineau, the druggist's wife, always stood close by to see that you didn't pocket any marbles without paying for them.

When school let out for Easter vacation Dad drove Mama and Olive and me with Aunt Hattie and Vesper to Grandpa's farm because Grandma had suffered a stroke. Mama told us strokes were common among people with diabetes. Early Good Friday morning, Aunt Dee came upstairs to tell us three kids that Grandma had gone to meet Jesus. After Grandma's body came back from the undertaker, her casket stood in Grandpa's parlor two days while neighbors came to pay their respects. The sight of Grandma in the casket and the smell of flowers nearby, just like the funeral service at Zion Church of the Brethren, gave me a strange, sickening feeling. That first funeral made me wish I'd never have to go to another one.

Not long after Easter, we moved from the downtown apartment into the home of Mrs. Skinner, because Mama was hired to be her full-time nurse. It was a nice big home, but Mrs. Skinner's daughter by her first marriage made my life there uneasy. Miss Laura Williams seemed sure she could improve Olive and me. She'd tell us what not to do as we ate. She'd tell us to leave our shoes in the entryway, and not to leave our fingerprints on the dusted furniture. She always asked me questions about school and made me look at pictures and her collections of stuff like lodge pins or political campaign buttons while she talked about their importance.

Though the move to the Skinner house gave me mixed feelings, the good thing about living there was being close to some great playmates. Melby Miller and his sister Ann lived just down the street. The three of us played we were knights who had to capture the barns behind homes on our block as castles. We traded Big Little Books, too. I soon decided that kids on the south side of town were a lot more fun than the northside kids. The Hinkle brothers, Jimmy, Stuart, and Pat, lived up on the corner and showed me how to make rubber guns to use in war games. John MacDonald lived only three blocks away, and John was always generous about sharing his wealth of toys and games.

After the city sewer system was all put in, Dad lost his PWA job, so he became a McConnon Home Products salesman. Dad put shelves in the back seat of our Dodge and drove all over Towner County selling spices, nectars, and other home and kitchen needs. After the school year ended, Dad said one day, "I'm going to be selling up around Rolette the next couple of days and can go to the farm where King lives now, if you want to go see him."

I was thrilled to think I could see King again. As soon as we drove up to Ralph Girard's farm, I could see it would be a happy place for King. All the farm buildings were in good shape, and the big farmhouse looked clean as a bone. Ralph Girard welcomed us and told me King was down in the pasture where Girard's son was fixing the fence. I asked if the pasture was close enough for King to hear me if I called to him, and Girard said, "Try it." I shouted toward the pasture, "Wah wah, wah wah, King." In a couple of minutes the collie I had trained and played with came running. He jumped up with his paws on my shoulders and licked my face. I pressed my face next to King's and hugged him and petted him with joy. Mr. Girard invited us to have

Rejoined with King on the Girard farm near Rollette

supper and spend the night at his farm, so I had several hours with King. Fourth grader Elise Girard told me she would always take good care of King.

That summer, since Mama was nursing Mrs. Skinner seven days a week and what seemed like all twenty-four hours each day, Olive and I spent much of the summer with Grandpa and Aunt Dee on the farm. While I missed playing with my friends in town, I liked being a farm boy again. One of my regular jobs was milking the Guernsey Daisy and feeding the chickens.

Grandpa carved me a whistle from a willow branch, which was a nice surprise gift.

At haying season, I earned my first pay as a farmhand. Ole Stenerson, Grandpa's renter, farming on shares, was haying on the home quarter. I went out to the field to watch, and Ole offered me the job of driving the horses that lifted the hay stacker. Ole's brother Oscar used the hay rake to pile the hay on the tines of the hay stacker, which was designed to lift the hay from the ground to build a stack. The first three times I drove the team very well, and Ole praised my work and gave me a quarter for a good job. But the very next time, I drove the team too fast and some of the hay was lifted right over the stack to fall on the other side. Ole said, "Give me back my quarter," laughing and not taking the quarter when I handed it to him. But he said Oscar should drive the stacker team.

The best thing about being on the farm that summer was riding Laura, the Morgan mare, who was a beautiful, smart old black horse with a star on her forehead. I could go to the pasture, grasp Laura above the nostrils, kiss her head, and lead her to a fence post. Climbing the fence, I could jump on Laura's back, and without bridle direct her with nudges from my knees to go where I wished. I could even lie down on her back and feel safe, knowing she would carry me gently to the barnyard. Unlike Laura Williams, this Morgan mare was the Laura I loved to be with.

Just before school started, the Schneider family moved into the house where the Hinkle boys had lived. When I met Grant Schneider, a year older than me, he asked me why the house across the alley from theirs was not being lived in. I told him the banker's family had lived there and maybe the new banker's family would soon move in. Grant suggested that the two of us build a cave in the space between the lilac hedge and the honeysuckles that ran along the alley. We dug a hole, covered it with boards and corrugated cardboard and old rugs and the sod we'd cut away, and had us a neat cave. When the banker's family moved in, their daughter, Marge Rendahl, same age as Grant, claimed the cave as hers, but said Grant and I could share it with her. We three became good pals.

Third grade brought Mildred Carter, a new teacher who had trouble keeping order. When students misbehaved, Miss Carter whacked their hands with a ruler or their butts with a yardstick. That kind of punishment wasn't to be accepted by Helen Lavendure one day. Helen's family was one of several Ojibwa families that had moved to Cando from the Turtle Mountain Reservation. When Miss Carter tried to whack her, Helen fought back, soon to be joined by her brother Francis. The two gave Miss Carter a tough fight, and Helen ran to the office for Superintendent Miller, who came to end the fight. I smiled when Superintendent Miller asked the Lavendure kids as well as Miss Carter to tell him what had happened. He did nothing to punish Helen and Francis for fighting with their teacher.

Superintendent Miller was as unusual a man as he was a superintendent. Because I was a friend of Melby and Ann, I visited the Miller home enough to get to know the whole Miller family. I learned that Paul Miller had graduated from Harvard, where he had been a track star, and was on the U.S. team in the Olympics of 1932 at Los Angeles.

He had a master's degree in education. What brought him to Cando was that he had married a Radcliffe student who was raised in Rolla, a town north of Cando. Melby had three pretty older sisters. The oldest sister, Betty, joined her parents in a string quartet that played for its own enjoyment. Superintendent and eighth grade teacher Ruth Linn played violin. Mrs. Miller played viola, and Betty played cello. Melby invited me to attend one of their home concerts. Hearing a live classical concert made me realize there was music more deeply beautiful than the hymns and popular songs I heard most of the time. That concert stirred my imagination about what I would most want to listen to in music.

Melby became the friend I spent most time with, much of that time spent working with him to follow directions from his erector set. We built many complicated little constructions we could make run with an electric motor.

My next most frequent playmate was John MacDonald. Besides sharing his many toy possessions, John and I would sometimes go to his dad's office on Main Street to ask for money for treats. If Doc MacDonald yielded us money, John and I would go to Tillie's Confectionery, not far from the doctor's office. I thought Tillie looked a little like the gypsy women I'd seen. She wore dangling earrings, long hanging necklaces, and many bracelets and rings. She wore lots of makeup, too. John told me Tillie was veterinarian Doc McPike's girlfriend, but that McPike's mother wouldn't let him marry Tillie. Often when we were sitting in Tillie's shop drinking a cherry Coke or lime phosphate, there'd be two or three young women dressed in pretty bathrobes at a nearby table drinking Cokes. John told me these were "call girls" who worked upstairs at Tillie's when men paid them to go to bed with them. I'd never known about "call girls" before.

Several things became important to me in third grade. Football, organized by us kids and played in some vacant lot, was a game I loved. Games were often put together spontaneously, having no adults to coach us or referee. We could always settle disputes by deciding what was fair. A few girls played football with us. One who played as well as any boy was Marge Rendahl. I knew I was one of many guys who wished Marge could be my sweetheart, but Marge insisted on being a friendly chum to everyone.

As a sports fan I went to all the home high school games. The Cubs weren't as good in either football or basketball as the year before, but like other kids, I cheered and admired them.

Important to me in school was having Loretta Murray, who taught seventh grade, change places when Miss Carter taught seventh grade music. Miss Murray, with bright red hair that matched her sparkly disposition, taught us nature study and art. One fine fall day, she took our class on a walking field trip to identify by leaf and bark and shape the various trees in Cando. Also that fall, when national elections drew near, Miss Murray had us hold a mock election. Before we voted, Miss Murray told us that Ben Lemke, North Dakota's U.S. Representative, was running for President on an independent party ticket. She suggested that loyal North Dakotans might want to vote for their own loyal son. But John MacDonald and I had already talked over the upcoming election and agreed that Franklin D. Roosevelt must be reelected, because Alf Landon would surely return the country to hard times. Most of our classmates voted for Landon, a few for Lemke, and Roosevelt got only a few votes, too.

I knew that except for Mom and Dad, all our other relatives thought Democrats were sinful and Republicans were good Christians. So I went to hear the campaign speeches of Republican candidates at the Memorial Building and learned that if Republicans were Christian, they were also hypocrites. I was given a card from the Republican Party that was supposed to be a joke about Senator Gerald P. Nye, who was supported by the Non-Partisan League. The card read, "Mrs. Nye won't let Gerald P(ee) in the house." Reading that made me disgusted with the Republican party.

Not long after Roosevelt was reelected, Aunt Hattie organized a butchering day on Grandpa's farm. Three of Grandpa's pigs were to be butchered, one for Aunt Hattie's family, one for our family, and one for Grandpa and Aunt Dee. Uncle Charlie and Dad were to do the butchering in trade for their pigs. I spent most of the day watching the pigs first get shot and their throats slit, then get scalded in boiling water to make it easier to scrape off their hair, and get split open to begin the butchering.

I saw something happen that helped me understand why Dad and Grandpa didn't easily get along. After Uncle Charlie shot his pig and handed the rifle to Dad for shooting his pig, Dad handed the rifle back to Charlie. I heard Grandpa say, "What kind of man are you, can't even kill a pig for your family?" But I knew Dad hated to kill anything and owned no guns for hunting, and I felt, even if Dad wasn't what Grandpa thought of as manly, he had the right feelings about animals.

Grandpa's main job on butchering day was heading the sausage making. So when the pigs were gutted, Grandpa cut away the flappy parts of the pigs' bellies for a pan that, with another pan filled with guts, was put on a sled to pull to the house where the sausage was made. Mom and Aunt Hattie scraped clean the pigs' guts and Aunt Dee helped Grandpa make the seasoned sausage at the sausage grinder. I watched the sausage making for a few minutes but went back where the scalded pigs were hanging to drain and cool in the air before being taken to the washhouse for cutting and wrapping as pork.

When Grandpa came back to get more meat and guts, I helped him load the pans on the sled. When he began pulling the sled, I decided to help him by pushing the sled as he pulled it.

On the icy path alongside the washhouse, Grandpa slipped and fell, crying out with pain. Dad and Uncle Charlie ran to him and sent me into the house for the women. Aunt Dee called Dr. Olafson, because Doc MacDonald had shot himself in the foot while duck hunting with Uncle Jesse.

As Dr. Olafson worked on Grandpa's broken thigh, I told everyone that I felt to blame for Grandpa's accident, saying that I'd maybe pushed the sled too hard as he pulled it. Dr. Olafson looked up from his work and turning to everyone watching, said, "Don't let that boy think he's to blame for his Grandpa's broken leg. That would be a hard thing for him to live with." I watched Dr. Olafson put Grandpa's leg in traction, rigging a rope with a bucket of sadirons across a two-by-four that rested on the headboard and footboard of the bed. The doctor said Grandpa's leg would mend so long as he kept his leg in traction. I told Dr. Olafson I wanted to be a doctor some day.

Cando had an indoor ice rink, and a men's independent hockey team that played other teams from North Dakota and Canada. Knowing that I wanted to skate, Aunt Ella gave me a pair of clamp skates that had been Rosamond's. So I learned to skate, even though my clamp skates often came unclamped from the soles of my laced boots. Jim Strachen, town constable, was also the ice rink caretaker. He organized hockey teams for third, fourth, fifth, and sixth graders and scheduled after-school games between the teams. Mom made me shin guards out of old overalls, with pocket inserts for board strips from peach crates. It was hard playing with clamp skates, but anyhow, I knew I'd never play hockey as well as football.

Cando also had a men's independent basketball team. The basketball team organized kids in grades three through six as "pee-wee teams" to play a short game before the regular games. I played, not very well, on the third grade team. But I liked going to games of both of the men's independent teams.

Walking to school against a north wind when it's fifty degrees below zero is bound to give a kid frostbite, and although I wore a thick stocking cap, my ears got frostbite one day. Teachers met all of us with frostbite at the school door where they had buckets of snow to rub on our frostbitten ears or cheeks to thaw them down slowly and make the frostbite less painful.

Spring at Cando School was always marked with a music festival presented in the theater of Cando Auditorium. This year, third and fourth grades together followed the theme of worldwide music with a song and dance that represented Holland. Our mothers used patterns to make us Dutch costumes. One song was about windmills, so we moved our arms like windmills, facing each other, and one song was about canals, so we moved across the floor as if we were couples skating. But the most fun of the festival was when we were waiting offstage during practice times. We had to sit on the few benches backstage, so girls had to sit on boys' laps. I was lucky to get Susanne Menness to sit on my lap.

We were all hoping for Grandpa's broken thigh to mend. And it did seem to be mending until one day when he was fed up with lying in bed. Grandpa undid the rope that gave his leg traction and shifted to the bed's edge to test his walking ability. He crashed to the floor and never got out of bed again.

In June after my third grade, Olive and I spent several weeks on Grandpa's farm. One day at Grandpa's bedside, Olive asked, "How do you feel, Grandpa?"

Grandpa smiled at her and said, "I feel with my fingers."

While there on the farm, I knew the fight between Joe Louis and heavyweight champion Jim Braddock was coming up. The closest neighbors, Gullicksons, had a good radio, so I asked if I could join them to listen to the fight. I was so excited when Joe Louis kayoed Braddock that I went back to Grandpa's and wrote in a notebook every round of the fight just as I remembered it. Boxing seemed to me the manliest of sports, and I thought Joe Louis the manliest of boxers.

Most of that summer, 1937, I spent in town. One day Melby and I were playing cowboys, making our pretend horses jump across pretend rocks as we'd seen them do in cowboy movies. We pretended a concrete flowerpot was a tall rock, and we both tried to jump it at the same time. Colliding with Melby, my forehead struck the concrete, giving me quite a cut. Paul Miller drove me to Doc MacDonald's office where I got seven stitches crossing my left eyebrow. The scar of that cut never really disappeared.

I spent a lot of time with Bobby and Dennis Brending that summer. Many days a bunch of us played stockyard tag, a game Bob Brending organized. When the stockyard along the railway was empty, we could swing the gates open or shut in the loading chute and between the pens. Swinging the gates to make escapes added to the fun. The rule was that we had to stay on the heavy wood plank walls and gates, never touching the ground. Each kid caught joined the guy who was it until everyone got caught.

Bob and Dennis Brending also led me to go swimming in Reid's coulee south of town. One day, before I learned to swim, I waded into a drop-off, and was rescued by Bob Brending. I vowed that day I'd learn to swim and became a swimmer before the summer was over.

Another thing I did with the Brendings was caddy at the golf course. Bob was Phil Belzer's favorite caddy, and since Phil often played with the Pederson brothers, Dennis and I caddied for Mel and Harry Pederson.

One highlight of the 1937 summer came in late July when Cando merchants held a "Thanks to Customers Day." A side street was blocked off, to serve big slices of free watermelons on a long wood tray. Merchants and their employees cut and passed out the watermelon, giving us kids slices as big as slices they gave grown-ups. The big event of the day was to let loose a greased pig that, if caught, became the property of whoever caught it. Lots of men tried, and most got greasy and dirty before someone held on to and won the pig. There were also competitions for eating raw eggs and baked pies. I watched one chicken farmer crack and swallow a dozen raw eggs at top speed to win that prize, and I watched several men and boys gobble down blueberry pies without holding onto the pie tin.

As always, John MacDonald shared what he had when I played with him. One day he let me take his bike for the afternoon. After supper when I was taking his bike back to him, I rode by Roy Canfield's house and was attacked by his dog. With a deep growl, the dog lunged up and sank his teeth into my left knee. Dad got Doc MacDonald to return to his office and take fourteen stitches in my knee. Doc followed the practice of having the dog tested for rabies before giving me a tetanus shot. Even though veterinarian McPike determined the dog wasn't rabid, Roy Canfield had McPike put the dog to sleep. I felt guilty that the dog had to die because of me.

The most memorable event of that summer was what happened after an evening of "tin can over." A bunch of kids often gathered to play after supper in the long daylight until the nine p.m. curfew whistle blew from the firehouse. One night the whistle blew right after we had all run to hide. I saw kids scatter to go home, but I ran in to kick the can anyhow. Just as I got there, Susanne Menness came running, too. We both laughed instead of kicking the can, and Susanne said, "I don't have to run home when the whistle blows." I said I didn't either.

Susanne's grandparents lived three and a half blocks from Mrs. Skinner's house where we were still living. So the two of us walked together to the Thompson house, but instead of going in, Susanne said, "Let's sit on the garden fence rail and talk for awhile." We had a lovely talk for about an hour. I told Susanne about living first on Grandpa's farm and about our trip to Arkansas. Susanne told me about her dad and mother getting a divorce and about her mother being a teacher in Fargo. She said she thought she was better off living with her grandparents right now, but that her mother came up often on weekends to be with her. Susanne said, "Well, I'm going in now, but I'll always remember this good talk we had."

As soon as Susanne was in the house, I broke into a joyous run, all the way to my bed in the barn behind Mrs. Skinner's house. I had talked Mom into convincing Laura Williams that I could make a bed in the barn loft filled with surplus furniture and sleep there that summer.

More than one night, I would go over the talk between Susanne and me, hearing in my mind everything we said to each other.

All in all, the summer of 1937 seemed to have been filled with events that made me happy and sure that I'd become a real Cando kid.

CHAPTER 10

Would I have to become *A Church Member*?

Towards the end of summer, Mrs. Skinner had another stroke and died. So Mama's nursing there ended, and we had to move from Laura Williams's house. While Dad was finding a new place for us to live, Mama was hired to nurse another old woman who had suffered a stroke and lived just a few miles south of Grandpa's farm. So Olive and I went back to the farm again.

Shortly before school began, Zion Church of the Brethren held a week of revival services led by an evangelist preacher from a Brethren college. Aunt Delia wanted us to go to the revival services every night, and Olive agreed to go and said I should go, too. One night Olive and other kids her age answered the evangelist's plea to come up to the altar. Kids twelve and up were expected to join the Brethren Church and be baptized, and that trip to the altar was like saying they'd join the church.

Olive was baptized the following Sunday afternoon in the coulee at Sam Burkhart's pasture. I watched as Olive waded into the coulee and was ducked three times by the church minister. Aunt Dee was very happy that Olive was baptized Brethren, and the following Sunday Olive joined all church members in the annual Brethren Love Feast. The Love Feast was the one day each year when Brethrens took communion of grape juice and unleavened bread. And before communion, each member washed the feet of another member. To me, joining the church and getting baptized seemed quite a stretch, and the Love Feast seemed to me silly.

We did find a place to live. It was the upstairs of a house that had years before been a neighborhood grocery, where the proprietor's family lived upstairs. It was into that upstairs that we moved, because the Trankinas lived downstairs. Pentecostal evangelist Joseph Trankina had moved to Cando from Chicago to be minister of the Gospel Tabernacle, the church that Aunt Hattie had helped start after she left the Brethren church. Trankina brought with him his weekly radio program called "Golden Moments," broadcast from the Mutual Broadcasting Station, KDLR, Devils Lake.

There were three Trankina sons, Vincent Anthony, fifteen, Anthony Joseph, twelve, and Joseph Vincent, eight. Joseph Vincent was twin to Nina, the only daughter. Mrs. Trankina was a wiry, fast-talking city woman who made sure her two older sons were kept from sin by whipping them with a razor strap every Saturday evening, telling everyone she met how she was raising her sons by strict rules.

The woman Mom was nursing in the country died, but almost as soon as we moved into our upstairs apartment, Mom took a nursing job on a farm near Edinburg. Twins had been born to a mother who was sick during pregnancy and almost died. So both the twins and mother needed a nurse. Dad, too, was away from home some of the time selling the McConnon products, so Olive sort of became cook and housekeeper. It made me think about Mom having to become cook and housekeeper when she was only twelve. Olive fixed good Campbell's soup and lots of toasted cheese sandwiches. We followed Mom's advice to eat fruit every day, and I drank lots of milk.

Dad drove us one weekend to visit Mom at the farm where she was nurse, and after a couple more weeks, Mom was back home with us.

That fall, Vince and Tony Trankina and their dad were all excited

Dad and me, in late summer when I was nine, just before entering fourth grade

because the Chicago Cubs were playing in the World Series. The Cubs lost to the Yankees, but the Trankina family still had something to be excited about. Two of Mrs. Trankina's nephews from Chicago came to live with her family in Cando. The hope was that a small town with a religious family would end the nephews' law-breaking habits. These two kids were not like any kids I'd known before. Their aunt's use of the razor strap did nothing to change their use of swearwords in everything they said, and being in a religious family didn't stop their shoplifting. Bruno, although fifteen, was in seventh grade but tough and fearless. I watched him one day run alongside an open farm truck, jump to grab the top plank of the truck box, and swing up into the truck box for a ride.

Bruno's seventh grade teacher, Loretta Murray, took it upon herself to coax both Chicago kids to be more respectable. But she had little effect on them. Shortly after Thanksgiving, Mrs. Trankina sent her nephews back to their parents in Chicago. I was happy to see them go, because the brothers dirtied the outdoor privy used by us as well as by the Trankinas. The brothers would squat rather than sit on the toilet seat and drop their crap on the seat instead of in the hole. I tried to think through what those two boys from Chicago imagined themselves to be. I guessed that they wanted to be as tough as Chicago gang members and to show they wouldn't follow the laws and expectations of the regular community. Of course they never talked about who they thought they were.

To help us avoid the messy toilet left by the Chicago brothers, Aunt Ella Mae said our family could use their indoor bathroom, including taking baths in their tub, which was a lot better than a spit bath with a wash basin or sitting in a washtub filled with water heated on the stove. Sometimes Aunt Ella would ask Olive and me to dinner and we'd have an evening with her and Uncle Jesse. That often meant I'd play checkers with Aunt Ella, and sometimes it meant Uncle Jesse would strap on his guitar and fasten his harmonica holder on his shoulders and give us a guitar and harmonica concert, usually songs he'd sing as he played. Uncle Jesse was maybe the most surprising person I knew, the way he'd be one kind of person today and a completely different person tomorrow.

Maybe it was being a whole year older, but I think it was mostly Miss Jolliffe that made me start thinking that I could be a really good student. My earlier teachers had always said I was a good student, but I had never thought about trying to be a good student until I was in fourth grade.

Teacher Evelyn Jolliffe, more than any of my other teachers, made learning and knowledge seem more important than anything else. I quickly realized she was the kind of person I wanted to become. Miss Jolliffe's bright brown eyes seemed to say, "What I see in the world makes me happy," and her thick, black, wavy hair seemed to say, "What's inside my head is even prettier." Miss Jolliffe had already had a big influence on what I read, because she was the school librarian who had suggested I read *David Copperfield,* which prompted me to read other adult books.

As a classroom teacher, Miss Jolliffe always made each school day seem new. She treated each of us students as someone she knew and wanted to help. She set up each school day to help us work fast and hard, then feel relaxed but not tired. She read aloud to us daily from books that made us sometimes laugh our sides out and sometimes want to cry. And every month when teachers got their checks, Miss Jolliffe sent some student from our class to the bank with her bank deposit book. She always paid the student who deposited her check twenty cents for their work.

Miss Jolliffe had us play a game that made history easy to remember. She had each student choose one of the persons we had studied about and tell the other students enough to help them guess who the person was. She had ways to make everything we learned seem real. When she told us about the trip she took to Canada the summer before, we fourth graders felt we could see the places she had visited.

One day she gave me a special assignment to write a report for her about British Columbia, a part of Canada she still wanted to visit. She said I could use a travel book, and the encyclopedia, and her book about the history of Canada, but to write the report in my own words. It was the best assignment I was ever given by a teacher, because it made me realize I could put together what I found in several different books and show how it all fit together to make sense

That Halloween, Cando firemen held a party at school for all kids in grade school. A volunteer fireman came to each classroom to talk about fire safety and to give each kid an apple and a bag of candy. Because Joyce Martin's dad was fire chief, he came to our classroom. He thanked us for not being out soaping windows or tipping outhouses, telling us we were part of the Cando community, and should always take care of our community. I thought Cando's fire chief was someone I wanted to be like when I grew up.

It had been Easter vacation of my second grade when Grandma died, and during Christmas vacation of my fourth grade, Grandpa died. His funeral was well attended, even in cold, cold weather. I was impressed that the Denny brothers had thawed the ground with a two-day coal fire so that his grave could be dug.

All four of Dad's Troyer cousins came to the funeral in Guy Troyer's big shiny Buick. I was sure the Troyers must be rich with their heavy gold rings set with jewels and their fancy tailored suits. After the funeral supper at Grandpa's farm, I asked Dad how his cousins had got rich. Dad said, "Selling bootleg whiskey and playing poker." Hearing that made me feel it was good that we'd never joined the Troyer brothers as citrus growers in Florida. I was suspicious of people who grew rich by taking advantage of others, and I knew gambling, like selling booze, made a few people rich while making a lot of people miserable.

That winter, snow fell for weeks, and winds left a long, tall snowbank behind the high school athletic field. It was up to ten feet high in places, and was an outright challenge for us kids. We made snow caves, some of them big enough for eight kids to sit on the snow benches we shaped in the caves. There were nine or ten caves, all connected by tunnels. We made the caves by pulling the snow out with our hands and pushing it out with our feet. We burrowed out the tunnels with our feet from each end until we had a connection. Candles from home with potatoes as candle-holders lit spaces that had no opening at the top. During the making, I'd go home with my pants frozen solid, but I wore long underwear and knee-high boots, so I never felt terribly cold from the fun work of building snow caves.

Another joy that winter was playing at the county fairgrounds. The horse-barn haymow was filled with fresh hay that we tunneled through to play tag. When we tired of playing in the hay we went to the judges' tower at the race track and jumped into the deep bank of snow on the track about ten feet below the tower where races were started and judged.

In spring, eighth grade teacher Ruth Linn asked me to be in the county declamation contest. She gave me a piece about a boy saving his dog from drowning in a well. It reminded me of King when he was a pup and had to be saved from the Kuhlbergs' biffy, so I delivered the declamation with genuine emotion for the contest at Rock Lake School. And I won a first-place blue ribbon. Susanne Menness won first place with a humorous declamation about being a flower girl at her aunt's wedding, and Donald Green won first place for his original oration about the value of taking jobs to earn money while still in grade school. Being a winner for Cando made me think that speaking in public was something I was good at and wanted to do again. We three winners were driven to the contest in Miss Linn's car. Susanne took the front seat on the way to the contest, but she made me happy by climbing into the back seat with me on the drive back to Cando.

My cousin Vesper, who was in seventh grade, was already playing piano for church services at the Gospel Tabernacle. Vesper had never had a piano lesson, but had taught herself piano, first playing by ear, but soon learning to read music and play from written music. It was just amazing how well she could play. Aunt Hattie said it was a "gift from God."

The summer after fourth grade, Mama and Aunt Hattie kept a promise to Aunt Dee that her younger nieces and nephews, when school was out, would keep Aunt Dee company now that she was alone on the farm. Aunt Hattie ordered new wallpaper for two of the upstairs bedrooms, letting us kids pick the wallpaper. Jimmy and I picked wallpaper with sports pictures for the room we'd share, and Vesper and Olive chose blue wallpaper with white stars for their room. Uncle Charlie made a dressing table from orange crates with a plywood top, and Mama and Aunt Hattie covered the table with cloth that matched the girls' room wallpaper. We four moved to the farm right after school ended.

Aunt Dee wanted her nieces and nephews to go to Daily Vacation Bible School at her Zion Church of the Brethren. She and Jimmy fixed up Grandma's old two-seat buggy for us to be pulled by Laura. Although Olive was the only one of us four who was a member of the Brethren church, we were all well accepted at Bible school. I liked getting to know Forrest Smeltzer and some of the other kids better, and Jimmy and I both liked playing kitten ball at Bible school.

The four Stong kids from the farm just south of Aunt Dee's used a buggy to get to Bible school, too. One day, Jimmy and Gerald Stong agreed to a race home from the church. Stong's buggy was to head south first and then east, while our buggy would head east first and then south to get to the corner of the road that led to both farms. Good old Laura showed her Morgan breeding and got us to the corner just ahead of the Stong buggy. Jimmy kept our buggy in front of Gerald's attempts to pass us, and when we told Aunt Dee about the race, she cheered our family victory.

After the two weeks' session, there was a Bible school performance for Sunday's church service, and I was asked to join Forrest Smeltzer and his cousin Beverly from our class to give Bible readings. I felt good that adults complimented my reading. Next day, when I was helping Aunt Hattie weed the garden she and Mom had planted, Aunt Hattie said I should become a preacher to pay back God for blessing me with a talent. But I was sure being a minister was a job I'd never want.

That summer Old Puss had three kittens. Jimmy and I convinced both Olive and Vesper that the kittens should be named after three women on the 1936 U.S. Olympics team. So the kittens were named Sonja Heinie, Babe Didrickson, and Kit Klein. Maybe because the kittens were often kept in Olive's and Vesper's bedroom, Old Tom, the yellow tabby who'd been on the farm since I was born, two times crapped on the girls' starred bedspread. The second time he did it, I caught Tom and smeared his face in his crap, then dropped him from the upstairs window. He landed on his feet, but must have understood his punishment, because he never crapped on their bed again.

At haying time, Ole Stenerson, Aunt Dee's partner farming on shares, cut and raked Aunt Dee's hay fields. But it was up to Jimmy and me to put the hay in the haymow for the next winter. Aunt Hattie arranged for Tony Trankina to join Jimmy and me. We three boys borrowed a team from Ole, and loading a hayrack, hauled the hay to the barn. The very first time we tried to use the hay slings to carry the hay into the haymow, the rope that lifted the hay slings broke. So we had to pitch the hay through two small hayloft doors, before moving the hay into a long stack for storage. It was awfully hard work, load after load, but the three of us managed to almost fill the haymow for winter.

When Aunt Dee bragged about our good work at the Brethren church, Elmer Smeltzer hired Jimmy for the rest of the summer as a farmhand, leaving Tony and me to do the daily chores for Aunt Dee.

Tony and I were having a good time as farm boys until one day Uncle Jesse showed up. Uncle Jesse had been sent to the Jamestown insane asylum for treatment to end his wild pranks on his drinking binges. He was given a couple of days to come home and set his finances in order, with a guard from the asylum. But he came to the farm without his guard and commanded Tony and me to climb ladders and trim the row of box elder trees, a job neither Tony nor I had ever done. When we finished tree trimming, Uncle Jesse took us to the grain elevator to sweep the dust and grain litter from the grain bins. We finished that job in time for lunch, but Uncle Jesse made Tony and me watch him shoot a blackbird from a tree with his six-shooter. Then he made us wash our hands and faces in a tub of floating dead flies in dirty wash water that was to be used to water the garden. When Tony and I hesitated to use the dirty wash water, Uncle Jesse fired bullets close to our feet to make us move to the tub.

Aunt Dee, who always had sympathy for Uncle Jesse, had fixed pork steak for noon dinner. Before coming to the table, Uncle Jesse went to his pickup, maybe to get a drink of booze. Tony used the opportunity to call his dad and tell him of our predicament. When Uncle Jesse came in for dinner, he took the platter of pork steak and fed it to the dog Jack, and to Old Puss and Tom, leaving us with fried potatoes and canned corn for dinner.

Not long after dinner, Reverend Trankina drove into the yard while Uncle Jesse was firing his six-gun at the windmill weather fan, shooting his initials in the fan. Tony and I ran to greet Tony's dad at his car, but he told us to go into the house while he dealt with Uncle Jesse. Trankina honked his Ford's horn and Uncle Jesse went to his car, carrying his six-gun. Tony learned later what happened between the two men. When Uncle Jesse came to Trankina's car, he saw Trankina twisting a short length of wire he'd taken from Uncle Jesse's pickup. It was wire used to start and stop windmills and was so heavy it ordinarily could be twisted only with pliers. It must have surprised Uncle Jesse to see the wire being twisted in Trankina's bare hands. Tony's dad told Uncle Jesse that he was twisting the wire for exercise, because at this time of day he would usually be using his punching bag to keep in shape. Uncle Jesse pushed his six-gun into the car, and Trankina grabbed Uncle Jesse's hand and forced his wrist down on the car door, making him drop the six-gun and yell with pain. Trankina convinced Uncle Jesse to drive back to town ahead of him and turned Uncle Jesse over to the guard from the Jamestown hospital.

We had a wonderful surprise celebration on the farm for the Fourth of July. Russell had bought a big older-model Lafayette sedan in Minneapolis and had driven it to Cando with David and Veora and three Bible college friends. He brought them all out to the farm—with fireworks and a croquet set. Those young folks were full of fun, especially a dark-haired young woman named Bonita, who was Veora's Bible college roommate. She and Veora and Olive and Vesper washed their hair in water from the rain barrel, and then Bonita insisted on washing Tony's and my hair because she thought rainwater was so special. Aunt Dee beat everyone in a croquet game, and the fireworks David and Russell shot off were grand.

In August Aunt Dee was visited by one of her cousins from Indiana, who was the cook and caretaker of two kids for a wealthy family in South Bend. During her visit she told Dad about a company in South Bend that made a powerful vacuum cleaner for cleaning furnaces. She told Dad he could make more money cleaning furnaces than selling McConnon products. Dad sent for information and bought a vacuum cleaner and a bundle of tools that went with it. He changed the back seat of the Dodge from a product display into a tool bin and began cleaning furnaces and chimneys in Cando and other nearby towns.

In the years before Dad began farming with Grandpa, Dad had had a business in Minot, North Dakota, selling and installing oil-burning furnaces. So his experience with heating systems made him start his own heating business for sales and services for heating systems to go with his furnace cleaning and repair work. He worked with that new business the rest of the summer, and made it pay better than anything he'd done since he had left his heating business in Minot years before.

While Grandpa was still living, Mom had used money she'd made nursing to buy Grandpa's tenant house we'd lived in when Dad farmed with him. Mama's buying that house moved Dad to buy a lot on the school street near the north edge of town, so we began looking forward to having our own home.

In the fall of 1938, we had a brand-new, beautiful school, built by Works Project Administration, to come to. It had been begun three years before, while we were still in the old three-story wood-frame school that had been in place for a long time, originally as both grade and high school. Our new grade school was built with all the most up-to-date construction materials, seeming to be fireproof and indestructible.

One new feature of our school was a two-way speaker system with controls in the superintendent's office. As soon as school began, we heard on our fifth grade room speaker our superintendent telling us how lucky we were to have such a fine school. When he finished talking, he played a phonograph record that he said was a Mozart piano concerto.

A few weeks later, we got a message that all boys were to come to the basement lunchroom for a meeting. There we were lectured by Superintendent Miller about standing close to the urinals. He said we were lucky to have private stalls, and as good citizens we should not pee on the floor. In the old school, where boys had to pee into a common trough, there had always been piss on the floor in front of the trough. Boys made it a game to see who could stand farthest back and still hit the trough. One day Francis Lavendure told those of us in the toilet that he was going to put his wet shoe prints on the ceiling. He jumped from a radiator to a wood crossbar and began swinging to get enough swing to touch his feet to the ceiling. But his hands slipped. He fell on his back in the shallow pool of piss, but, amazingly, got up and went home to change clothes. I think those of us who saw Francis fall were happy to use the private stalls and stand close to the urinals.

Behind the new school was a hill of excavated dirt from construction where we played king of the hill until the hill was trucked away. Also behind the school were six box elder trees, growing close enough together for us to play tree tag at recess. The rule was that you could not touch the ground, but could go from tree to tree to escape whoever was it. One day after rain, I jumped to catch the wet branch of another tree and slipped to fall on my back, knocking my breath out. I lay there feeling I might never get up again, until my breath came back.

Our fifth grade teacher was Katherine McDonald, a pretty young woman with curly reddish-brown hair. She made sure we knew that MacDonald spelled Mac was Scot, but Mc names were Irish.

That fall something happened that made me know I didn't want to be identified with a church. Eloise Maust, a high school girl and member of the Zion Church of the Brethren, called me to the hallway. She told me Beverly and Forrest Smeltzer were going to be baptized and become church members, and I should get baptized, too. I told her I couldn't do that, because I didn't feel any need to be a church member. She came back the next day to say I should meet with the minister to sort out what I believe, but I told her, "No. I know I'm not ready to be baptized or to join any church. I'm not sure what I believe, but I don't want any minister to tell me what I believe, either."

The claim that a person becomes better by joining a church didn't seem convincing to me, and I didn't feel like I belonged to any church. Part of my feeling, I know, was because of seeing Olive and other kids go up to the altar before she was baptized. I thought the two hymns they chose at that time sort of forced the kids to go to the altar. One of the hymns was "Softly and Tenderly, Jesus Is Calling," and the other one was "Just as I Am, Without One Plea." I think the words and music to those hymns were used to stir up kids' emotions, and make them think they were doing God a big favor if they became church members.

CHAPTER 11

How did I get to be *A Bad Kid*?

I couldn't help but wonder, when I was eleven, if I was naturally bad or naturally good. I felt sure that becoming a church member wouldn't change what I was by nature.

But I did some things that year that made me think I had become a bad kid. The trouble was, I couldn't say how that came to be.

For instance, one day Loyal Bjornstad passed me a note applying the F word to me and one of our girl classmates. I knew Loyal was only teasing, but he made me mad, so I sent him back a note on the same paper saying, "Not so, you do-do! Don't spread your bullshit here!" Miss McDonald intercepted the note and kept Loyal and me both after school. She gave us a shaming lecture about using nasty language and being bad.

I didn't much feel like a bad kid that day, but after Halloween, I had reason to think I had become a bad kid. Bob Brending passed the word around for us kids to show we were just as tough as kids in the past had been. First thing we did was start with the alley at the west edge of town and flip over every outhouse. After tipping more than a dozen, we came to the block where the town constable lived. We weren't about to risk tipping Jim Strachen's biffy, so we stopped there and ran downtown. At the corner of City Auditorium, Bob Brending said, "Let's go up this street, letting the air out of the tires of every parked car." After leaving a number of tires flat, we felt like doing something more risky, so we pushed a car away from the curb to block the street. Right then some high school boys came along to tell us they had blocked the east road into town with gravel wagons stored at the edge of town, and that they had been chased by the sheriff's car. Now they were trying to hide from him.

That scared us younger kids enough to break up and go home. Olive asked me where I'd been, and I told her I'd just been playing with a bunch of friends. I felt dumb about what I had really been doing and felt ashamed of the lie I told my sister.

The next day at school I felt more dumb and ashamed. I was called to the classroom door to be challenged by Norm Holien and Sterling Weiker. They told me they knew I had been with Bob Brending Halloween night, doing a lot of damage around town. They wanted me to give them the names of all the other kids in our bunch. I said I couldn't do that. Norm said the city attorney told him there was an estimate of four hundred dollars' damage, and that parents of every kid involved would have to pay for the damage.

I felt dizzy and sick to my stomach hearing about that cost, but I couldn't be a sneak and give Norm and Sterling any names. Norm said, "Well, when we get all the names we can, we'll let you know how much you have to pay. We have twenty names now, so that'd be about twenty bucks each kid pays. You think about it, and we'll see you tomorrow." Next day I learned that H. L. Conway, the manager of Towner County Co-op Elevator, had paid the four hundred dollars to the city attorney, saying that he'd been a kid once himself. That was a big relief, but I still felt guilty, and wondered if I'd do something bad again to show I was tough like other kids.

Next Sunday, when Olive and I had supper at Aunt Hattie's, there was talk about Conway's paying off the kids' Halloween pranks. I was scared I'd be asked if I'd been on the list of bad kids, but no one asked, because Uncle Charlie told us what he and other kids in his day had done on Halloween. He said they had pulled the high school principal's Model T up the flagpole to hang there, and that they drove a cow up three flights of stairs to the stage in the auditorium. The only way the cow could be taken back downstairs was to use a block and tackle with a veterinarian's sling under the cow's belly and let her down from the fire escape door and balcony. Aunt Hattie seemed pretty disgusted with Uncle Charlie for laughing as he told his stories, showing that kids in his day took bigger risks than we did on Halloween.

The next Wednesday at the public library I checked out two books and promised myself to read two books a week to keep me busy instead of doing more bad things. But I broke my promise to read by taking time off to build an electric motor. I'd found the directions in one of Aunt Dee's magazines so I scrounged up the parts from the local telephone office shed and from Sitz Hardware. I built the motor and made it run on a six-volt dry cell.

Olive was proud of my work and told her ninth grade science teacher about my motor. He asked me to bring the motor to his science class and talk about it. That made me proud, but it was a big letdown when ninth grade boys didn't seem at all impressed by my work. Some grinned at each other, and some just yawned and giggled. I said, "I'd like to see you guys make something electrical, but you're all maybe too lazy or dumb." I knew that was a bad thing to say, and felt ashamed that I probably made my sister feel ashamed for me.

Just before Christmas, though, I helped make something that was appreciated. John MacDonald and Melby Miller and I built a little clubhouse from a refrigerator box and scrap lumber that even had a window and a door that swung on hinges. Melby bragged about our clubhouse to his sister Ann, and Ann brought her friends Marge Rendahl and Susanne Menness to see it. The girls suggested a pre-Christmas party for the clubhouse and wrote names to put in a hat for us all to draw and exchange presents. When we had the party and we opened our exchange presents, Susanne right away pinned on the silver wings I had bought her. I opened my gift from Susanne, a model kit for building a British Spitfire fighting plane. Susanne squeezed my hand and touched her head to mine and said, "See. We're like twins again, drawing each other's names and both giving presents about flying." Right then, I fell in love and for days imagined how great it would be to put my arms around Susanne and kiss her and kiss her and kiss her. Then I began feeling stupid and ashamed of what I was imagining, sure that Susanne would think I was silly if she knew of my daydreams.

I felt my daydreams were bad, but not as bad as my wayward tongue. After Christmas, when John invited me over to play with some of the things he'd got as presents, we put on his boxing gloves and went at it. Mrs. MacDonald, with sparkling brown eyes and red hair, kept watch, telling John not to hurt me as I was punching him out. When we took our break from boxing, and John's mother gave us milk and cookies, I wanted to show Mrs. MacDonald gratitude so I said, "It must be nice to have a mother who doesn't have to work away from home all the time." Right away, I knew I had said something bad, sounding as if I wasn't happy with my mother. On my walk home, I felt so ashamed, I had to wipe tears from my eyes and blow my nose.

While I could see it was hard not to be a bad kid, I wasn't at all convinced that kids who were more religious were not just as bad as I was. The Trankinas lived downstairs, making it easy for Tony and me to spend time together. One thing we did was pore over the *Spors Catalog*, thinking of what we'd like to buy. I mostly wanted a microscope, a telescope, and model toys that ran with electric motors. Tony said he'd like a whoopee cushion, some stink bombs, a flower that would spray water on its sniffer, and playing cards backed by photos of naked women. Tony liked to sing mocking words to hymns, like "Jesus, lover of my soul, hang me on a telephone pole," and "At the bar, at the bar, where I smoked my first cigar."

One night Tony came up to our apartment because Reverend Trankina was holding a prayer meeting downstairs. The prayer meeting was full of women's voices, and one woman's voice was very loud. Tony said, "Hey, listen. She's gonna come through pretty soon." It sounded to me like the woman's cries became wildly happy just when Tony said, "There. She just had her climax." I didn't know what Tony meant, so he said, "It's like when you jack off." After her wild, happy cries, the woman voiced a rattle of short syllables that sounded like talk from the jungle people in a Tarzan movie. Tony said, "There. Now she's talking in tongues. They often do that after they come through."

I'd heard about Pentecostals talking in tongues, so that by itself wasn't surprising. But her voice sounded crazy, and what Tony said about her "climax" seemed vulgar.

The Pentecostal religion seemed really confusing to me, because it seemed Pentecostals didn't mind their own rules in what they'd say or do. One night, Tony and I were both at the Kensingers'. At this time, Uncle Charlie was working for WPA, building outdoor privies. Tony said, "It really stinks that Roosevelt makes men like you build outhouses. Roosevelt should get factories going and give you a decent job."

Uncle Charlie started talking fast, waving his arms as he said, "Decent job? In a factory? On a production line? Listen, boy. At WPA I build a really good toilet. I make the whole thing myself, not putting it together piece by piece with other fellows. Every one I build, I can be proud of. I'd go crazy working in a factory."

Now, I knew Uncle Charlie had called Roosevelt's New Deal

wicked and he said one day that the NRA sign with an eagle holding a torch was "a sign of the anti-Christ." So I was surprised when he spoke so well of his WPA job and, it seemed to me, defended Roosevelt's New Deal, even if his church had convinced him to think it was wicked.

That spring of 1939, Reverend Trankina announced that Jesus would come back to earth on a day very soon, that he named. It didn't happen, of course, and Reverend Trankina gave up being minister for the Gospel Tabernacle. Trankina kept his radio program called Golden Moments, and Uncle Charlie often sang on that program, even though he stayed with the Gospel Tabernacle church.

Members of the church voted to join the Assemblies of God, but Reverend Trankina said he wanted to remain independent. So the Gospel Tabernacle began a search for a new leader and hired my cousin Russell as temporary minister. Russell had graduated from his Bible college and was waiting for a call to head an Assemblies of God church somewhere. He and his wife Gladys, along with Fern Duffy, started a kid's Bible study at the Gospel Tabernacle, just across the street from the high school. Aunt Hattie talked Mom into sending Olive and me to our cousin's Bible study for kids. I remembered Dad saying, "I started to read the Bible once, but it had this so and so begat so and so who begat someone who begat another, just going on and on. It didn't make any sense to me."

I didn't want to go to Russell's Bible class. I admired my cousin Russell, because I knew he was very smart, but I tried to hide my attending my cousin's Bible study from all my friends. And I didn't know why I didn't want anyone to know that my cousin was a minister.

Even sports caused me to feel like I was sometimes a bad kid. In spring I won the fifth grade high jump and broad jump and felt proud to be Cando's entry at Towner County Play Day. When I lost both events to a kid from Rock Lake, I hated that kid for beating me. But then I felt ashamed about hating him. I knew it was bad to feel like you had to be the winner, if someone was better than you.

A big change that spring made me feel good. Dad, with help from men he had hired, dug the basement for our new home. So he hired some Mennonite house movers from Wolford to move the house on a Saturday from Grandpa's farm into town. I went with Dad in our car to be sure our house was moved okay. It was slow going, because any time we came to telephone wires that were too low for the house to pass under, a telephone linesman had to free the line and raise it. But I was thrilled to see the house get placed on its foundation. That meant our family would before long move to our own home. Our having to move from place to place had made me feel our family was unsettled and unsure of itself.

The day after the house was moved, I helped Dad plant four little trees in our yard. Planting those trees made me feel really good, because I knew some day those trees would grow big. And then the next week, Dad hired our neighbor Andy to plow up part of our backyard for garden. Helping Mom and Dad plant potatoes and other vegetables made me feel good, too. Planting and caring for garden was the one thing Mom and Dad liked to do together. Working with them made me feel like our family was going to be closer now.

Midsummer after fifth grade, Owen Stong called and asked me if I would herd his cows. Aunt Dee drove into town and took Olive and me to the farm. I was so excited about herding cattle, I ran most of the half mile to Stong's farm. Owen told me I could have Colonel, the Shetland pony, for herding the cows and took me to the barn where I put a bridle on Colonel and rode him to Aunt Dee's barn. Next day, right after breakfast, I rode Colonel back to Stongs. Ethel put a lunch for me in a cotton bag tied to a half-gallon jug of water for hanging across Colonel's neck. Owen pointed out the cut hayfield to take the cows where there was fresh growth for grazing.

For five weeks I herded cows six days a week from about eight in the morning to about six in the evening before herding the cows back to the barnyard. Each day in the field, I'd sing and talk to Colonel, and sometimes hug his neck and kiss his head for being such a good pony. Owen had told me Colonel was so ornery, he couldn't let his daughter Eulalie ride him. But Colonel seemed always happy with me that summer. We easily kept those twenty-eight cows in control. Each evening I curried and brushed Colonel down as he ate the measure of oats I put in his grain box. I felt sure animals are a lot like people. If you expect them to be good, they will be good. I said to myself, keep expecting yourself to be good and you won't have to join some church to stop being bad.

After five weeks, Stongs began threshing, and Owen moved his cows into a fenced-in, harvested grain field. Owen paid me twenty cents a day for herding his cows six weeks, so I had earned six dollars being a cowboy.

That weekend Aunt Dee drove Olive and me to town for Cando merchants' "Customers' Day." In addition to free watermelon, there was a greased pig to catch and contests for eating raw eggs and berry pies. What was different this year were carnival rides in one block of Main Street. When I went to ride the Ferris wheel, I saw Laddie, a golden retriever whose owner was Roy Miller, publisher of the *Cando Record*, sitting on a Ferris wheel seat riding all by himself. When I handed my ticket to the guy running the Ferris wheel, he told me he was letting Laddie ride free for as long as he wanted, because Laddie was a good dog.

Next week I got another farm job. Ole Stenerson was starting to thresh the crops on Aunt Dee's three quarter sections. He told me he'd pay me a dollar a day to keep the grain from the threshing machine level as it was dumped into grain wagons, and to shift the grain spout to an empty wagon when one wagon was full.

Ole Stenerson made me think of Vikings I'd read about. He had only one eye and a withered socket where the destroyed eye had been. Ole was about six and a half feet tall, and maybe the strongest man I'd ever seen. I'd watched him pitch a fork full of three bundles of wheat into hayracks that hauled to the threshing machine, and I knew those three bundles weighed about a hundred fifty pounds. One day a harvest hand, the guy who swaggered around acting tough and bragged he had boxed for a carnival fight tent, pitched bundles from his hayrack crosswise, stuffing the feeder and clogging the threshing machine to stop it, so he'd get a bit of rest while the thresher was cleared of its jammed bundles. Ole was on top of the threshing machine at the time, and saw the tough guy shut down the work. Ole strode across the top of the threshing machine, grabbed the tough guy by an arm and the seat of his pants and threw him to the ground, yelling, "You're fired, you lunkard! Go to the missus and get your pay." The crew around the machine all yelled, "Way to go, Ole."

So, after two farm jobs, I'd earned eleven dollars. John MacDonald had just been given a new bicycle and still had his old bike. I asked him if I could buy his old bike, and John said we had to ask his dad. We rode the two bikes to the doctor's office and when Doc had time to see us, we asked if I could buy John's old bike. Doc said, "How much are you willing to pay for it?" and I told him ten bucks. He said, "Okay. Give the money to John right now, because when you leave here, he might let you have it for less." I gave John two five-dollar bills and Doc MacDonald said, "Okay. Business over." I was as happy as I could be. It was a good bike, even if it wasn't new. When I showed Dad my bike and told him how I paid for it, Dad gave me a ten-dollar bill and said he was happy to buy me a bike that only cost ten bucks.

That summer, Uncle Jesse went on a binge again, driving all over the region scaring people. Stories about his rampages were town gossip. He had a federal government contract to drill wells on the Belcourt Indian Reservation in the Turtle Mountains. One night he shut down a dance hall at gunpoint, saying it was too late for all the noise the dance band made. When he was closing the door to the dance pavilion, a deputy sheriff placed a gun in his back and told Uncle Jesse to give up his gun. Uncle Jesse showed him the gun wasn't loaded.

While he was still drilling wells on the reservation Uncle Jesse called Aunt Ella to bring up a box of dynamite for blasting through rocks where he was drilling. Aunt Ella asked Olive and me and a neighbor girl, June, to go with her. Uncle Jesse gave us all quite an adventure on Gordon Lake where he'd rented a cabin. A brisk wind on the lake made the waves high, and the boat we were in was leaky. Neither Uncle Jesse nor I caught any fish where he had me row the boat. When Uncle Jesse took over to row to a new location, Aunt Ella was pulling up the anchor. As Uncle Jesse jerked the boat with the oars, Aunt Ella fell overboard. Uncle Jesse jumped in the lake to help her and showed her that she could stand up where she was. An Ojibwa man whose cabin was nearby rowed his boat out to help us, and we learned that he and Uncle Jesse were acquainted. We went to his cabin, where his wife gave Aunt Ella a blanket to warm her. The Ojibwa couple had a five- or six-year-old boy. To further upset Aunt Ella, Uncle Jesse said that he was the little boy's dad. That made the woman angry and made the Ojibwa man sneer at Uncle Jesse. Aunt Ella drove home in a mighty huff, and I wondered how Uncle Jesse could live with himself, being so mean and crazy.

Shortly before school began, John MacDonald's mother died when a blood clot cut off blood to her brain. That was terrible, and I felt so sorry for John. I knew he must feel his world had fallen apart, but I didn't know what to say as comfort, so I didn't say anything. That made me know I was not being a good friend. And though I knew that was bad, I didn't know what to say.

During the first week of school, Dad got a call from Rugby, telling him his cousin George Troyer had been shot by two guys when they tried to rob his saloon in Wolford. George died on the way to the Rugby Hospital. I went with Dad to the funeral where George's wife Hazel, who was always very good to Olive and me, seemed to be in a terrible shock of silence. All efforts to find the killers failed. Not even any suspects. As time went on, Dad told me he believed George had shot himself, but the Troyer brothers covered up his suicide so Hazel would get his insurance.

When school started, Roy Baney hadn't yet finished the carpentry on our house, but because the Baneys lived just two houses from ours, Roy Baney said we should move into their home until ours was ready. His wife, Etta, was teaching far enough from Cando to rent a room and come home only on weekends. Roy and Etta had adopted two nieces, both in high school, whose mother had died. Living in the Baney house began a strong friendship between Olive and the Baney sisters.

We finally moved into our own home, and were all wildly happy. Mom looked more pleased than I'd ever seen her, and Dad gave all his spare time to making improvements in the house. Olive and I each had our own bedroom at opposite corners of our house. I put up posters on my wall and bought a little radio at a rummage sale to listen to before falling asleep. What I most appreciated was being able to read as late as I wanted without disturbing anyone with my light.

We had a big harvest from our garden, and Mom canned a lot of chard and spinach and tomatoes to add to the pears and peaches she had canned while still at Baneys'. Dad had made one corner of our basement a root cellar, and we stored cabbage, parsnips, beets, rutabagas, squash, and potatoes in it. Harvesting the garden made me feel like I was shedding some of my bad-boy problem.

I learned that fall that a gift can change someone's life. Dad gave Olive the surprise of paying for her to take voice lessons from Grace Harris. Mrs. Harris had been an opera soloist when Dr. Harris convinced her to marry him and move to Cando. Olive had a pretty soprano voice, and Dad bought a secondhand piano so Olive could accompany herself as she practiced her songs. Her lessons made singing Olive's great passion. I found my sister's singing a joy to listen to, and Olive always told me about the arias and art songs Mrs. Harris asked her to learn. I felt as if I had my own music appreciation class right at home.

Olive had begun singing with the Baney girls as a trio, and decided to join the Methodist church choir. Sometimes their trio sang a special number at church, so I decided I'd follow Olive and switch from attending the Brethren church. Olive and I knew we would make Aunt Dee feel bad that we left the Brethren church, but we felt more at ease with the Methodists. It seemed to me that where you felt most at ease was where you should go to church, if you went at all.

So I entered sixth grade feeling I wasn't such a bad kid after all. But it wasn't long before my teacher labeled me a bad kid. As soon as I saw Genevieve Lester, I knew I was headed for trouble, and it began in music class. Because she could play piano, Miss Lester taught us music herself. One day she told us to sing a song about a daisy telling a robin she was thirsty. When we were to sing the song, I didn't join in. Miss Lester saw I wasn't singing and asked me why. I answered, "Because it's a silly, stupid song, not fit for sixth graders to sing." I was sent up to the classroom for the rest of the music class, and when recess came, I was told to stay in my seat.

That day I vowed to get even with Miss Lester and almost every day I thought of something to say or do to annoy her. I had hardly any recess that year, and for "Deportment" my report card listed me as "disrespectful and troublesome."

In one way, not having recess was good for me. We'd been given new world history textbooks, so during recess I read my world history textbook all the way through. One day when Miss Lester left me all alone, I discovered that last year's world history texts were still in our classroom. So I planted a book in my desk and read that world history book all the way through, too. I was amazed that the two books disagreed so much about the past. Each told a different history of the Roman Empire and reasons for its fall. Each book presented the medieval and the Renaissance periods differently, and each told a different story about the Reformation and emerging nationalism. They sort of agreed about colonization of the Americas, but not about colonization in Africa, India, and the South Pacific. Learning that history books tell different histories was a good thing to know.

After my scare from being a bad kid at Halloween, I was grateful when Marge Rendahl gathered about eight of us in her yard for an early bonfire and wiener roast. Marge suggested that we do what kids do back east and go to the biggest homes in town and knock on their doors and say "Trick or Treat." When we did, we collected more than three dollars in coins, so we took the money to Blackburn's Drug and had ice cream sodas, much better than tipping outhouses.

When Christmas vacation came, Mom and I were invited by Mary Emily Smeltzer to visit their farm home for a couple of days. Prairie Rose School was still going, and I walked with Forrest one cold morning to see what school would be like if I had stayed at Prairie Rose. Both evenings Forrest and I helped his dad Willard with chores.

Willard Smeltzer was way ahead of most farmers. Electricity on his farm was from his own wind power generator. He had built an underground icehouse that kept ice all summer. And maybe most inventive of all, he played radio music through loudspeakers to his cows when they were in the barn for milking, claiming that the music made them give more milk. I liked talking with Willard both evenings. Besides being smart and inventive, he knew how to be funny. I found his face fascinating, because hours of work in the sun had made his face as red and wrinkled as a turkey tom's neck, and as he talked, those wrinkles were in constant change.

That year, during high school basketball season, I went to all home games. One night after a game, Grant Schneider led a bunch of us to climb onto the roof of Sitz Hardware on Main Street. Grant led us to climb or jump from one roof to the next, all the way down the block. We were quiet as we could be moving from roof to roof. Before we broke up to go home, Grant said, "Next week, we'll go across the roofs on the block towards the railroad." That stretch of buildings were the tallest on Main Street and I had no idea how we'd even get on top of the bank on the closest corner. But it was a thrill to follow Grant, and by the end of basketball season we had been on top of almost every downtown building. Often after climbing across the stores we'd gather behind a building and chatter about how hard it had been, never admitting how scared we often were. Of course our parents had no notion of those climbing nights, and no one downtown seemed to know either. We felt as proud and brave as that gang of tough kids in the movies.

Superintendent Miller made good use of our public address system that year. He turned on the speakers in grades four through six to a program from NBC in New York with Walter Damrosch conducting the NBC orchestra and teaching students about music. One day he featured arias from Puccini operas. A girl in our class screeched to mock a soprano's voice and said, "Why do we have to listen to this stuff?"

I said, "If you'd listen and not act so dumb, Darlene, you'd be able to tell it's beautiful music." When a lot of kids laughed, Darlene started to cry.

Miss Lester kept me in from recess and said, "I can't understand why you always have to be so bad."

So I was determined to meet Miss Lester's expectations, and the next week found a chance to be really bad. Miss Lester read aloud to us Joyce Kilmer's "Trees" from our language book. She told us we should illustrate the poem to show we understood it. My drawing showed I thought the poem was silly and stupid. I drew a number of eyes at the tops of branches that were shaped like leafy human arms, shaped to suggest they were praying. I drew a breast-shaped mound that had a tree-mouth pressed against a nipple and had milk dripping down from the mouth. In the upper left corner, I gave the tree hair that held a robin's nest. In the lower right corner I drew rain from a cloud pouring down the trunk into a snow bank.

When Miss Lester picked up my drawing, her face turned red. She held it up for the class to see, saying, "This is a vulgar, mean drawing by someone who doesn't understand poetry at all. He just wants to show off how bad he can be." But I was happy that some of the kids snickered as she held up my illustration of "Trees," and I was happy to meet Miss Lester's expectation as a really bad kid.

I decided that sometimes I was bad even when I wasn't expected to be, because I'd do something bad without meaning to. I also decided that bad things I had done weren't any worse than things kids did who had joined some church. So I was convinced that even if I became a church member I'd probably be just as bad as I was naturally.

CHAPTER 12

Could I become *Trustworthy*?

I decided I needed some spending money, so I answered an ad to sell and deliver *Saturday Evening Post* and *Ladies Home Journal* magazines. I found customers in downtown stores and at the county courthouse, ten each week for the *Post* and twelve each month for the *Journal*. That gave me almost two dollars a month for the easiest paying job I'd ever had.

Missing sixth grade recess had more than one good result. Besides giving me the chance to read two world history books that each told a different story, I discovered *Boys Life Magazine*. Superintendent Miller had ordered it for our classroom and reading it made me want to become a Boy Scout. Miss Jolliffe showed me there was a copy of *Handbook for Boys* in the school library, so I checked it out and read the official scout manual cover to cover. I began learning all the requirements for Tenderfoot, to be ready to pass the test. On my twelfth birthday, I went to the Congregational church parsonage to see scoutmaster Amel Whitwer, and told him I was ready for the Tenderfoot test. He asked me to come back the next day, and after I passed the test he said I'd be given my Tenderfoot badge the next week at a court of honor. Now I had the Scout's oath and the twelve Scout laws to help me become a better person. I especially felt the first Scout law, "A Scout is Trustworthy," was what I wanted to become.

Cando was lucky to have Amel Whitwer for scoutmaster. Besides being highly intelligent, he was a wholly experienced camper and woodsman from New England. I quickly made him my model to grow toward. I knew Superintendent Miller was also from New England, and wondered if all men from New England were as good and intelligent as those two.

Troop 82 hadn't been active for several years, so it had to be reorganized. Reverend Whitwer counted us off into three patrols and told

Proud to be a Second Class Scout

each patrol to elect a patrol leader. John Gibbens, Art Torkelson, both eighth graders, and I were elected. Scout uniforms could be bought at a department store in Devils Lake, but I asked Reverend Whitwer if he thought any of the former scouts might have had uniforms. He told me Bruce Stevens had been a scout, and he thought I might be able to buy a uniform from Mrs. Stevens. I called Mrs. Stevens and was told I could buy whatever she could find. She found only the scout shirt, which she sold to me for fifty cents and gave me Bruce's *Handbook for Boys* to boot.

When Troop 82 went on an overnight hike in early June to a grove east of town, I passed my first two Second Class tests. Following the directions in *Handbook for Boys*, I showed I knew the rules for hiking and how to prepare a meal in the open. I followed directions from a story in *Boys Life* to make a kind of sleeping bag out of two blankets to sleep in under the stars. Around the campfire that night, Reverend Whitwer led us in funny songs such as "My Name is Yon Yonson," and he told us a scary ghost story. He also announced that we'd have a weeklong summer camp at Lake Upsilon in the Turtle Mountains the last week of June. When I told Mom and Dad about the upcoming troop camp, Dad gave me the money to go.

Our camp at Lake Upsilon belonged to the Isaac Walton League of North Dakota and had a one-room cabin for shelter. It had a dirt floor, a fireplace, and some tables and benches. Some scouts had brought tents to sleep in, but others of us slept on the floor in the cabin. Reverend Whitwer built himself a lean-to and slept in it.

One evening at camp we heard in the distance repeated grunts and thumps. Reverend Whitwer called us to follow him to the fenced-in bison preserve. There we crouched behind bushes to watch two buffalo bulls run and smash their heads into each other. I hoped one wouldn't kill the other, and after ten or more minutes, they turned from each other and ran off in separate directions. Reverend Whitwer told us that the bison were trying to declare which one was the alpha male to lead the herd.

I made it my purpose to pass all requirements for Second Class during camp week, and did. But one chilly night I made the foolish mistake of stacking my clothes on my shoes by my pillow before going to sleep in front of the burning fireplace. While I was asleep a charred log rolled out on top of my clothes, burning them and my shoes. Next day, Reverend Whitwer drove me to Rolla and bought me a pair of high-top farmer work shoes. Dad gave me the money to pay back Reverend Whitwer and I felt lucky that my scoutmaster hadn't made a big deal over my failing to be prepared, which, of course, is the basic Scouts motto.

After troop camp I felt even more loyal to Boy Scouts. Those of us who passed our Second Class tests were awarded in a court of honor by one of the Lake Agassiz Region directors. I began right away to work on my First Class requirements, and searched for everything to read that was related to camping.

Olive also went to camp that summer, but it was to Methodist Epworth League camp where she and the Baney girls were the camp's designated trio, singing at every camp service. Heading their camp was an evangelist called "Daddy" Moon, a minister in his fifties who preached to the young people about youthful sins and dangers, especially the danger of dancing. When Olive returned from camp she told me how "Daddy" Moon demonstrated the danger of dancing. He took Peggy Baney in his arms in a cheek-to-cheek dance embrace, pulling her body tight against his and telling the girls, "You see the desire it makes you feel? That's natural, and dancing makes it worse."

A natural danger more scary than dancing occurred in late summer when our scout troop took another overnight hike. Before the hike we met at Reverend Whitwer's backyard and were told that we'd have to make the hike without our scoutmaster because he had to visit a parishioner who was near death. He said he'd come out to the campground about nine o'clock. We hiked the three miles to the grove through muggy heat, pitched our tents, and fixed our suppers. As we gathered around our campfire, the sky grew black with clouds and we put out the campfire and prepared to take shelter in our tents. Reverend Whitwer drove up and told us we had to leave where we were tented because the radio had warned of a coming tornado, and big trees near our tents would crush us if they were blown down on us. There were two buildings in the grove, a ramshackle animal shed and what had once been a garage, that had no door. Reverend Whitwer led us to the garage and told us that he had to return to town to be with his family when the tornado came.

When the storm began, Vernon Hagen sang a song from a movie that went, "Fight on for Newton High, fight on, to do or to die." Being amused gave us courage until the tornado began sweeping through the grove. It just skirted the garage, but it flattened the animal shed and several of the big trees where we had pitched our tents. We were soaking wet, but no one was hurt. John Edward Stutzman's dad owned the farm just east of the grove, so after the tornado passed, John Edward led us to where the Roberts family lived as farm renters. We saw the barn had been demolished and saw a two-by-four from the barn jammed into the farmhouse dining room like a spear. Mrs. Roberts found dry clothes for every one of us. She put us to sleep, several in a bed.

John Edward called Reverend Whitwer, and he called all our parents to tell them we were all safe. In the morning Mrs. Roberts fixed us breakfast, and when Reverend Whitwer drove out, he loaded his car with scouts, and Mr. Roberts said he had to go to town and drove the rest of us and our gear back to town in his truck. The tornado had blown down trees in town and had demolished the chimney and one of the towers on the courthouse. A few homes had bad damage, but no one was hurt, and most of the town had been spared.

In late summer, 1940, Dad asked me to go with him to Rugby to help him clean furnaces. We worked in some of the downtown businesses and in some of Rugby's homes. My job would be to clean out all the ashes, then brush down the firebox and vacuum up the soot while Dad cleaned the furnace pipes and chimney. I didn't mind the work, but I hated getting so dirty. It was hard to get clean again in the hotel bathtub, and there was no shower in the one bathroom.

One of Dad's cousins, Guy Troyer, owned the theater in Rugby. He told the manager of the theater to let me go to movies free any night I wanted. One evening I met a couple of Rugby kids and asked them if they'd like to go to the show with me, telling them I could get them in free. When I asked the manager for tickets for me and my friends, he was not happy, but he did let us all in free. Another of Dad's cousins, Oscar Troyer, owned the beer joint and pool hall on Rugby's main street. Oscar's son, a high school kid named R.B., taught me to play pool and gave me Coca Cola from the bar.

When harvest time came, I asked Ole Stenerson if he'd hire me again to take care of the grain wagons. But Ole told me needed me instead to herd his cows. I borrowed Stong's Colonel again, and for three weeks herded Ole's cows and young stock in the fields that had been harvested. What I couldn't understand was that Colonel seemed unhappy and kind of ornery all three weeks. I thought it was because he was with cattle and in fields that were strange to him, but I wished Colonel could tell me what was bothering him.

Harvest-time Saturday nights in Cando were always fun for us boys, because we could usually catch a fight between two men in the alley behind Uncle Jesse's saloon. One Saturday night after watching a fight, Grant Schneider almost had a fight with a kid from Egeland. He was watching the fight, too, and told Grant and me his name was Ray. As we walked back towards the center of downtown, the three of us talked about how England was being bombed every night. Ray said the war was England's fault and that Germans were a lot better people than the English. Although Grant had a German name, he was on the side of the English and asked Ray if he wanted to fight for the Germans. Ray was smart to say no.

Mom took a job nursing Mrs. Madson in her home after she had a stroke. Mrs. Madson hired me to put on her storm windows. While I was working for her, Mrs. Madson called me to her bedside and handed me a revolver. She said, "I want you to throw this down the toilet hole. It has already done more harm than it should have, and I want it destroyed." I did what she said, although I sure would have liked to take that revolver home with me as my own. But I wanted to be trustworthy, like a good scout. Mom said Mrs. Madson had a wild imagination and told the minister when he called on her that she had broken every one of the Ten Commandments. The poor woman didn't live very long.

I felt a huge disappointment that fall, because Superintendent Miller had been hired away to be superintendent of New Rockford

Schools. Besides having to give up the friendship of Melby and Ann, I knew Superintendent Miller had done so much good for Cando Schools. Before leaving, though, Miller had assigned two teachers instead of one for both seventh and eighth grades to make those grades more like junior highs in bigger schools. Loretta Murray would have seventh grade homeroom, but would teach math and science to both seventh and eighth grades. Ruth Linn, who was Ruth Linn Williams from her marriage the spring before, had eighth grade homeroom and taught English and social studies for seventh and eighth grades. Miss Murray's red hair and green eyes showed both her sense of fun and her temper. Mrs. Williams, tall, vivacious, and pretty, always wore hand-knit dresses. I thought Mrs. Williams had the most musical speaking voice I'd ever heard.

Miss Murray taught math with lots of physical activities, sending us to the blackboard for drills and teaching us to chart ground plots with compass and protractor, then taking us outdoors to measure and check our plots. In earth science, Miss Murray liked to give us quizzes without warning. One such quiz had the question, "In what state is the Grand Canyon?" I couldn't recall whether it was in Colorado or Arizona, so I answered, "In the state of erosion." Miss Murray read my answer to the class and told them it was correct. We students remembered what we called "Murray's Sayings." One saying, to stop kids from writing on desks or walls, was, "Fools' names and fools' faces always appear in public places." Another saying, "Empty wagons rattle most," was to stop kids from yapping.

Miss Murray decided that all seventh graders should learn to knit. She brought us knitting needles, but told us we had to buy our own yarn, and to carry our knitting with us to work at whenever we had time. I had taken on a paper route, and one day I had to collect from Coach Kilpatrick during basketball practice. The team was being run through some screen plays when I got there, so I sat on the players' bench and began knitting. When Coach halted practice and came over to me, the team followed and howled with ridicule at the sissy with knitting needles. Coach Kilpatrick sat down beside me and said, "Have you learned how to purl yet? I'll show you." When he picked up the knitting and began to purl, he put a quick end to the wisecracks.

Mrs. Williams made sure we learned grammar and could apply the rules of English to our writing. She taught us verb tenses, subject-verb agreement, and the parts of speech, and had us apply the grammar in writing our own paragraphs, letters, and various longer pieces. She taught us to recognize exposition, characterization, and plot development in stories, and she had us memorize poems that we read in literature. She also taught us to prepare and deliver informative speeches. She taught us Roberts Rules of Order by having us elect class officers and hold class meetings. She had us organize a local chapter of the North Dakota Young Citizens League. That year in late autumn, our chapter hosted the YCL's regional convention. As the elected president of our YCL, I conducted meetings at the convention. I liked getting to know kids from other schools and soon learned that other seventh graders knew more than I did about a lot of things.

The last nice thing Mrs. Williams did for me was to ask me to be in a panel with high school senior Vernon Pearson and eighth grader Susanne Menness at a PTA meeting. We were to talk about how to apply history and social studies to our lives. Vernon Pearson was on the debate team and he spoke about the importance of following the war in Europe. Susanne talked about how we are really a small planet, living closer than it seems to other parts of the world. She mentioned that Russia, which was then invading Finland, had sold us Alaska, and was only twenty-seven miles from our territory across the Bering Strait. When it was my turn, I told how I had read two world history texts in sixth grade and was surprised to learn that they told two different histories of the world. I felt my talk was pretty lame compared to Vernon's and Susanne's, but Mrs. Williams and some of the PTA members praised us all three.

During Christmas vacation I had reason to be disappointed by Dad. Troop 82 was to have a one-week winter camp at Lake Upsilon during vacation, and when I asked Dad for the twenty-four-dollar camp fee, he turned me down. I felt Dad was being stingy and cheating me out of an important experience.

So when Aunt Dee drove into town and asked if I'd come out with her and shoot jackrabbits that were eating the new trees in her shelterbelt, I said sure, right away. I told Dad I was going to Grandpa's farm to shoot jackrabbits for Aunt Dee. Dad said, "I don't like you going to shoot rabbits, and besides, it's not Grandpa's farm, since he's dead and gone."

Aunt Dee heard Dad and said, "To the grandkids it'll always be

Grandpa's farm," and Mom added that she thought I should go help out my aunt. I felt I'd won that disagreement.

I had Floyd Jorgenson sub for my *Devils Lake Journal* route and went to the farm with Aunt Dee. It was a gray, windy day, getting colder by the minute when we got to the farm about an hour past noon. With Grandpa's 22 Winchester and a box of cartridges, I headed into the shelterbelt. I shot two jackrabbits before coming back in for noon dinner. Walking back the mile length of the shelterbelt, I was facing the north wind and before I'd gone a hundred yards, snow began coming horizontally right at my face. I could hardly see my way, and three times I stumbled and fell into the snow. By the time I got to the house I was caked with snow and cold to the bone. Aunt Dee asked me to go to the woodpile and bring in a couple of armloads of kindling for the cook stove. Then she sent me to the cellar to bring up two scuttles of soft coal and about ten smaller chunks of lignite for the cooking range. She was afraid the oil heater might not keep the house warm enough.

By this time I had broken into a sweat, but still I was shivering. When I told Aunt Dee I felt like I might faint, she felt my forehead. "I think you have a fever. You should lie down on the couch in the dining room and cover up good." I soon fell asleep. I woke up when it was pitch dark, but I could see through the bay window we were in the midst of a nasty blizzard. The wind was howling and I could hear Aunt Dee snoring in her bedroom off the dining room. My mouth was so dry my tongue was stuck to the top of my mouth. I could tell I had a high fever. I went to the kitchen for a drink of water and threw some lignite chunks into the kitchen range. Through the kitchen window I could see that the blizzard had already laid a high bank between the house and the pump house. I felt dizzy again, and got back to the couch with my water, covered up with the quilts, and went back to sleep.

It was dim morning when I woke up again with my mouth all sticky dry. My throat felt swollen shut, and I felt I was burning with fever. I heard Aunt Dee at the kitchen stove and tried to call her, but couldn't make my tongue work very well. Aunt Dee heard my sounds, though, and came, looking very worried. "Telephone lines blew down, so I can't call out. I made it down to the mailbox with a note in case the mailman comes. You're a sick boy, Wallace, and I think Doc MacDonald ought to see you."

Mailman George Williams did come to the house and followed

Aunt Dee in to the couch where I was. He felt my forehead and said, "Whew! He's on fire all right. I'll go to Noah's place soon as I get to town. I got stuck a couple of times already, but I'll make it to town. Maybe MacDonald can get out here in his Green Hornet. By the time I get to town, roads are bound to be too drifted for car travel."

In my mind I could see Doc MacDonald's Green Hornet. He and Uncle Jesse and Ed Crume had rebuilt a Model A with caterpiller treads and ski runners, so it could go where cars couldn't go.

Aunt Dee kept giving me aspirin every several hours, usually waking me up for me to take them. I tried to keep my throat open with water, but man, it was hard to even get the aspirin swallowed.

Night passed, but I was so sick, I hardly knew when morning came. Aunt Dee fixed me some tea, and I did get some down, but I quickly faded back into sleep. In late afternoon, I heard Dad's voice right by my couch. "How's my dear boy? I got some sulfa capsules from Doc MacDonald that he says will fix what you got. He better be right." Dad held a glass of water and popped two capsules into my mouth, and somehow I washed them down. I took two more a couple of hours later, and by the time Aunt Dee was ready for bed, I was feeling not quite on fire. Dad sat by my couch, covered with a quilt, and he told me next morning he had gotten some sleep.

"Doc thought you probably have strep throat, and said by now your fever might break." Dad felt my face and forehead and said, "By God, I think the sulfa did it."

Dad told me Doc MacDonald's Green Hornet had burned out a wheel bearing, so he had slogged on foot through the snowdrifts the seven and a half miles to the farm. "Doc told me I'd better get to my boy, by horse or by foot, and I didn't have a horse. But here I am, and I think you're gonna get well." That was Saturday, and by Monday the telephone lines were working again. By Tuesday, the roads were plowed clear, and Dad and Aunt Dee and I got back to Cando in Aunt Dee's V-8. I sure lost my resentment of Dad for not giving me money for winter camp. I knew now that my dad was truly trustworthy.

When school began again, Mrs. Williams didn't return because she was going to have a baby. Mrs. Kilpatrick was the first substitute teacher, and I hoped Mrs. Kilpatrick would stay as replacement, because she was witty. One day, giving us spelling, she said, "Concrete. Anything you can touch is concrete," as she touched Stuart Hinkle's head. But Mrs. Kilpatrick didn't want full-time work, and the replacement teacher we got wasn't any match to Mrs. Williams. I felt I was missing a lot of English and social studies.

Not long after Christmas, Art Torkelson, who delivered the *Grand Forks Herald*, said he'd like me to take the south half of town while he kept the north half. Delivering the *Herald* would make me much more money than delivering the *Devils Lake Journal*, but the problem was that to deliver the *Herald* you had to put up a fifty-dollar bond, and Dad couldn't afford it that winter. Art said, "Let's go talk to my dad."

I had talked more than once with Torkel Torkelson. He was the town's major shoemaker. Once when I had him put half soles on my boots, he was making an amazing wood carving of a ball in a cage of four connected posts. I asked Torkel how he had learned to carve like that, and he told me he'd learned it in Norway. Art had sometime earlier made my imagination soar by telling me about the Torkelson family taking a ship from New York City to Norway a couple of summers before. They spent a month following their cousins' goats up the mountains, making cheese along the way and picking up the ripe cheese on the way back down. What a fabulous adventure!

When I went with Art to Torkel's shoe shop, Art explained about my not having the money for the bond. Torkel asked Art, "You trust him?" When Art said he did, Torkel said, "Okay, I'll pay for the bond, but if Wallace is dishonest, I get the money back from you." Art laughed and said, "That's a deal." I kept that paper route through ninth grade and liked getting to know the more than thirty families on my route.

The new Peavey Elevator man moved to town with two boys who became my friends. Walt Brower lived right across the street from the grade school, and his son Willard was in eighth grade, while Roger was in sixth. Mrs. Brower seemed to like her sons bringing home friends, and the Brower family were always playing cards or board games together, so it was fun to visit there.

Walt Brower had been a minor league baseball pitcher. He taught Willard to pitch baseball and to throw a beautiful football pass. Roger was a comic book nut who knew more about comic books than any other kid, and was generous in lending his massive collection. So he got me reading comic books for a while.

A major change at our home came when Dr. MacDonald talked

Mom into taking an asthmatic sufferer as a patient into our home. Lillian Hunt was an unmarried woman, maybe ten years younger than Mom, but frail and subject to frequent bouts with breathlessness. Mom was paid by the county, but Doc MacDonald said it was federal money that paid for her care. Miss Hunt moved into Mom and Dad's bedroom, so that meant Dad would sleep with me, and Mom with Olive, an arrangement we'd followed before. Miss Hunt had to inhale an awful smelly powder when she had her asthma attacks, but otherwise she was a pleasant member of the household. Doc MacDonald came to see Miss Hunt every week, and Mom seemed to like having an "in-house" patient. We were all glad it meant Mom didn't have to go to someone else's home to be a nurse.

Miss Hunt had been raised in Canada, and was a very loyal British subject. One day I brought Willard Brower and Grant Schneider home for dinner. After my friends left, Miss Hunt said to me, "Brower? Schneider? They're foreigners, aren't they?" I assured Miss Hunt that my friends and their parents were all American citizens. I was pretty sure Miss Hunt hadn't really been asking a question, but was showing her distrust of anyone who didn't have an English, Scottish, Irish, or Welsh name.

At the Memorial Day program, I was asked to recite, "The Flag Is Passing By." I admit I felt honored to speak before about a hundred people.

Also that spring Mom rented a vacant lot near our home to give us an even bigger garden. Dad and I helped her plant that lot full of corn and potatoes and squash as well as other vegetables. I took the responsibility of keeping the corn and potatoes hilled up and weeding the whole garden—part of following the Scout law, "A Scout is Helpful." Now that Mom didn't have to be nurse outside our home, she gave lots of attention to cooking vegetables. I decided that vegetables have more flavor than any other kind of food.

I answered an ad in *Boys Life* for a down-filled sleeping bag. As a birthday present, Dad gave me half the money I needed for the sleeping bag, and I took the other thirty-four dollars from my savings from delivering the *Herald*. It was a beautiful sleeping bag with a strong waterproof khaki cover. I began sleeping under the stars on our lawn the night after it arrived. North Dakota from late May through August has splendid weather for sleeping outdoors without a tent, unless it rains. I loved to sleep under the star-filled sky for many nights through the summers after seventh, eighth, and ninth grades.

That summer of 1941 our scout troop went to the Lake Agassiz Council Camp at Wood Lake south of Devils Lake. Our troop had the camp all to ourselves, with Reverend Whitwer in charge, assisted by Homer Rendahl and John Vaughn, two former Cando scouts, as counselors. Again our main focus was to pass our scout requirements. Several of us were now working for First Class. I passed my swimming, my tracking, my signaling, mapping, and life-saving tests, as well as my pioneering merit badge requirements.

One day we hiked to the bluff called Devil's Heart. We passed a burial ground still in use by Dakota Sioux Indians. Reverend Whitwer told us a story about the Dakota tradition to place food on graves. He told us a white man once asked a Dakota, "When will your relatives come up from their graves to eat that food?" The Dakota answered, "When your relatives come up to smell the flowers you put on their graves." I was happy Reverend Whitwer admired American Indians. I'd been reading about them and I admired their knowledge of the earth and their reverence for everything in nature. To me Indian reverence for the earth best represented the Scout law, "A Scout is Reverent."

Friday before the camp was to end on Sunday, my cousin Russell, who was preaching then at the Assembly of God Church Camp at Lakewood Park near Devils Lake, came to take me home for Uncle Jesse's Saturday funeral. I had known Uncle Jesse had cancer, but I didn't expect him to die so soon. Just a month before, his daughter Rosamond had come home from her job in Washington, D.C., to die of congestive heart failure.

I was somewhat surprised at how sad I felt about Uncle Jesse's death. Part of that sadness, I think, was for Aunt Ella Mae. I wondered if she would stay much longer in her home after losing her daughter and her husband. Sure enough, not long after the funeral, Aunt Ella began to prepare for a sale of Uncle Jesse's tools and well equipment, and not long after that, she had a sale of all her household goods. She sold her home and moved to be near her relatives in Thief River Falls, Minnesota. Uncle Jesse and Aunt Ella being gone seemed to take a big chunk out of my life.

And then I learned that Susanne Menness's mother had remarried and wanted Susanne to come live with her and her new husband in

Fargo. The last time I saw Susanne was to watch her play table tennis with Vernon Pearson in the backyard of the Methodist parsonage, a popular play site for kids of all ages. The Pearson boys were sons of the minister. Claude was already in college. Vernon was graduating from high school, and Richard was two years older than me. Vernon had asked Susanne over to play table tennis. Susanne was in shorts and a low-cut blouse and already looked like a beautiful young woman. I knew she had far outgrown me, but I still felt miserable about her leaving town.

I had just reached thirteen, and I felt a bit scared about those teen years. I thought, overall, as a twelve-year-old I had made some progress at being trustworthy, and knew better what being trustworthy could mean. I hoped I could obey the Scout Laws and sustain all the good values I was learning as a Boy Scout.

CHAPTER 13

Can a teen still be *A Good Kid*?

I kept trying to follow the Scout laws and be a good kid, but I kept doing things I knew I shouldn't do. Sometimes I wondered if I was in charge of who I was, or if circumstances managed my life. For instance, when we went swimming in the coulee at Reid's pasture, we boys always swam naked. One day, a bunch of girls drove up to the coulee bank. Instead of staying covered by the water when the girls got out of the car, we all rushed out at the girls. They jumped back in the car and drove away. I was sure the girls thought we were crude. I wasn't sure why I'd joined the other guys to do something I knew was bad and had broken the law "A Scout is Brave" when I yielded to the coaxing or pressures of others.

Also, swimming at the coulee, some guy would share a pack of cigarettes he'd hooked from home, and we'd all light up and smoke. I'd go along with that, because smoking was supposed to be manly. And I guess it was to feel manly that made us guys at the swimming hole kill gophers the way we did. There were a number of gopher holes along the coulee. By filling a leaky milk bucket we found in the pasture with coulee water and pouring it down a gopher hole, we'd force the gopher out of the hole. Standing around the hole with sticks, we'd all club the escaping gopher to death. I always felt torn inside between doing what other guys did to feel manly, and my own values not to be a smoker and not to be cruel to animals, but to follow the law "A Scout is Kind." Pretending I was manly was not making me the kind of person I wanted to be.

But that question of whether I could be in charge of my actions kept coming. I had been hired to take care of Mrs. Noyes's big yard that summer. It usually took me a whole day to mow the lawn, water the flowers, and pick up fallen refuse from rain and wind. Gladys Frost, who had been my second grade teacher, had always had an apartment in Mrs. Noyes's house upstairs. I had liked her as my teacher, and I could remember May Day when, responding to the May basket I left in the doorway leading upstairs, Miss Frost chased me, caught me, and kissed me. One day when I came to take care of the Noyes yard, I saw a panel truck advertising coffee parked in the back driveway. Not long after, I saw Gladys Frost and the coffee man at the panel truck embrace and kiss like lovers do in movies. I felt happy that Miss Frost had a boyfriend.

After I finished the Noyes yard, I took a long ride on my bike on Highway 281 south of town. Coming back, at the edge of town I saw Betty mowing the Belzer lawn, and rode my bike in to say Hi. It was in Miss Frost's class that I met Betty, so I told her about seeing Miss Frost kiss the coffee man. Betty said, "Oh, I've heard all about that. He's from Devils Lake. He's a married man with kids. Miss Frost is screwing around with a married man."

I thought, What? How can my classmate know so much about the private lives of grown-ups? I left there feeling ashamed that I'd been the carrier of nasty gossip and was not keeping the Scout laws, to be Trustworthy, Loyal, and Courteous.

That summer I'd had a continuing sore throat, and not wanting a return of strep throat, Mom decided I should have Dr. Olafson remove my tonsils. Ordinarily I went to Dr. MacDonald for everything, but he had done such a bad job removing Olive's tonsils, Mom sent me to Dr. Olafson. He set me in a chair like dentists use, injected some novacaine, and cut out my tonsils. He had me rest on a cot off his treatment room for about an hour before Dad picked me up and drove me home. Then Dad drove to Blackburn's Drug and brought me back a milkshake to comfort the soreness in my throat.

Next day my cousin Veora had a tonsillectomy from Dr. Olafson, too, and Dad brought Veora to our house to recover, so Mom could be her nurse if need be. Veora was Mom's patient in Olive's bedroom off our living room, where I was a patient on the sofa. Being close enough to talk in spite of our sore throats, Veora and I had a long visit the day we spent in recovery. Veora told me about having been jilted in love, talking to me as if I were no longer a kid. She talked about a lot of things she had learned as telephone operator about Cando citizens. Some things people did were not very nice. It made me feel more grown up to be talked to as a grown-up. Now that I was thirteen, going into eighth grade, I was feeling older. But I wondered if growing older would make me see the bad in other people, as Veora and Betty did.

When school began, I could see what I thought was bad about eighth grade girls. For one thing, they had outgrown us guys, most of them now taller than we were. And their taking on womanly shape seemed to have made them act as tough as boys. Besides, they seemed too interested in sex. Adult books I'd been reading for several years often described love affairs, but not in sexy language. Eighth grade girls, though, seemed to find adult books that described sex in full details. One book they were passing around was *Sorrell and Son*, a best seller. In it, they had marked the more vividly sexy passages, and were now passing it around to us guys. When one of the girls handed me the novel, she said, "I guess you'll read the whole book, but you might want to read the marked passages first."

A brother and sister, Neil and Marjorie McLean, moved from Egeland to Cando into an apartment just three doors from our house. We three began walking to school together, and soon became friends. Marge, a ninth grader, was almost as pretty as Susanne Menness, but I could tell Marge thought me just a kid like her little brother. Neil was small for his age, but lacked nothing in challenge and daring. He spent lots of weekends hunting with his dad, Hector, and other men. Neil would pass along the raunchiest songs and stories I'd ever heard. But the language used by most eighth graders made me believe that being a teen turns your talk nastier.

Our eighth grade teachers seemed to expect us all to be bad kids. It reminded me that kids, like farm animals, usually do what's expected of them.

Our new superintendent, Mr. Stewart, had hired all new eighth grade teachers. Miss Gilbert, a large, heavy-footed woman, had taken Mrs. Williams's place for social studies. She'd spend most of every day writing outlines of our social studies textbook on the blackboard, telling us to copy every word, because what was in those outlines would be on our tests.

And instead of Miss Murray for math and science, the high school band teacher, Harvey Retzlaff, was our teacher. He never really taught us math, just assigned us pages from our math book, and had us trade papers to grade our work. He never taught science either, but seemed to think science should be taught as a health course pointing out the falseness of advertising. He'd bring a toothpaste ad to read aloud and say, "They just want to get you hooked on their product. Now you should know that baking soda is a better tooth cleaner than Colgates or Ipana." Kids reacted to Retzlaff saying, "*Rats Laugh* has such bad breath, he must never brush his teeth with anything." Earth science was supposed to be what we were learning, but it was taught as false advertising, too. He'd bring ads from farm magazines to ridicule, never giving us time to discuss the textbook chapters he told us to read, just giving us true-false tests over the chapter. I was reading lots of science books and knew for sure that earth science was not a question of true or false, but was full of uncertainties. Until eighth grade (except for Miss Lester), I had always liked my teachers. Gilbert and Retzlaff were making me hate teachers, and I didn't like that feeling.

No one could hate our English teacher, only laugh at her or feel sorry for her. Miss Tollefson had just finished St. Olaf College, and seemed scared to death of us. She also taught English in high school, and had to share the desk in our classroom with Gilbert and Retzlaff. She'd come into the classroom, usually a few minutes late, out of breath from her fast walk from the high school and from carrying a load of books and papers she had to correct. She'd look for a place on the shared teachers' desk to set things down, and often would drop some of her armload on the floor.

One day Miss Tollefson arrived with an unwrapped condom on top of her load of books and papers. She held up the condom and said, "Someone left this big balloon on my desk, but didn't yet blow it up." Of course the class howled with laughter, but she could never maintain class order anyhow.

Tough-talking, strutting Less Mellors had replaced Coach Kilpatrick, who had been well liked and admired. Kilpatrick had been preparing us junior high kids in phys ed with good fundamentals in all sports. Now we were treated like scum. At phys ed, Mellors would give us the equipment, tell us to choose sides and go at it. He'd sit on a bench at the side of the field, reading a newspaper or a magazine. We knew from reports by high school kids that Mellors and Miss Rollestad, the giggly vocal-music teacher, were necking almost nightly in Mellors's parked car. At Christmas vacation, they both left Cando Schools and got married. No one was sorry to see those two go.

Superintendent Stewart, who had replaced Paul Miller, and had hired that bunch of crummy teachers, would strut down the hall mornings towards his office, and kids standing along the walls of the hallway would call out, "Jeep, Jeep, Jeep, Jeep," as he passed by. He couldn't tell who was saying it, and pretended he didn't hear it. Kids gave him the name Jeep as soon as they saw him, thinking he looked like the character of that name in the funnies. But I never joined the kids calling him Jeep, because Olive worked as Stewart's secretary part of each day in the Student Work Program of the National Youth Administration. Olive insisted that I not make fun of Stewart for her job's sake. Even so I despised him for hiring the teachers he'd brought to our school.

Boy Scouts was still what I used to try to keep my life on course to be a good kid. I passed all my First Class tests by the end of September, the last test being the fourteen-mile hike. Art Torkelson picked up a township map at the courthouse and he and I plotted our trip to follow coulees north and west of town. We filled the requirement one Saturday before our papers came in at the depot for delivery. John Edward Stutzman joined Art and me as the first First Class scouts in the revived Troop 82.

I started to work on my merit badges right away after the court of honor. Because the Art Merit Badge was among the first listed, I studied the merit badge booklet for art and went to Miss Murray after school to ask if she would be my examiner. I knew that she painted and seemed to know about works of art and artists. She said she'd be honored to be my examiner, and asked me how I liked eighth grade. I complained about every one of my eighth grade teachers. Miss Murray said, "Don't be too hard on them. They've all been given jobs that are anything but easy, having to teach classes in both high school and eighth grade. I have it easier with all four subjects for seventh grade. It's not the fun it was, teaching both seventh and eighth grades with Ruth Linn Williams, but our new superintendent has his own ideas. We all miss Superintendent Miller." I felt better, hearing a teacher I admired tell me that it wasn't only students who thought Cando School was no longer as good as it was before.

That fall, Coach Mellors never gave us eighth graders any football instruction in phys ed, but would simply toss us a football and tell us to choose up and play touch ball. We wanted to play tackle, not touch ball, so we did what we'd done when we were younger kids. We put together our own football team, but being older, we organized our team with set plays and positions. I was halfback as both running back and blocking back, and played either linebacker or safety on defense. We chose our best players, Grant Schneider and Willard Brower, as co-captains. Brower could throw a pass thirty yards or more to Schneider, who rarely missed a catch.

Grant had a friend at the Devils Lake parochial school and arranged for us to play St. Mary's eighth grade team on a Sunday. When they arrived in a farm truck, we saw that most of their team were taller and heavier than we were. They smeared us, tackling Brower before he could get off a pass, and always had Schneider covered. They scored easily on end runs with two guys running interference and getting great blocking from their linesmen.

Both teams played without uniforms or any protective gear. After we were trailing twenty-eight to nothing, I was determined as linebacker to stop their scoring another end run. I felt by faking out one of their interference runners, I could tackle the ball carrier. I was able to dodge the lead interference and with all my strength, lunged at the ball carrier. I brought him down, but his knee slammed the top of my head. I woke up on the sidelines, seeing the driver of St. Mary school's truck laying a damp handkerchief on my forehead. He told me I had stopped their team from making another touchdown. I faded out knowing our team had the ball, and was later told that Brower had hit Schneider for one touchdown, so at least we weren't skunked.

I walked home with a mean headache and right away lay down in bed. John MacDonald went home to tell Doc about my being knocked out at the game. Dr. MacDonald came to our house, and after first checking on Miss Hunt, came to examine me. He said I had a pretty severe concussion and bawled me out for playing without any equipment.

Eighth grade had seemed to put an end to the great group of kids who had lots of fun together. Now we were all acting as if we had to prove we were each better and separate from everyone else. I think I did a lot of things just to be defiant; then after doing them, I'd feel ashamed. It didn't help that the more physically developed girls acted as if they were in charge of us guys' social life. Their parties were marked by games that made us do what the girls wanted.

Phyllis Burkhart had a Halloween party at her home, but the only game that seemed to mark Halloween was ducking in a tub to grab apples with our teeth. One game that embarrassed me was passing a cabbage head from boy to girl without hands, holding the cabbage under our chins so we had to push up close, chest to chest. Another game was spin the bottle, with the rule that at your turn to spin it, you had to kiss the person of the opposite sex that the bottle stopped to point at.

Another party was at the home of a new girl in our class, Joanne Peterson, whose dad took over as manager of the J. C. Penney store. Her party in early winter had most of the same games as the Halloween party, but added the game of post office. I took advantage of one rule of that game, just to be spiteful, I guess. The rule was, if you got a letter from a girl requesting a kiss, you could trade the letter with some other guy for a piece of candy. I traded all my letters, three of which were from Joanne Peterson. When I learned after the party that Joanne had a crush on me, I felt stupid for acting so defiant at her party.

Heavy snowfall early in that school year meant that many country kids had to move into homes of friends in town. Olive's best friend, Mary Converse, came to stay at our home and share Olive's bedroom. I liked to hear Mary talk about her older brothers. The oldest, Sheldon, had been a Navy air force pilot, but became a test pilot for Grumman Aircraft. Chesterfield cigarettes paid him to be on an advertisement, and Mary had a poster of the ad. Her other brothers, Ralph and Duane, were both in college, and Duane was a track star on his college team.

One day Mary accidentally gave me quite a surprise. I was in the girls' bedroom talking to Olive. Mary came to the room after her bath and with her mind occupied, peeled off her bathrobe to stand in front of me bare. It was my first frontal glimpse of a totally naked woman, and Mary had a tall, elegant figure. She laughed and apologized as she put her robe back on. I felt somewhat embarrassed, but I sure wasn't offended. I wished it might happen again to give me more time to look at Mary's bare body.

On Sunday, December 7, 1941, I was building a model airplane and listening to the broadcast of "Kay Kaiser's Musical College" on NBC. Dad was at his desk working on business and I told him what was being broadcast, so he joined me to listen to the shocking reports. Olive and Mary had been out for a walk and when they joined Dad and me at the radio, Mary was almost in tears, worried that her brothers would have to go to war. In several months both Ralph and Duane were being trained to be officers in the Navy and Army. Sheldon continued to be a test pilot. I felt envious, thinking it would be so brave to be fighting for the U.S.

That year Olive and Mary Converse had become their senior class leaders with Mary class president and Olive glee club president. Mary said their class was so full of duds, if those two didn't take leadership, nothing would get done. So Olive and Mary took responsibility for planning their commencement, too. But of course they couldn't be responsible for North Dakota weather on their prom night, May 8. A heavy snowstorm almost ruined the girls' fancy gowns and slippers.

At school the day after Pearl Harbor, Mr. Retzlaff asked me what I thought about the attack by the Japanese. I told him I thought World War II would be over in a couple of months, now that the U.S. had joined the Allies. Retzlaff didn't agree with me, but said he was afraid he'd soon be drafted. He wasn't drafted during the school year, but enlisted when school was out.

Many Cando men in the headquarters company of North Dakota National Guard were called to war right away. The guard was headed by Captain Roy Miller, editor and publisher of the *Cando Record,* and by Lieutenant Bill Considine, who managed the county welfare office. There were about fifty men in the headquarters company, and they were moved in early January to Bismarck for quick training. They then became the lead platoon of the 164th Infantry, sent to the South Pacific. There were many anxious Cando families whose husbands and sons were fighting in that first infantry division called on to take back South Pacific islands from the Japanese. It wasn't long before Rollie Andricks was the first casualty of the Cando National Guard company.

Mary's aunt taught school in the little town of Calio, and because of heavy snow, had to stop driving from Cando to work and rented a room in Calio. Her husband was mail carrier on a star route to transfer mail to and from smaller towns by car, and he often could not get home until long after dark. So Mary's eleven-year-old nephew, Dalton, came to live with us, too. I felt Dalton was annoying because he wanted so much attention from me, but when he started building model airplanes with skill, I grew to like him. The trouble was, our home had before seemed just the right size for our family, but now there was someone sleeping in every room except the kitchen. Miss Hunt had her bedroom, and Olive and Mary had theirs. Dad slept with me, and Mama slept on a couch in the dining room. Dalton had the sofa in the living room as his bed.

Elgie Jacobson showed me that it's sometimes hard to know when you've done something that's bad. Elgie's parents were among my *Grand Forks Herald* customers. One day when I stopped at their house to collect, Mrs. Jacobson and her friends were having a card party with drinks on their front porch and used me for a laugh. When I said I'd come to collect for the *Herald*, Mrs. Jacobson said, "Maybe you'd like to collect in trade? Would you rather have me or Elgie?" Her friends whooped as I blushed but didn't answer. I was stupid to tell what happened, but I told Neil McLean. A day or so later, Elgie attacked me in the classroom with no teacher present. I felt I couldn't even try to defend myself, but let Elgie pummel me as long as she wanted. I knew I'd been as bad to tell Neil what Mrs. Jacobson said as she had been in using me for her joke, and more bad than Elgie for beating up on me.

In early 1942 I had the good luck to find a new friendship. The youngest and maybe the smartest of the talented Pearson brothers was Richard. Richard was missing school, recovering at home from rheumatic fever. After church one day, Reverend Pearson told me Dick was feeling lonely. When I went to visit Richard, I took along a copy of *Popular Mechanics Magazine* with directions for making a powerful capacitor like those used by the U.S. Army to make static on enemy radio reception. Dick was excited to get the directions and told me to come back in three days when he'd have made the capacitor. Dick had a shop in the parsonage basement where he worked with chemistry and electricity. I was sure he knew more about those subjects than any other kid in town. I watched Dick turn on the capacitor and heard the Pearsons' radio upstairs blare static. Dick said he'd most likely made static on radios in the whole neighborhood. I learned a lot from Dick as he let me help him in his shop.

That spring Reverend and Mrs. Pearson asked Olive and me to go with them and Dick to Jamestown College to see Claude and Vernon Pearson play in *Macbeth*. Claude was Macduff and Vernon was Banquo. I thought everyone in that college play was fantastic and I was eager to read Shakespeare's plays after seeing *Macbeth*.

On that trip, Dick showed me he had other talents besides science. On weekends college students who went home left room in the boys' dormitory for Dick and me to sleep. Two students still in the dorm began talking about Catholic priests and nuns having sex together. One guy said a plumber had to be called to open the sewer from the nuns' quarters and found the sewer line clogged with condoms. I was so proud of Dick's courage when he said to the college guys, "You two should be ashamed. You know that's nasty gossip and not true. Priests and nuns are good, devout Christians. You should respect them, not show your ignorant Protestant prejudice." I decided right then I wanted to spend more time with Dick Pearson, and when my voice changed, I joined Dick to sing bass in the Methodist choir.

I had already made singing part of my life right after Christmas when Violet Peterson replaced Miss Rollestad as vocal music teacher. Miss Peterson brought back Cando School's strong music tradition with girls' glee club and a big mixed-voice chorus. She also started a male chorus for junior and senior high, giving us music written for boys' choirs with soprano and alto as well as tenor and bass parts. Miss Peterson knew how to make kids love singing, and being in male chorus gave me a sense of belonging that was strong and spirit-fulfilling.

I felt the war was having bad effects on our little town. Besides the National Guard and draft taking so many men from Cando, war jobs attracted families to move to the west coast. I knew I'd miss the Brendings and the Schneiders when they moved west. And then Walt Brower took an elevator job in a town in the Red River Valley. Bob and Dennis Brending, Grant Schneider, and Willard Brower were going to leave a terrible gap in Cando sports teams.

I felt I'd miss Grant Schneider most of all, since he and I had built a cave together, and I'd climbed atop nearly every building on Main Street with him. But in ninth grade Grant changed so much, I didn't see much of him any more. Always before a natural leader, Grant had become a loner. One day he told me what had changed him. He said he was spending almost every evening with his ninth grade English teacher, a pretty recent university graduate. He said he'd sneak into her apartment through a basement window so neighbors wouldn't see him. I wasn't sure I believed what Grant told me about things he and his teacher did, but it sounded both exciting and risky. I wondered if Grant and his teacher took those risks for love, or if they had become part of the mood of war, to take advantage of the uncertainties about the time you have.

When summer came, the new John Deere dealer brought sons

Mike and Arlo Westmiller to town, giving Cando athletics some gain against all the loss from other guys' departures. And then Joe Welch moved from Rugby when his dad took over Cando Bakery and I knew Joe was good at basketball.

That summer our Troop 82 was again at Lake Upsilon's Isaac Walton Campground. Weather almost shut down our camp activities with two days and nights of heavy rain. I learned that even digging a trench around a tent can't keep out water if the tent is on slanted ground. My tent mates John Schaeffer and Billy Schwartz and I had soaked bedding until the rain stopped. But getting to know those younger guys better, especially Billy Schwartz, was a real gain. Though I was two years older than Billy, he became as good a friend as Art Torkelson and Dick Pearson, who were two years older than me. Billy was a smart kid who read lots of science and said he wanted to become a doctor, just as I did.

We never expected the war's national security rules would affect our family, but they gave us a nasty surprise in late summer, 1942. Mom got a phone call from Dad that he had taken the weekend from work to go fishing in Canada with a Rolla businessman. On their return at the border entry station, Dad was refused reentry. Dad had become a Canadian citizen years before in order to get a Canadian homestead. When he moved back to the U.S. he had never reclaimed his U.S. citizenship. All August, Dad had to stay in Canada, getting some work as a farmhand, but his lack of furnace work put a hard strain on our family. Attorney Clarence Joseph got Dad papers for proof of birth, work, marriage, and home ownership, so finally Dad was permitted to return home and then he again became a U.S. citizen.

CHAPTER 14

When did I become *An Adolescent*?

Man alive! When school started in the fall of '42, I had grown three or four inches. With my added height and weight, I made the football team, though only as a substitute guard. Even so, I was glad to be on the team, and Dewey King, who played center and was team captain, gave me tips on how to improve my play as a linesman.

Besides those changes in height and weight, I could tell my attitudes were changing, too. I wasn't worrying as much about always being a good kid. In fact, I was feeling that for a ninth grader in a small town, I was kind of a big shot.

When I showed I could sluff off chipping half of one of my top front teeth, I felt I was pretty tough, too. One day at practice, John Gibbens

Cando Cubs football team, 1942

and I were sent to tackle running back Donald Green. We both hit him at the same time with so much speed we swung around, and my mouth slammed against Gibbens's helmet. So besides the team letter I got that year, I got a gold crown for my upper right front tooth. It took some bravery to pass dentist Johnson's tedious, long-lasting procedure for that gold crown. His old equipment meant that he used an inch-diameter grindstone to give the broken tooth an even edge, and he used a hand-sprayed atomizer when the tooth grew too hot from grinding. I thought I was plenty tough to refuse novocaine, but it took four hour-long sittings to prepare the tooth for its crown. I didn't even feel guilty about what the dentist charged Dad.

Neither did I feel guilty about taking part in the swagger and loud banter in the locker room after practice. It helped me feel like a real jock. As I'd shed my stinking sweatshirt and jock strap, I'd head into the locker room joining teammates to sing raunchy made-up words to current pop love songs such as, "I'll be seizing you in all those unfamiliar places, that my dream of you embraces all night through." One day Miss McConnell, whose business ed classroom was right next to the locker room, came to the wall of the locker room to shout, "Boys! Stop that vulgar singing, right now, or I'll report you." We stopped right then, but were at it next day again, because to us Old Maid McConnell never had sex herself, so she didn't even get the humor we felt about sex.

It was obvious I'd become an adolescent because sex was on my mind, more often than once in a while. The major subject of that interest was Peggy Baney.

When Roy and Etta Baney moved to California to take war plant jobs, they left their adopted daughters in Cando with our family until Roy and Etta could get settled. Marilyn soon married soldier Bud Cartwright, and left with him for Fort Leavenworth. But Peggy stayed with us to wait for her folks to send for her.

At first Peggy charmed me with stories about her year at the University of North Dakota. One story gave me mixed feelings. At Epworth League Camp Peggy had been offered room and board in exchange for babysitting and some housework in the home of the minister who headed Wesley College, located near the university. When the minister's wife took their children to visit her mother, the minister told Peggy she should move into his bed. Peggy told me her refusal of his invitation made the minister mad as hops, and he asked her why she thought she'd been given the room and board job, anyhow. That story reminded me of Olive's story about the minister Daddy Moon and his demonstration of the dangers of dancing. Peggy's story made me wonder if trying to seduce young women was a typical minister's calling. But the story also made me fantasize about getting Peggy into my bed.

Peggy showed me enough of herself to make me very horny. When Peggy moved in, Mother offered her Olive's bedroom, but Peggy said that Mom and Dad should keep that bed, and she would sleep on the couch in the dining room. That was a treat for me. From my bed through the open door I had dimly lighted views of Peggy as she changed into her pajamas. Sometimes in full light I'd see her without blouse as she ironed her clothes wearing a slip or half-slip and brassiere. I knew the look of her breasts so well I could see them in my mind's eye.

One day, Mom's friend Mrs. Swenson phoned to say her oldest son was home on leave. He'd been at Pearl Harbor when the Japanese attacked. Mrs. Swenson wondered if her son might take Olive to a movie. Mom explained that Olive was at college in Minot, but asked Peggy if she'd like a date. The night Peggy dated sailor Swenson, she came home while I was still reading in bed. She went to the bathroom and came to my room to say Mom was snoring away so loud it sounded like Dad. But Dad was in Rugby installing a furnace.

Peggy closed the door to my room and sat on the edge of the bed. I asked her about her date with the sailor. Her answer was a sigh and a comment that sailor Swenson was a chain smoker who must not have found her attractive. I said Swenson must be blind not to find her attractive, and Peggy stretched across the bed, touched my face with her lips, and said, "I sure wish you were old enough to be my date." Then she kissed me open-mouthed with her tongue flickering in my mouth. The way she kissed gave me courage to pull her to me. Peggy kicked off her shoes and slipped under the covers. We kissed again and again, while she guided my hand through her unbuttoned blouse to the snap at the front of her brassiere. She said, "A snap in front is easier to handle if you have big boobs like mine. You should learn how to unsnap a bra." I learned, right away.

Feeling Peggy's bare breasts was more than I had ever hoped. She also let me unsnap her garter belt from her stockings so I could caress her bare legs, but she pulled my hand back when I reached too high. After a couple more exciting kisses, Peggy said, "That's all for tonight, but I'll be back again some time soon."

Every night for the next week I waited for Peggy to keep her promise. But about two weeks after her visit to my bed she showed me a letter she had just received from Olive. It was short, in purple ink, with every word underlined. "Leave my baby brother alone! Don't you dare ruin his innocence!" I felt deceived and embarrassed, and most of all disappointed. Why would Peggy write my sister to tell her about our secret petting session? Many nights until Peggy left for the west coast, I'd lie in bed, recalling that one special night, keeping my eye on the couch where Peggy slept.

As the ninth grade year progressed, another woman stirred my desire. Our teacher of English and social studies was Helen Handy, a first-year teacher out of Moorhead State College. She was five foot two, eyes of blue, with a figure like a movie star. She obviously wanted her students to like her, and I tried to show her I did.

Miss Handy told the class she had a boyfriend in the Air Force, and she said the war was always on her mind. One day she read to the class a chapter from the novel *They Were Expendable*. She read us the description of General MacArthur leaving doctors, nurses, and medical corpsmen in the Philippines to be captured or killed by the Japanese as they watched MacArthur load one small ship with his furniture and with other family possessions and then watched the general chug away in another ship with his family, his riding horses, and his dogs.

I was incensed. I raised my hand to ask Miss Handy, "If that's the kind of man General MacArthur is, why are we fighting this war, anyhow?"

Miss Handy said, "Do you really want to know why?" and I answered that I sure did.

Miss Handy sent me to the library for John Gunther's *Inside Europe*, and told me that might help me understand the why of the war. When I finished Gunther's history of political events from World War I to 1936, Miss Handy loaned me her own copy of William Shirer's *Berlin Diary*. Shirer's day-by-day account of the German people accepting Adolph Hitler's values of racial superiority and hatred of Jews was fresh news to me. Miss Handy followed Shirer's book with *Saw-*

dust Caesar, that told how Mussolini created a fascist state in economically depressed Italy, which helped me see how a tyrant can use propaganda to bring a nation under his total control. The next book was *Out of the Night* by German communist Eugene Krebs, who, writing as Jan Valtin, told of punishment dealt to him as a political prisoner in Nazi Germany. Finally, Miss Handy gave me her copy of *Mein Kampf*, and I read the cunning and fearful plans of Der Führer, to learn how fear and hatred are used to justify anything a dictator coaxes people to accept.

By the time I finished those five books, I had become so aware of tyrannical nationalism, I could recognize its appeals in propaganda from our side as well as our enemy's. Fascistic behavior became a constant reference for me, and I began to see that some bigotry and ugly meanness in our own society mirrored the politics of Hitler and Mussolini. I was also convinced that we were fighting a noble cause, and I followed news of the war with a passion for our side to win.

But my desire for Miss Handy came from giving oral reports of each book. Because I had football practice right after school, we arranged for those reports on evenings when she was working in our classroom. Miss Handy was good at asking questions that helped clarify the political ideologies I had read about. At each report, she asked me what my feelings were about the immediate news of World War II. Through the readings and the reports, I had changed in the way I looked at the world and at the ideology of nationalism. I felt Miss Handy and I had a special understanding, and I felt I had fallen in love. During my report sessions, I'd pull my chair close to her, and I had soaked up the sight and sound and aroma of Helen Handy so well, I could fantasize about loving her.

The crush on my teacher was hard to bear. When football season ended, I took back my *Grand Forks Herald* route. Miss Handy was a customer, and I hoped I might have some intimate encounter with her in her room at the Cando Hotel. No such luck. I tried to be satisfied with seeing her a couple hours daily at school. Sometimes I'd raise my hand during quiet work sessions to pretend I needed help, hoping to get her to lean over my shoulder so I could feel her touch me.

Shortly before Christmas vacation, the girls persuaded Miss Handy to chaperone a ninth grade dance. We held the dance in the school lunchroom, with a record player. Miss Handy let guys dance with her, and when I danced with her I told her how happy I was to have a pretty young teacher to dance with. Shortly after we danced, Miss Handy asked me to go with her to our classroom and carry down the piano bench, because the girls wanted to sing popular songs. Up in the classroom Miss Handy ran her hands down her dress and said, "Look. My dress seems to be changing color under these lights." As she stroked her dress, I was struck by the way her dress fit her body. I took a step towards her, looking in her eyes, and Miss Handy opened her arms to me. We embraced and kissed. It wasn't a kiss like Peggy's, and Miss Handy pulled away quickly to say, "That can never happen again. Let's go back downstairs." Okay. I knew I'd never be able to kiss my teacher again, but did she have to say it? I didn't dance with Miss Handy again at the party.

As we readied to leave for Christmas break, an excited Miss Handy told us she'd be seeing her Air Force boyfriend, and would possibly not return as our teacher. I felt envious and jealous of the boyfriend. But Miss Handy returned from vacation, seeming utterly sad. After a few days, a sub teacher took her place for more than a week. When Miss Handy returned to teach us, she acted like a different person. She no longer acted as if she wanted to be liked, and made me wonder if she no longer liked teaching.

In midwinter, a death shocked all of Cando. Dr. Olafson committed suicide in his garage from carbon monoxide. Town gossip said it was no accident, because the doctor's wife had acquired the reputation of being available for sex with lots of men in town. I wondered why the good doctor would kill himself over a woman who was called a town tart.

"Town tart" was soon what Helen Handy was being called. By late winter, kids talked about Miss Handy and the woman who ran Cando Hotel while her husband was away at war. The talk was about the two women being dates for the businessmen who stopped at the hotel. Shortly, there was gossip about Miss Handy dating the owner of a bar and bowling alley. That was really scandalous, because the bar owner's wife was then hospitalized for a nervous breakdown. Miss Handy's behavior made me feel stupid for feeling at one time that I was in love with her.

The obviously troubled teacher brought an end to her teaching in Cando when she attended the annual spring prom, an event produced by the high school junior class as a public dance to make money. Miss Handy came with her friend who ran Cando Hotel, obviously after having too many drinks. When she was jitterbugging with Francis Lavendure, an Ojibwa dropout student, she was jigging so fast, one of her breasts popped out of her gown. That drew guffaws and hisses from everyone nearby. My cousin Veora was working then as night telephone operator. Veora told me that on Sunday evening after the prom, the president of the school board phoned Miss Handy to tell her he wanted her resignation by Monday. Without it, she would be fired and a warning to schools would be sent to keep her from ever being hired to teach again in North Dakota.

My last interaction with Miss Handy was at our ninth grade commencement. I was to sing in a duet that she would accompany at the piano. She came to my seat in the front row of the high school auditorium and whispered, "Let me hold on to your arm when we go up the steps to the stage." I could smell booze on her breath and felt sorry for her. I gave her my arm with my fullest courtesy, and she made no mistakes when playing for the duet.

Ninth grade commencement had puzzled me, though. My report card grades at first semester had made me pretty sure they were best in our class. But I was named neither valedictorian nor salutatorian. Years later, Betty, with good humor, told me why I'd been passed over. Miss Handy kept Betty after school, and the two began an argument about Betty's behavior. Betty was sharp. She told Miss Handy that she planned to tell everyone she knew about Miss Handy's sleeping with the married bar owner. Betty said Miss Handy blanched and asked what Betty wanted of her. Betty told me she answered, "I want you to make me valedictorian."

And yeah, when I got my final report card, I saw that Miss Handy had dropped my grades for both English and social studies. But I remembered the books Miss Handy had introduced me to, and how much I had learned from reading them. I'd learned how dictators changed every part of society in Germany and Italy, so that traditions of freedom that had taken so many generations to build had been squelched. I'd learned to recognize oppression's cruelties, and for all that, I was truly grateful. I'd learned, too, that someone you feel you know might be changed by circumstances.

The school year closed right before Memorial Day. Reverend Whitwer spoke at the service and his talk made the war seem necessary and honorable. His talk reinforced my hope that I could fight in the war, too. I was asked to recite "In Flanders Field" at the service, and I felt I gave a strong emotional tone to the poem.

In early June, Reverend Whitwer was called to be minister for the Congregational church in Minot. I felt I lost my best guide and model for becoming a better person. After Reverend Whitwer left, his successor as minister became scoutmaster, but for only several months because he was called to be an army chaplain. Our next scoutmaster was Mr. Bowman, a farm implement salesman whose oldest son had been an Eagle Scout. Mr. Bowman persuaded the commercial club to buy Troop 82 a little one-room house to be set on its own lot next to the tourist park. Our troop had become smaller, but those of us in it now had our own meeting space. A big disappointment, though, was that the change of scoutmasters had prevented our getting scheduled for a summer camp that year.

CHAPTER 15

Can I become *A Really Good Son?*

Since I'd have no scout camp that summer, Dad asked me to help with his furnace work. Dad had made our family much better off with his furnace business. He'd built up a territory that ran east north of State Highway 17 into Minnesota and west north of U.S. Highway 2 to the Montana border. I'd helped Dad before for a couple of weeks in Leeds and Rugby, and felt I might prove I was a good son by working with him that summer after ninth grade.

While I didn't really like the work that made me get dirty, I did like traveling with Dad. Nearly every evening after supper Dad would talk to me about his boyhood, beginning with his life on the farm near Kokomo, Indiana, that his mother's grandparents had given to her. Dad described a life full of aunts, uncles, and cousins, and until he was eight, a life with a little brother and two little sisters.

Sobbing with tears, Dad told me about the deaths in two days of Joseph, Ardella, and Amelia from scarlet fever. And his telling was so clear I cried, too, feeling I was there with Dad. Dad said the deaths of his younger brother and two sisters was the turning point in his life. "When Mother lost her three little ones, it seemed she lost me, too. She never was the same mother after that." Dad explained that Grandma was already expecting Jesse. Two years after Jesse's birth, Delia was born, and in another two years, Hattie. "The second three babies came in the same order as the first three, a boy first, then two girls, as if they were replacements. But the second three never replaced the love I'd felt for the three little ones who died. And the second three never got the love and care Mother gave the three little ones. Mother could never get over her grief."

Those deaths, Dad said, made his joyous boyhood turn into a lonely sadness. And the loneliness grew sadder, Dad said, because he could never feel sure of Grandpa's love. " A big part of the trouble between Pa and me was Pa's buying a steam-driven tractor. More than anything in the world, I wanted to drive that tractor, but Pa kept saying I wasn't old enough. 'Not 'til you're fourteen,' Pa would say."

An almost tragic butchering day made Dad's relationship with Grandpa worse. Grandpa's job that day was to stand on the planks between two saw horses to lower the killed pigs into a copper kettle of boiling water so the hair on the pigs could more easily be scraped off. A neighbor's son, about Dad's age, asked Grandpa to let him help scald the pigs, and in one effort, lost his balance and fell into the scald tank. "Pa seemed to think it was his fault the boy got burned, 'cause he'd go over to visit that boy when he was in bed getting well." The steam-driven tractor came into play the next spring when Grandpa let that boy drive the tractor before he let Dad drive it. "I was sure, then, that Pa had no love for me, so I swiped Pa's canvas satchel from the storeroom, packed my clothes, and walked into Kokomo after midnight to catch the morning train to Peru."

The story of losing his little brother and sisters in two days and the story about how Dad was treated as a boy by Grandpa made me feel very close to Dad. Those talks with me were so full of feeling as Dad told me about the events in detail. Those talks were the beginning of Dad's life history.

As we worked in towns moving east along Highway 17, Dad kept telling me his life history. He told me about beginning to earn his own way as a helper at the steam-driven electric power plant in Peru. Then he moved to Wabash and became an apprentice steam engineer with the machines in a gravel pit. He worked there to become a journeyman and finally got his certificate as a steam engineer. All this time, he stayed away from the farm near Kokomo. It was seven years between his running away from home and his return to the farm near Kokomo, when the family was about to move to North Dakota. Dad said Grandpa asked him to go along to North Dakota, but Dad wanted to stay in Indiana where he could do engineer's work instead of farm work.

Maybe in telling his life history, Dad tried to prepare me for adolescent sex, because he told me lots of stories about his girlfriends in Wabash. I laughed hard when he said, "You know, a buggy sure beat a car for diddling a girl, especially if it was a buggy from the girl's family. Driving home from an evening at church, you could pull down the curtains, tie a knot in the reins, and trust the horse to take you on a slow walk to the girl's home, leaving both hands free for your fun." His stories were always about sex as fun, making me envy that attitude. To me, having sex with girls my age was too filled with consequences for me to pull it off.

In our work that summer, we planned a longer stop in Grafton, because Dad was contracted to install a new boiler furnace in a drugstore. In Grafton, I learned the misery of making up a lie. One evening I met a group of friendly Grafton kids, and I told them I was from Texas. Maybe I was embarrassed to tell them I was helping my dad work with furnaces, or maybe I wanted to see if I could use a convincing Texas drawl. They seemed to accept my lie, because they invited me to go swimming the next morning with them. At breakfast next morning I asked Dad if I could take a couple hours before going to work to go swimming, and Dad was generous.

I stayed at the river swimming beach with the Grafton kids all morning, and feeling guilty for staying so long, I made up another stupid lie. I told Dad I had met Ruth Linn Williams when she was giving her toddler a ride in his buggy. I said she asked me to walk along and tell her what was happening now in Cando School. I was caught in that lie because at the post office that afternoon, Dad saw Bill Williams and told him how glad I was to see my former teacher. Bill Williams told Dad that his wife and son were visiting grandparents in Rock Lake. Dad told me he was so embarrassed he didn't know what to say. He was almost in tears as he asked me why I'd lied to him. I confessed my finding kids as friends in Grafton and Dad said, "My God. Why didn't you just tell me that instead of a lie?"

Dad had agreed that I should go back home the last weekend of July to collect from my *Grand Forks Herald* customers and send my monthly payment to the *Herald* business office. To get home, I had to take a train from Grafton to Grand Forks, but stay overnight before catching a train to Devils Lake where I'd change to the train to Cando. I said goodbye to Dad, feeling horrible about my lie to him. I got a room at the Grand Forks Dakota Hotel and caught a city bus to the city park swimming pool where I spent the afternoon. I came back to the hotel to find I had a message from the druggist where Dad was installing the new furnace. The message said Dad had been taken to the Grafton hospital and that I should call the hospital's number.

I felt panic as I phoned the hospital. I was told Dad had had an emergency appendectomy and was in the recovery ward asleep. I said I'd catch the morning train to Grafton, and asked them to give Dad that message. I phoned Mom and learned the druggist had called her, too. That night I was in total misery, afraid for Dad, and full of shame for my lie to him. I think it was the first time I felt I had to pray, and prayed hard that Dad would be okay.

Next day when I got to the Grafton hospital, Dad was on a regular ward, feeling sore and weak, but out of danger. He gave me the keys to the Chevy van, telling me to go home and take care of my paper business and to assure Mom and Olive that he was all right. I was only fifteen, but in 1942, North Dakota let kids get a driving license at fourteen, so I drove home. About a week later, I drove back to Grafton to bring Dad home to rest and to recuperate under Mom's care.

There at home, one of Olive's college roommates came to visit. Evie appealed to me because she was athletic, and I borrowed the archery set from Troop 82 to see her outshoot me with bow and arrow. She and Olive went with me to Carlson's coulee to swim. Evie let me demonstrate the life-saving carry, and holding her with most of my body beneath her was a real treat.

That same week, Mary Converse brought her cousin and his friend from Alexandria, Virginia, to meet us. Roland and Bruce were still in high school but had come to visit Mary and her mother and to work in the harvest fields. They drove me with them to the Leeds swimming pool. I sure envied the way Leeds girls were attracted to Roland and Bruce, and wished I could be as smooth with girls as those guys were.

I wanted to work in the harvest fields, too, so I went to the men's store where Sammy Schwartz kept listings of help wanted. I got a job as field shocker on the Mulcrone farm northwest of town. When I arrived there, I found that Kenny Gilchrist had just begun work there, too. Oats was the first field Kenny and I shocked, which was good, because oats is the least heavy grain, and setting a shock in place with twelve bundles wasn't hard. When we moved to a barley field, we had more weight and found that the barley beards scratched our lower arms. When we got to the heavier durum wheat field, our final assignment, we were ready for the really hard work.

Potato harvest was also beginning, and Neil McLean told me his sister Marge and the Belzer girls and Marge Rendahl wanted Neil and me to pick potatoes at the Parker and Miller fields. Phyllis Belzer drove us out to the work field each morning and we picked spuds all day. That was backbreaking work, bending over to shove potatoes into burlap bags for eight hours.

Football practice began a week before school started, so I quit picking spuds and checked out my uniform to go to practice from two to five each afternoon. Vernon Hagen, our captain, was optimistic about our team as we spent the first week getting into condition. I was to play a regular guard on offense and to pull out for interference on end runs. Because I was good at anticipating the other team's offense, I got to play linebacker on defense. Tackling was what I liked best about football.

Our coach Pat Reilly had been deferred from the draft because of a severe foot injury. He organized a good practice, but wasn't such a good play strategist. We lost in consecutive games to Devils Lake St. Mary's, Rugby, and New Rockford, so overall, the season was disappointing.

And then I had another disappointment. I missed the last game of the season when I came down with the measles. I ran a high fever and had a nasty itch on my neck and chest. Doc MacDonald said it was only rubeola or German measles, but mine was a rough case. Because it lasted six days, I knew I'd miss tryouts for the basketball team. I never expected to make the starting five, but had hopes of making the traveling squad.

But maybe it was luck that I missed basketball team tryouts. Bob Torson brought the groceries to our house when I was eating lunch in the kitchen. He sympathized with me for missing the tryouts, because he thought we'd have a good coach in Bruce McVey, who had played with Bob in both high school and college. But Bob also brought me a surprise. He asked me if I'd like to work at Torson's grocery, delivering the groceries Tuesday afternoons and Saturdays with the delivery pickup, and in general helping with everything in the store. I was hired to get to work at seven Monday through Saturday mornings, and to help clean up and close at six-thirty evenings, except Saturdays, when we'd close at 9 p.m. Some nights I'd be called back to help unload the semitruck's delivery from Minneapolis, and every other month on Sunday, I'd help scrub and oil the floor. I became a valued store worker, well trained by the Torsons. Joe, Bob's dad, was the store's owner. Bob and his wife Florence helped Joe manage the store.

My working hours gave me a new schedule. I'd get up each day at six and be at work by seven to set out the store's produce. At 8:45, I'd rush from downtown to school, spend the morning in classes, walk home for noon lunch, and be back for classes from one to three-thirty. Then I'd work again until 6:30. It wasn't long before teachers and people in and out of town identified me with Torson's Grocery, and I learned to know the many folks who bought their groceries there. When winter came, I learned how to drive on ice and snow with Torson's delivery pickup. I also learned to know the kitchens and families of maybe half of Cando's homes when I stacked the delivered groceries on cupboards or kitchen tables. I got a kick out of some of the families.

One family that amused me was the Armeys. Both father and mother worked at the Cando grain elevator, leaving the Armey kids alone at home. One of the kids was Richard Armey, who, with his brothers and sisters, would grab a box of cereal as fast as I'd unload the delivery basket, tear open the cereal box and eat the dry cereal by the handful. I never suspected little Richard would one day become a U.S. Representative from Texas, and the GOP's majority whip.

Tenth grade brought a whole set of new teachers. Egil Hovey, the principal, was also world history teacher. He taught history the way I understood it to be taught in college, with daily lectures, drop quizzes over assigned readings, and short essay questions in tests to supplement the multiple-choice questions. Miss Selfridge was librarian, who taught biology and tenth grade English. I liked her English classes, but she worked exclusively out of the textbook in biology. She was a very helpful librarian, too. The new superintendent, Stensland, taught geometry, but from a workbook, keeping the subject more boring than it should be.

My favorite subject was Latin, taught by Loretta Murray. She sent us to the board each day for board drill with verbs, nouns, adjectives, and new vocabulary. The faster you finished the drill, the farther you could move to the left at the blackboard. I worked to get to the far left edge where the attractive eleventh graders Marge Rendahl and Lorraine Brightbill usually stood. Miss Murray had us read Latin aloud daily and translate as we read aloud. She gave us short compositions in Latin each day. Best of all, Miss Murray taught us much about Italy and the Romans.

A new classmate arrived when Dr. Palmer took the place of Olafson. In early winter I asked his daughter Olive to go to a movie with me. We sat on the opposite side of the movie house from the crowd of kids from high school to avoid being razzed as a dating couple. I gathered the courage to hold Olive's hand, and that seemed acceptable, but not as exciting as I'd hoped. After the movie, Olive invited me to come into her home where Dr. Palmer had his clinic upstairs. To my surprise, Olive said she'd make us roast beef sandwiches to go with cookies and milk. While waiting for my treat, I looked at the books on shelves between the kitchen and dining room and found a set of Rudyard Kipling. While Olive and I were eating the treat she'd made, Dr. Palmer came into the kitchen and introduced himself. I mentioned the books by Kipling and learned that he liked reading Kipling, too, so we had a good talk about favorite books we'd read. When I recognized it was time to leave, I sensed that Olive was disgusted with me for giving all my attention to her dad and Kipling. When I reached for a goodnight kiss, Olive backed away.

I began singing bass in Methodist choir with Dick Pearson, and during his dad's sermons, Dick often pointed out sexy passages in the Old Testament to keep us amused. Being in choir was my only access to music because wartime had ended both band and chorus at the high school. I inquired of Grace Harris if I could be her student, and she seemed happy to teach me singing. Those lessons were broadening in several ways. Mrs. Harris painted and so did her daughter Lucille, so I often had new paintings to peruse. The two women had traveled a lot, and after my voice lessons they would serve me milk and cookies and show me photos and brochures of places they had visited. Lucille Harris was also librarian for the city library, and she had often steered me to good books.

Richard Halliburton's adventures were among my favorite books that year, and I read Paul de Kruiff's writings on science. Having been introduced to Shakespeare by the Jamestown College production of *Macbeth*, I decided to read a book of Shakespeare's poems. Of course I read novels and became fascinated with *The Picture of Dorian Gray*. The witty dialogue of Wilde's characters in that novel prompted me to read *The Importance of Being Earnest* and *Lady Windermere's Fan*. The only other book by Wilde I could find was a collection of his poetry. Reading that book in study hall one day, I was aware that our principal, Egil Hovey, was looking over my shoulder. Mr. Hovey asked if I enjoyed reading Oscar Wilde, and I named the works I'd read. Then

Hovey asked, "Did you know Oscar Wilde was a homosexual?" and walked away, leaving me to ponder that bit of information.

Since no one was writing about basketball games for the paper, I asked Bob Denison, publisher and editor of the *Towner County Record Herald*, if I could report the basketball games for his paper. I began with home games of course, and I guess my reports improved, because before long I was traveling with the team to write about all the games. The team members were good critics of my writing, and I think I wrote better sports copy as the season went on.

My work at Torson's Grocery kept me busy, too, being given more responsibilities as I grew more acquainted with the store's operations. One day, Bob Torson was opening a box of cookies with a butcher's slicing knife, pulling the knife across the box towards himself. The knife slipped to cut into Bob's groin. He was rushed to the hospital in Devils Lake where they found Bob had cut several arteries and nerves. The outcome was that Bob had one leg amputated at the knee. It was a couple of months before Bob came back to work on crutches, waiting for his artificial leg.

Back the year before, Mom had started a regular correspondence with her cousin Carrie Lanter in Fort Worth, Texas. Mom told me Carrie had moved to Fort Worth to teach junior high English because her rancher husband Jim had died of a heart attack. Mom suggested that I might like to write to Carrie's eighth grade daughter Jim Carrie, and I began a correspondence with my third cousin while I was in ninth grade. Our correspondence led Jim Carrie to say that she wished I would come visit in Texas. That led Carrie to ask Mom if she and Olive and I would all pay them a visit, saying that her mother and father, in whose home she and Jim Carrie lived, were planning a visit to California the coming summer, and there'd be ample room for us. Mom didn't feel she could make the trip because of her in-house patient Lillian Hunt, but when Mom told Dad about the invitation, Dad said he'd pay the way for Olive and me to visit Mom's Texas relatives.

I had to wonder if I'd been a good enough son to deserve such a gift from Dad. One thing I'd learned as a tenth grader was that I had started to feel like I was growing up, and didn't feel that I was still a totally impetuous adolescent.

CHAPTER 16

Who says I'm *A Damn Yankee*?

After Olive received her teacher's certificate from Minot State and when Cando High was dismissed for the year, Dad drove Olive and me to Devils Lake to catch the Greyhound bus for Fort Worth. It was a beautiful sunny morning when we bid Mom goodbye at home and when we thanked Dad and said goodbye to him in Devils Lake. We had a lunch stop in Fargo's bus station and headed into the lake country of Minnesota, watching the prairie turn into thick groves on fields spotted with lakes. As we entered northwest Minneapolis we saw that summer had already brought bright green lawns, thickly leafed trees, and multicolored flowerbeds in tidy yards. As we neared downtown, Olive pointed out the obvious marks of poverty in the crowded, run-down row houses. We had supper and changed buses at the big Minneapolis bus depot, filled with noisy travelers.

It was dusk when we came to Owatonna, but I was struck with how attractive a small Minnesota town could be with its big stately homes and handsome downtown business section. By the time we reached Iowa it was dark, and I fell asleep until Des Moines. Pulling out of that city we were greeted with heavy rain. All the way to Kansas City, the rain was so fierce I was afraid the bus driver couldn't see the road. I offered to wipe off the fogged windshield with my handkerchief, but the driver told me to go back to my seat where I'd be safe. That bus driver took us through the rainstorm skillfully, and we pulled into the Kansas City bus depot for breakfast.

We had almost a two-hour wait for a bus change, so Olive and I went for a walk downtown. Kansas City seemed bigger and prettier than it had nine years earlier when we passed through it on our way back from Arkansas. Back waiting for our bus to leave, we saw dozens of servicemen waiting for their buses, too.

Our trip south from Kansas City turned hot, suggesting that we were already down south. Small towns looked less prosperous than in the upper midwest, and people who got on the bus seemed kind of down and out. In Oklahoma the bus passengers got noisy, and their chatter made them sound less educated. By the time we reached Fort Worth, we knew we'd have to listen carefully to catch what people were saying.

Olive phoned Ludvil Lindsay's home where Carrie lived. Carrie said we should take a cab to 1610 Jennings Avenue. A big-bellied driver threw our suitcases in the cab trunk and bragged about Fort Worth all the way to our destination, which wasn't far from downtown. We were greeted with big hugs from mother's cousin Carrie, a pretty, trim, well-spoken woman with dark red hair. I was impressed with how attractive thirteen-year-old Jim Carrie was. She looked at least fifteen, with beautiful light-red hair, a pretty freckled face, and a slim, womanly figure. We looked each other over with what I knew to be admiration on my part. I was wishing for a big hug from Jim Carrie, but knew it wasn't the right time to show each other that much affection.

"Aunt Carrie," as she wanted us to call her, assured us we'd get to visit with all the other Lindsay relatives, too. She said they'd planned a picnic for the very next evening with the families of Mother's cousins Hague and Lancelot. Carrie fixed us greens and black-eyed peas and cornbread for supper with a yellow cake for dessert, and we had a happy, lively conversation with everyone getting acquainted. I knew right away I was going to like the junior high English teacher Carrie, and I felt a strong attraction for her vivacious daughter, Miss Jimmy.

At the picnic next evening in Forest Park near Texas Christian University, we met Lance and his wife Margaret and their seventeen-year-old son, Jack. We also met Hague and his wife Reba and their daughters La Faun, twenty-one, and Lenore, nineteen, both students at Abilene Christian College for Women. Hague's son, Hague Junior, or Sonny, as he was called, was a year younger than me and seemed eager to get acquainted. Our picnic of hot dogs and baked beans and coleslaw had been bought at a store, but Margaret had baked a big pan of peach cobbler "with peaches from our own backyard," she told us. It was delicious with the iced tea.

During the picnic, Olive took me aside and told me not to pay so much attention to Jim Carrie and mingle more with Jack and Sonny.

She said La Faun and Lenore had told her Jim Carrie and I seemed much too friendly. Olive's rebuke was embarrassing, because I knew I had a strong crush on my third cousin. By the end of the next day, I was sure Jim Carrie felt the same about me, and we had found private times in the yard among the peach trees to steal some hugs and kisses.

Sonny and Jim Carrie took me Friday to the Forest Park pool, and on the bus going there they taught me some songs that were popular in Texas, but never heard in North Dakota. One song, "Beautiful Brown Eyes," was typical. It was about a guy who staggered down by the barn, fell down by the door, and got his marriage called off. He protested that "Liquor has kept us apart," and his sweetheart vowed she'd "Never love blue eyes again." It was obvious that Sonny and Jim Carrie considered the song very funny. During our swim, Jim Carrie and I restrained ourselves from being too physically connected, so we wouldn't alarm Sonny. After the swim Sonny told me that the public pool was always closed on Wednesdays because Tuesday was the day colored people could use the pool, so on Wednesdays the pool had to be drained and scrubbed. I said I thought that was a silly practice, but Sonny said, "Us Texans know how to handle the colored."

Because Mom was from Texas and probably the kindest, most generous person I knew, I was amazed to learn my Texas cousins had values that seemed to me unlike Mom's and even un-American. When Olive and I had dinner at Lance's home, Jack showed me a closet holding rifles, shotguns, and revolvers. "Those are to be ready for the nigger rebellion that's bound to come once the war's over. They've learned to be biggety in the army and navy and are gonna want things we're not about to give 'em."

Back in Cando, I'd closely followed the war in Europe and the South Pacific, through radio news and through *Time* and *Life* magazines, mainly. But I didn't see much interest in war news by my Texas relatives. *The Fort Worth Star Telegram* was delivered daily to Aunt Carrie, and I read it to keep up with news. There were so many murders reported daily in the *Star Telegram* there wasn't a lot of space for other news. When I asked Sonny why so many murders, he said, "Well, there are other papers for the colored, and they tell about a lot more killings of those people."

Sunday we went with Carrie and Miss Jimmy to what was called the Christian Church. I was puzzled by its name until I thought of

Texas Christian University. Hague's family was there, too. But their church seemed strange to me. Hymns were sung without organ or piano, and the only participation by the congregation was to read the Psalms. The sermon was a reminder of how easily we fall into sin followed by a long prayer to ask that we all be forgiven. After church we were driven to Hague's home for Sunday dinner. Hague was assistant principal of one of the biggest high schools in Little Rock, but he talked more about his temporary summer job, selling auto parts for his brother-in-law, whose Dallas business was the largest auto parts dealer in north Texas. He bragged about his sales the past month earning him more than he made in two months with his assistant principal's salary.

It seemed to me Hague should have become a businessman of some kind. He asked me lots of questions about how much North Dakotans made in various kinds of work. When I told him Dad's business was selling, repairing, and cleaning furnaces, Hague said, "Oh, that kind of work is for the colored in Texas." He seemed pleased when I told him I had herded cows and worked on farms. He said, "You knew Carrie's husband Jim Lanter was a rancher, didn't you? And your grandpa Lindsay was a farmer near Weatherford. We'll have to make a trip out Weatherford way and show you where your mother grew up." I told him Olive and I would like very much to make that trip. I knew that the hard work I was proud of back in North Dakota was something my Texas relatives had never done. They didn't even mow their own lawns.

Back at 1610 Jennings Avenue Olive told me her cousins La Faun and Lenore seemed to think they were much better than her because she went to a state college and they went to a private women's college. But later that week when Carrie invited Hague's family for dessert and asked Olive to sing for everyone, Olive had a chance to show her talents. She accompanied herself at the piano and sang several of the art songs she had sung with the college choir. La Faun and Lenore looked displeased when their dad praised Olive for her singing. That day, Jack had come with Hague's family for dessert, and he and Sonny talked about Jim Carrie in ways that made me know I could never feel close to them. They both told me, "Miss Jimmy doesn't sit like a lady, but crosses her legs to show them almost clear up to her crotch." To me their concern about how Jim Carrie sat only showed what nasty minds they had.

But I began to feel less close to Jim Carrie, too. She arranged for me to spend an evening with her and some of her pals. The girls about her age were physically much more womanly than girls that age up north. Mainly, though, I was amazed to hear them talk so proudly about their recent petting and sex experiences. Then when some boys obviously older than any of the girls came with beer and cigarettes they passed around, I felt I was in a rougher crowd than I was used to. Jim Carrie didn't smoke or take a beer, but other girls did, with lots of laughing and talk. Back at her home, Jim Carrie and I talked about the evening. I said I thought the boys were too old for her and her friends. Jim Carrie laughed and said, "That's how things are down here, that's all."

I asked how, with the war enforcing gas rationing, the boys had gas for driving all around Fort Worth. Jim Carrie said, "Oh, Texas has lots of oil wells, you know. The boys just pay a little more at the gas station. No one here gives much heed to rules about gas rationing."

We had heard Mom often talk about her cousin Irene, and finally Olive and I visited her, although she seemed to have no association with her other cousins. Irene had a small home in a newer, modest part of Fort Worth. She had no children, just her husband, "Sweetie boy, Charlie."

Irene asked Olive and me to go with her to her Seventh Day Adventist church, and Olive said she knew Mom would want us to do that. I learned that many Seventh Day Adventist young men were conscientious objectors. A young sailor who was in the Navy Hospital Corps spoke at church about the Hospital Corps being an acceptable alternative to being a C. O., because Corpsmen never carry weapons. I was also impressed because the Hospital Corps seemed a good way to gain medical experience if you wanted to become a doctor.

Hague kept his promise to drive Olive and me out past Weatherford to the spot where Grandpa Lindsay and Mom had lived. The house and farm buildings were all gone, and the land seemed not to have been farmed for quite some time. It was overgrown with wild grasses. Hague also drove us into Weatherford, and he went to the courthouse to see if there was any information about Mom's older brother George, but he learned nothing about the man who had gone away after his father died.

Another of Mom's cousins was Lula, who lived with her husband George in a downtown apartment. Both Olive and I felt more comfortable with Lula than with any of Mom's cousins except Carrie. Lula and George seemed genuinely interested in North Dakota and in our relatives there. They seemed to like us a lot, even if we were Yankees. But we also met Lula's father, Mom's uncle George. He was in his late eighties and blind. When we were introduced to him as Hadie's children visiting from North Dakota, he said, "North Dakota? Yankee soldiers killed our pap at Vicksburg. A squad of them bluecoats came to our farm in Kentucky and stole all our horses and butchered all but one of our cows. I was too young to kill any of them Yankees, but when I was a Texas Ranger, I killed a passel of Mexicans."

After a week or so, the wealthiest of Mom's first cousins came over from Dallas with her daughter Sarah. It was Muriel's husband who owned the biggest auto parts dealership in north Texas. Their son Richard was away in the Navy, but their seventeen-year-old Sarah was a blue-eyed blond with what I'd heard described as "bee-stung lips." Muriel seemed very impressed with Olive's singing. She said Olive and I, with La Faun and Lenore and Jack and Sonny, should all come to Dallas for a long weekend visit at her home.

I wondered why she hadn't invited Jim Carrie, too, and I could tell that both Carrie and Jim Carrie felt hurt about Jim Carrie being left out. The day we all took the bus to Dallas, Jim Carrie went on the same bus to visit a friend in Dallas. I sat beside Jim Carrie as she tried to hold back her tears. She said this wasn't the first time she'd felt rejected by her other cousins and couldn't know why they treated her like an outsider.

Richard Meggs, with only one leg, used a crutch with dexterity when he picked us up at the Dallas bus depot. I was amazed at the Meggs home in the White Rock neighborhood of Dallas. It stood far back on a corner lot a half-block wide on Mercedes Avenue. The yard was well landscaped, and we soon learned it was cared for daily by a black gardener.

Muriel told us proudly that she herself had designed their home with its long, sweeping second-floor verandah. Downstairs was a huge, richly furnished living room with a grand piano. There were two dining rooms, one for formal dining and one for daily use next to a large kitchen that ran the width of the house, and there was even another small eating accommodation for the gardener and the two black women who worked in the house daily. There were two half-baths

With Texas cousins Jack and Sonny Lindsay in front of the Meggs home

downstairs and a huge bathroom-dressing room in the master bedroom. The upstairs was designed for Richard and Sarah. Above the living room was a game room with piano, pool table, tennis table, two desks, many filled bookshelves, a fireplace, and lounge furniture. One door from the game room was to the hall and the other door opened onto the verandah. The first bedroom next to the game room was Richard Junior's, furnished with a desk and lounge furniture, three twin beds, and its own full bathroom with a shower. Then came Sarah's bedroom, which had two twin beds, a regular-size bed, lounge furniture, a desk, and a luxurious bath and shower. The verandah had wicker lounge furniture all along its length.

Events for our visit in Dallas seemed planned to match the wealth apparent in the Meggs home. Richard arranged for a vice president of the bank in the tallest building in downtown Dallas to take us on a tour of that skyscraper. We went for rides at the state fairgrounds one afternoon followed by an evening outdoor performance of *The Merry Widow* in a pavilion. The next night we had dinner at Sammy's, the most fancy restaurant I'd ever been in. On Saturday afternoon we kids all went with Richard and Muriel for an overnight at Robertson Park on Lake Hubbard, where he had rented cabins for his young people's Bible class and for us visitors. I was impressed with the ease and good humor he showed leading the service for his Bible class.

Muriel was so impressed with Olive's voice that she phoned a society reporter from the *Dallas Morning News* to write an account of our visit, with a photo of Olive and a description of Olive's solo work at college. And Muriel liked Olive so much she told her that it was acceptable for third cousins to marry, and she would be happy to have Olive as daughter-in-law.

But Jack told me, almost in tears, that it was just unfair that first cousins couldn't marry. He told me he knew he could never love anyone as much as he loved Sarah. It didn't surprise me that he was in love with Sarah, who seemed the classic Southern belle with blonde hair, creamy complexion, and full bosom. I was attracted to Sarah, too, and felt kind of guilty for thinking she was maybe more attractive than Jim Carrie.

A week after our return to Fort Worth, I was ready to return home, but Olive had taken a job as secretary to an executive at McDonald Douglas Aircraft. She was going to stay with Lula and George, where there was room for her, so she could earn some of the good salary paid at a war plant. Just before I left, Carrie arranged for her younger brother, Lud Junior, to visit Olive and me. Lud was a men's clothier salesman who drove out in his convertible and fancy outfit for supper. He proved as charming as Jim Carrie said he was. He'd been married, but was divorced with lots of girlfriends, according to Jim Carrie. I thought he was handsome and smooth enough to play a southern gentleman in a movie.

Muriel had suggested that I spend one more day and night in Dallas, so my bus stopped there first on my trip home. Sarah drove me out to White Rock Lake where we swam and played in the water so intimately I grew a painful hard-on. When we went back from the swim, Sarah said she wanted to take a nap and invited me to nap on the rug by her bed and hold her hand until she fell asleep. I held her hand, and my mind had too many erotic thoughts for me to take a nap.

Three days and nights on the Greyhound bus took me back to Devils Lake, and Mom arranged for my friend Norval Garber to drive me back to Cando. I had a good time telling Mom all about our visit with her Texas cousins, except I left out my disapproving judgments of them and didn't mention my sexy feelings for Jim Carrie and Sarah.

Mom was concerned about Olive's job at the aircraft company, afraid Olive might not take the teaching job she'd been promised in Montana. Olive made Mom and me both anxious when she wrote to say she had met an army veteran who was driving the Fort Worth city bus she took to work. She wrote that the bus driver told her he had fallen in love with her. I was annoyed, feeling sure that no man from Texas was good enough for my sister, especially no bus driver. Lula and the bus driver's regular girlfriend convinced Olive that she should break off from that guy. When Olive got home she had another adventure to tell me about. The aircraft company exec she was secretary for came on to her one day when he kept her late at the office, and she had to persuade him he wasn't being true to his wife and children. It wasn't long after Olive got home that she left for Culbertson, Montana, to teach music and high school English.

What did I conclude about our trip to Texas? I felt it had been a glorious adventure, and that I'd learned a lot of things, including more about myself. I decided I was lucky to be growing up in a small town in North Dakota. Guys growing up in Texas cities seemed to know nothing of hard, outdoor work. They seemed to leave all the hard work outdoors to black men, and they seemed to me afraid of the black men. Kids there seemed to lack the easy comradeship boys and girls in Cando had from working and playing together. And though Mom's relatives seemed very committed to their religion, that church I went to with them didn't seem committed to the kind of Christian love and generosity to all people that seemed a strong part of both the Brethren and Methodist churches I'd been to in Cando. It seemed that Mom's relatives weren't nearly as good as she was, so I concluded that Texans and North Dakotans just have different values. But I also wondered, if I'd visited small towns in Texas, would folks there be more like folks in Cando?

I wrote letters of thanks to Carrie and Muriel, but decided that writing to Jim Carrie or Sarah would be too strange to be enjoyable. I didn't feel close enough to Sonny or Jack to write them, either, so I sort of felt my connection to Mom's Texas relatives was over when my visit ended. It was a different experience, feeling like an outsider during my Texas visit. Though no one called me a damn Yankee, not even Mom's old uncle George who made no secret of his hatred of Yankees, I felt separate enough there to know it wouldn't be easy for me to be a Texan.

CHAPTER 17

Now I want to prove I'm truly
A Grateful Son

While Olive was still in Fort Worth, almost as soon as I got home Dad phoned from Hallock, Minnesota, where he was working. He called to welcome me home and to say I should persuade Mom to take some time off so she and I could join him for fishing at a lake in Minnesota.

It wasn't easy to convince Mom to have Miss Hunt move while we'd be gone to Doc MacDonald's hospital just across the alley from our house. But when Aunt Dee agreed to drive us where we were going, Mom said she would make the trip.

What dismayed me is that Mom asked Laura Williams to make the trip with us. I had never liked Laura Williams and I could never understand why Mom and Dad did like her. The year before Uncle Jesse died, Aunt Ella had told Mom that she suspected Dad and Laura Williams were having an affair. Mom only laughed at that, but I knew there must have been talk by neighbors about the number of times Dad went to Laura's house. Dad said it was to read and relax in a quiet place. It was hard, I knew, for Dad to find his own space in our home with Mary and Dalton Converse boarding there before Olive had yet gone to college. But suspecting that people might have been talking about Dad and Laura Williams was creepy to me, and I was really annoyed that Mom asked Laura Williams to be part of our family vacation.

So in reaction, I asked Dick Pearson to join us for our fishing trip. We all piled into Aunt Dee's '37 V-8, Mom in front with Aunt Dee, and Dick and I forced to share the back seat with Laura Williams. I was glad I'd brought Dick along when he grew annoyed at the constancy of Laura Williams's loud raspy voice. When she began to blame President Roosevelt for forcing the U.S. into war, Dick said, "I don't think you know what you're talking about, Miss Williams." She was shocked and told Dick he was rude and should have been raised to respect his elders. Dick's response to her was, "Respect has to be earned."

Mom tried to make the rest of our trip less contentious, but Dick had at least turned down the frequency and high volume of Laura Williams. I think Dad was shocked to see the addition of Laura Williams and Dick Pearson for our family vacation, but he accepted it courteously and drove us first to Lake Bronson, a newly opened Minnesota State Park. The lake had been recently stocked with fish,

At the cabin on Lake of the Woods, near end of summer, 1944

but wasn't yet open to fishing, so Dad drove us on to Lake of the Woods. Dad knew a commercial fisherman there named Aaron Hoover. Hoover had been a farmer in the Zion community until during the depression when he moved to Lake of the Woods, where by the time we got there he had a big, prosperous operation with his home, fish house, fishing boats, and boat pier.

Dad rented a cabin for us less than a half mile from Hoover's place, and when Dick and I went over to Hoover's with Dad, Aaron Hoover invited Dad to go out next day in his fishing boat to be part of the commercial fishing. Hoover said Dick and I could use his rowboat to fish in big Lake of the Woods that spread up into Canada. Dad brought fish from Hoover's catch to the cabin for supper, and when he learned that Dick and I had caught nothing in our outing, he took us back over to Hoover's after supper and got an invitation from Hoover to take Dick and me on the commercial catch the next day.

Going out on the trawler with Aaron Hoover and his grown son was an unexpected adventure. We left the Hoover pier about seven a.m., being told they would set out two half-mile-long seines, and then pick up two seines they had set the day before. Aaron Hoover told us his commercial license gave him a territory on the lake, and we watched as he let out the seine while his son slowly drove the trawler down a straight line between marked buoys. Hoover told Dick and me we could let out the second seine. As we did that, Dick accidentally knocked Hoover's metal identification tag off the seine into the water. Hoover said, "If a game warden should inspect this seine and find no identification tag, I could lose my commercial license." Dick began to apologize, but Hoover's son cut him off with, "Ah, it's no big deal. The game wardens know this is the territory where Hoover holds the license and that sometimes tags fall off."

Dick and I helped pull in the two heavy seines full of fish, freeing the snagged fish from the seine to drop them in the tub-shape of the trawler with the other fish that were the approved size for selling. Any fish too small or too large were thrown quickly back into the lake. Back at the pier, Hoover's son brought down to the boat a wheelbarrow with wooden boxes half full of ice, and Dick and I helped sort the fish to fill the boxes. The full boxes were wheeled into the icehouse to wait for the truck, which would deliver the fish to a fish market in the Twin Cities.

Besides his fishing business, Aaron Hoover had a mink farm and showed us the cages where he raised the mink until they were ready to be slaughtered for their furs. Hoover told us he was also the official airplane spotter for the government, reporting every plane that passed over that bay of the Lake of the Woods.

While Mom and Aunt Dee didn't do much except fix our meals and sit on the screen porch talking with Laura Williams, they both seemed to like their time to relax. I agreed with Dick that fishing in a commercial fishing trawler was great fun. I felt grateful for the vacation Dad had given us, but I felt guilty that I'd not given Dad any of my time to be with him. So when Dad came home from Hallock and asked if I could help him with his work, I said yes right away.

We went first to Starkweather, the first town east of Cando on Highway 17. My part of cleaning a furnace was first to clean out the ash pit. Next, I'd brush down the firebox and the drum that circulates heat before the smoke moves towards the chimney. Dad would use extension rods with a big brush to clean the chimney and the smokestack that ran to the chimney, and replace any parts of the smokestack that were worn out. Sometimes shape or size required cleaning a chimney from the top, and often Dad would let me go up on the roof for that job. Working as a team, we usually finished a job in less than two hours.

Dad kept a record of earnings from every job as well as full records of all expenses. His goal was to take in more than a hundred dollars each day and to keep expenses low enough to net about seventy dollars a day. At the end of each day we had to spend a long time washing off the soot, then head to a restaurant for a big supper.

From Starkweather we headed towards Park River, and I fell asleep. When I woke up it was night, and we were in a hotel room. I felt pain in my chin and mouth and I said to Dad sitting next to the bed, "I think I chewed through my lower lip."

Dad said, "That's the third time you said that. It's all stitched up now and the doc said you're going to be all right. I fell asleep after you did and ran into the ditch and hit a culvert at a crossroad. The panel truck is in the body shop and you'll need a couple days rest before you're ready to work again. The doc said he'd take the stitches out Thursday." Dad spent the next couple of days lining up work, and I spent part of each day walking out to the city park along the river. When the panel truck was ready for work, I was ready, too.

After a week in Park River, we were to go to Pembina. I talked Dad into letting me call Willard Brower in St. Thomas to ask if we could stop in to visit Sunday. We were invited for Sunday noon dinner, and after dinner Willard and Roger took me to meet friends who had a war scheduled with another set of guys. Weapons for the war were railroad spikes taken from kegs sitting by the depot. The railroad spikes were hurled at opponents with a short loop of binder twine. Garbage can lids were used as shields, so it was a noisy war, and luckily, no one was wounded.

We drove to Pembina late afternoon and checked into a handsome old hotel where we were served a family-style supper with other hotel guests. Evenings after supper, Dad resumed his life stories, a continuing account from day to day, ending when we were both ready to fall asleep in the bed we shared. I looked forward to Dad's stories, rather than going to a movie or walking around downtown. His stories made his early life come alive for me, and made him seem like a friend as well as my dad.

From Pembina we crossed the Red River and drove to Hallock, where Dad was to put in a new boiler furnace in the hotel where we stayed. In Dad's story sequence, he told me about his marriage to his first wife, Lil, and their move to the province Saskatchewan, where Dad had contracted with the Canadian government to drill wells for homesteaders. Dad laughed as he told me, "Lil opened her own beauty shop in Moosejaw, and I was moving from homestead to homestead with my well rig. After about six weeks, when I went back to Moosejaw, I found that Lil had moved a local barber into our apartment. Seemed to me he'd make a better fit with Lil than I ever would, so we got a divorce." Dad told me his contract for drilling was for two years, so after his contract expired, he decided to be a homesteader himself. "That's why I became a Canadian citizen. John Donahue, another homesteader, and I built a house we set half on each homestead, 'cause government requirements said every homesteader had to build a house on his land."

Dad told me his next two years farming his homestead were also spent drawing full plans for a tractor that could push instead of pull a drill, a cultivator, and other equipment, so the driver could see what was in front and wouldn't have to turn to see his work.

The next evening Dad told about a visit that was still very moving in his memory. Uncle Jesse brought his wife and baby to Dad's homestead near Swift Current. Uncle Jesse had sold his homestead near Wolf Point, Montana, and was moving back to Cando. Dad had to wipe away sniffles when he said, "It was really the very first time I'd spent with my brother, and we had a good long talk about Pa and Mother. Jess said Pa had made his farm a real showplace, but Mother was traveling everywhere for doctor help, taking Delia with her, and that was costing Pa a bundle. Then he told me trying to have a well business partnership with Pa didn't work. That's why he went to Montana. He said he was going to set up a well business for himself in Cando. It was some satisfaction to know I wasn't the only son that couldn't get along with Pa. But all in all, that was one welcome visit."

As we worked our way back towards home, Dad's stories took his life from Canada to Detroit, where he worked for Henry Ford and tried to get Ford to manufacture his tractor. But the World War had turned the Ford plant into war production, so Ford couldn't get interested then in tractors. Dad said he knew he had to patent his invention, so he went to Washington, D.C., and got a job selling real estate while he waited for his patent to get registered. Then Dad went back to Indiana and sold his patent to the Hart Company. He said, "Old man Hart wanted me to marry his invalid daughter and be a partner in the company, but I told him if I ever marry again, it will be because I want to be a father."

Dad's next adventure was to drill oil wells near Shawnee, Oklahoma, where he was hired by a Cherokee woman to head the drilling on her land. He said that the Cherokee woman was smart and beautiful as well as rich. He said he might have married her, except she couldn't have children. "When I explained I wanted to have a family, Marie said we could adopt children. Guess I said the wrong thing when I told her I wanted the children to be of my own blood. Marie thought I was saying I wanted a pure white child, and told me I should move on."

The last of Dad's stories that summer was about meeting Mom after he had started his own oil drilling outside Mineral Wells, Texas. Mom was then living with her nearly blind father on their farm near Weatherford. "Soon as I got to know her, I knew she was the one I wanted to be mother to my kids, and I talked her into marrying me." Dad told me about their first baby not living at birth, and while Mom had told me about that, too, Dad was very emotional in his telling of it.

Dad's stories about his life affected me deeply, making me realize that even though Dad was fifty years older than me, his stories made him feel like the best chum I'd ever had. I was really grateful to know how he had dealt with his life.

At home, Dad said I'd better get back to work at Torson's grocery, so I could keep my job there. He said he could get along without me, but in mid-August his arthritis flared up

Olive on the lawn of our home in Cando, 1944

badly, and he again needed my help. Torsons were understanding and hired John Schaeffer again to take my place while I'd be helping Dad. We went back to Leeds, where Dad had been working, and in a few days, Dad's arthritis seemed better. He agreed to repair the chimney of the home where we were working. I carried up the bucket of mixed cement and the bricks Dad would need.

I stayed up on the roof with Dad, handing him the bricks as he cemented them in place. Dad said the roof flashing for around the chimney should be replaced, and sent me with it to the hardware store for them to make the metal flashing. When I got back, Dad was lying in the shade of a tree, not awake, and breathing fast. As soon as I felt his forehead I knew from Boy Scout first aid that he had heat exhaustion, maybe heat stroke. I covered him with a blanket from the panel truck. Then I went in the house and called the office of the one doctor in Leeds. The doctor was at Rugby Hospital delivering a baby, so I went back to Dad with a glass of water and decided to drive him back to the hotel. Dad was disoriented, a symptom of heat stroke. When I got him to our room I convinced him to take a cool bath. The cool water lowered his body temperature, and I kept giving him glasses of water.

I brought Dad supper from the café across from the hotel, and it wasn't long before the desk clerk told me I had a message from the Leeds doctor. I called the doctor and he came to see Dad. He said it looked like heat stroke all right, and said Dad should go home and rest up. We checked out of the hotel and I told the people where we'd been working what the doctor said. I drove Dad home where I knew he'd recover under Mom's good nursing care.

Dad's rest after the heat stroke was just what he needed, and he told me his arthritis was gone enough for him to get along without me. I told him I'd go back to Leeds with him, anyhow, and help finish up the chimney repair.

Olive had just come home from Texas and was getting ready to go to Culbertson, Montana. I told her how I felt about Dad's generosity in paying for our trip to Texas, and about how Dad had told me loads of stories about his life when I was working with him. It felt good to tell my sister how close I now felt to Dad, and made me feel I had made some progress towards being a really grateful son.

CHAPTER 18

When will I know I'm *The Real Me*?

When eleventh grade began, I felt confused about the kind of person I really was. And though a lot happened in my junior year of high school, nothing seemed to clear up my confusion. I continued to read, especially books about science, but school had less appeal for me than it always had before. Our new principal, Don McKechnie, taught English with enough flair to make literature come alive. I liked chemistry too, and our chemistry teacher, Miss Torgerson, let Roy Pile and me set up the labs. She was also advisor to the school paper, and I decided to be part of the school news staff. I was appointed assistant editor to Marge Rendahl.

One subject totally plagued me. I'd signed up for typing because I wanted to type instead of doing all my writing by hand. The trouble was, Miss McConnell assigned daily office projects, which meant we had to turn in each day a body of work as if we were stenographers. Those projects were too long to finish in the minutes we were given during class, but Miss McConnell insisted that they be turned in each day, even if it meant working after school. My job at Torson's Grocery gave me no time after school, and besides, I thought the projects were a waste of my time. Miss McConnell, of course, felt otherwise. She gave me a final typing grade of seventy-five (a D).

Olive had always been a favorite student of Miss McConnell, not only in typing and shorthand, but in school plays Miss McConnell directed. But there again, I fell far back of my sister in Miss McConnell's opinion. When she announced tryouts for the school play, Neil and Marge McLean said they were going to tryouts, so I went, too. We were all cast in a silly play about a high school boy who overcame his lack of popularity. John MacDonald and Lorraine Brightbill were also in the cast, with Clyde Stebbleton, who played the lead. I was cast as the harsh and unlikable high school principal. Most of the time on stage was given to Clyde and John, who played the good teacher who helped Clyde become popular. While waiting backstage, Marge and Lorraine and Neil and I used our time to have fun. One thing we did was to try to stretch a man's shirtsleeve garter around the remarkably slender waists of Marge and Lorraine. When Miss McConnell discovered our antics, she kicked us out of the cast and called off the play, saying the cast was not dependable. I didn't mind not being in the play, but I felt some guilt about not being dependable.

My greatest disappointment with school that fall was that our football season was cancelled. All coach-type men had gone to war. We weren't the only school in our part of North Dakota that cancelled football season that year. But when Olive urged me to make a short visit to her in Culbertson, Montana, I saw Culbertson had a coach who was draft-deferred because his eyes were not good enough for military service. I arrived on the Empire Builder at about two a.m. and was met by Olive and Coach Sheldon. They took me to the Oliver Lab home where they both roomed, and I shared Coach Sheldon's bed. Next morning Mrs. Lab fixed us all a great breakfast, and I was warmly welcomed by Oliver Lab and son Ralph, who was a couple of years younger than me.

Thursday, I sat in on Olive's chorus rehearsal and English class, then went to other classes with a Culbertson student that Olive chose to be my guide. I was eager for school to be over, because Coach Sheldon had invited me to work out with the Culbertson six-man football team. I had fun at practice, playing a running back and giving the Culbertson defensive players more than they could handle. When I was on defense, I showed I could tackle the ball carrier before he got to the scrimmage line. After practice, several team members and Coach Sheldon tried to coax me to move to Culbertson and join their team, but I laughed off the invitation. Next day, though, when Culbertson played Plentywood's team, Coach Sheldon asked me to be line judge. So I had a short but fun two-day football season for my junior year.

Several of the team members invited me to bring Olive to a party on Friday night. I grew annoyed when some of the high school boys flirted with Olive more than I thought they should, even though I knew I would have flirted with her myself if she weren't my sister. The girl who gave the party asked me if I had been out to see the Missouri River west of Culbertson and invited me to take a hike with her Saturday. Coach Sheldon took me with him to hunt coyotes early morning, so I got to see some of the rolling prairie outside Culbertson. I met the girl kids called "Ma" before noon, because she said she'd fix a picnic lunch for our hike. "Ma" told me she had been a waitress in Great Falls the summer before, and that she'd dated about fifty guys. Man, I felt unready to be compared to fifty other guys, especially the ones in the Air Force she said she'd dated. "Ma" from Montana was too much for me. As we were eating our lunch on the rocky bluff above the river, "Ma" pointed out that she liked her zipper opening in the front of her skirt, because it was so handy to open. I got the implication, but I was too unsure of myself to touch the zipper in that corduroy skirt.

Wanting football where I could find it, I talked Arlo and Mike Westmiller, Neil McLean, and Bud Garber into going with me to Minneapolis to see University of Minnesota play Ohio State. We took the train, stayed in a cheap Minneapolis hotel, watched the Gophers get trounced by the Buckeyes, rode the streetcar all the way to and from the airport, went dancing in St. Paul's Marigold Ballroom, and bought leather flight jackets at Dayton's department store. We tried to go into Moby Dick's bar on Hennepin Avenue, but were bounced out right away.

That winter, as the war wore on, high school seemed to me a sorry second best to being a serviceman overseas. I followed the war news with intensity, excited to see that the battles were starting to be won by our troops, not by the Germans and the Japanese.

I continued to report the basketball games for the *Cando Record-Herald*, and found the whole process of putting together a student newspaper kind of fascinating. Editor Marge Rendahl asked me to write an editorial, so I wrote my opinion that having more girls in the cheerleading squad than there were guys on the basketball team was absurd. I argued that the cheerleaders should watch the game more closely and make cheers spontaneously, instead of using cheers designed to show off the cheerleaders. Not a popular opinion. My editorial made me probably the most unpopular guy in high school. I had to wonder if the reaction to my editorial was really a reaction to me.

Sometimes, girls put together a party at someone's home after basketball games. In study hall, one of the Cub's best basketball players, Joe Welch, called out in a loud voice on Monday morning after a Friday night party, "Hey Garber, I hear you tried to touch Joyce's titty. Better keep your hands off, 'cause she told on you." I thought what Joe said was a lot more offensive than my editorial, but Joe didn't seem to offend anyone.

Olive Palmer's mother made the '44-45 school year a lot less boring, and indirectly kind of restored my feeling of being respected by other kids. Mrs. Palmer announced a meeting after school for kids and told us that she had a promise from the Commercial Club to support a teen canteen if we students organized and ran it. She said that Devils Lake had a teen canteen that we could learn from. Those of us at the meeting decided to organize right then, and elected a committee to get things started. Senior Phyllis Belzer was voted committee chair, and Olive Palmer, Bud Garber, and I were also elected. The four of us were to go to the Devils Lake teen center to learn how to put our teen center into place.

Phyllis got permission for our visit, and Bud drove us in his sister's Oldsmobile to Devils Lake the following Saturday night. The Devils Lake teen center was in the downtown Moose Lodge, and kids had been given help from their commercial club to decorate the rent-free space for use on Saturdays and special occasions. The Coca-Cola bottling company in Devils Lake had helped with free posters and the loan of a cooler and reduced prices for soda pop. The kitchen of the Moose Lodge was used to cook wieners and the teen center sold hot dogs and popcorn and soda at low prices. They had a jukebox for music, and besides dancing and food, had tables for cards and board games.

I had fun dancing with one of the girls on their governing committee, asking her questions about everything I could think of about running their center. I also told her that Cando had only the Odd Fellows Lodge, which had card parties and dancing for members every Saturday night. I said, "To be frank, I doubt if we can find any building in Cando for our teen center."

The girl was quick as a steel trap. She came back with, "Okay, Buddy, you can be Frank, and I'll be Earnest. You won't ever get a teen center with that kind of attitude." So the four of us left Devils Lake with a can-do attitude for the Cando teen center. The night was viciously cold, and just as we passed through Churchs Ferry to join U.S. 281, we hit a stretch of ice and went into a spin. Bud turned the Olds into the spin and we stayed out of the ditch. We all figured with that kind of luck, we could make the teen center happen.

Within a week we had school board permission to use the elementary school basement for our center on Saturday nights. Torson's Grocery agreed to sell us buns and wieners and popcorn at cost. Through Jeannine Gleeson's mother, who'd become manager of Cando Hotel, we got a popcorn machine and jukebox on loan because the hotel no longer used them. Devils Lake's Coca-Cola not only loaned us a cooler, but gave us dozens of posters to help decorate. Lots of families loaned us card tables, card decks, and board games. We decided not to ask parents to be chaperones, but to ask young married couples, and got promises for all school weekends ahead. A contest to name the center resulted in Marlyss Kling's suggestion of name, "The Jam Jar."

We drew up a set of governing rules and voted our organizing committee to be the governing board. We had a set of rules, including signing in and out with no permission to return after signing out. That rule was to guard against kids going out to get a smoke or a drink. Our teen center was a great success, and besides Saturday nights, we several times got permission to open on a Friday night after a basketball game, inviting kids from the opponents' town to come to our center.

The new assistant depot agent, Dennis Mattson, was still a teen, so he came to the Jam Jar and became the most popular guy to dance with. I heard girls say, "Dennis is not just the best jitterbugger, he's neater than any other guy. He's always scrubbed clean, just like his clothes." Dennis and I became friends, so I learned he'd earned his job by taking a quick telegraphy course at a Minneapolis technical school. He rented a room above a store downtown and ate in restaurants.

One day Dennis came by Torson's at closing time and told me to phone Mom and say I was having dinner with him that evening. At Hansen's Café Dennis told me that he had sent a telegram to the sons of Dr. Harris, telling them their father had died and that they must return for the funeral and to settle a half-million-dollar estate. Dennis knew I took voice lessons from Mrs. Harris and thought I should know right away what he knew. Until Dennis told me, I hadn't even heard of Dr. Harris' death, and had no idea the Harris wealth was so great.

It was odd, but in all my visits for voice lessons in the Harris home, I'd never even seen Dr. Harris. But one evening I heard his voice. After my lesson, I was talking to Lucille and Mrs. Harris about my hope to attend medical school at the University of Colorado, because I wanted to live in Colorado to practice medicine. I heard the voice of Dr. Harris call out from his office at the front of the house. He said, "Don't be a fool, boy. You come back here to practice medicine and you'll make a lot more money." He kind of shocked me, because I'd never thought of being a doctor to get rich. From what I knew of Doctors MacDonald and Palmer, they practiced medicine to help the sick, not to get rich. Dr. Harris made me think that the jukebox song, "Money is the Root of All Evil," told a lot of truth.

One night that winter Dad helped me confirm that making a lot of money was not one of my ambitions. Kenny Gilchrist was a projectionist at Lyle Brightbill's movie house, and also was a passionate photographer. Kenny had been given permission to use Frank Parker's darkroom in the *Record Herald* building's basement while Frank was in the army. Another of Kenny's passions was to play poker, so he invited guys to join him nights for poker in the darkroom when there were no movies. One night I got home almost at midnight, and Dad was still up waiting for me. He asked, "You got some girl that keeps you out so late?" I explained that I'd been playing poker. Dad said, "Poker! That's how my Troyer cousins got their money. You want to turn out like them?" That was a powerful thing to say to me, because while I knew the Troyer cousins were rich compared to Dad, I also knew Dad was a much better man than any of them.

On New Year's Eve, I found out Dad could still surprise us. The first day of 1945 was a Monday, so New Year's Eve was celebrated Saturday, at least in Cando. Dad had gone downtown Saturday afternoon, but didn't come home for supper. Mom had given me most of our wartime meat stamps to turn in for a pork loin roast so Dad could have his favorite dish on New Year's Eve. Mom waited supper until after seven p.m., but when Dad didn't come home, Mom and Miss Hunt and I had a delicious meal. I could tell Mom was worried that Dad hadn't come home, and at about ten that night, she could no longer hold back her anxiety. "I think you should go downtown to look for your dad" sent me downtown right away. The only places to look for Dad were in the bars, so I checked Gordy's bar first, then the City Bar across the street. There were two other possibilities, the Green Lantern restaurant which often stayed open till midnight, and Mel's bar, which had originally been Uncle Jesse's Rex Bar and Billiard Hall. The Green Lantern was closed, so I went into Mel's bar.

Not much of a crowd in Mel's, but in a booth with Mr. and Mrs. Carmichael, the owners of the Green Lantern, was Dad, with a glass of whiskey in front of him. As I went to the booth, Dad started to stand up, but sank back down in the seat and pulled me to him in a hug. "Hey, my buddy boy. Wallace, you know Archie and Minnie Carmichael? They been keeping me company after they closed shop and Doc MacDonald petered out."

I said hello to the Carmichaels and told Dad he should come home with me now. "Oh, I will, just a minute. First, I want my friends to know I have the best and dearest boy in the whole world," pulling me to a hug again, and making me sit to keep my balance.

Mrs. Carmichael said, "Your dad's been telling us how proud he is of you and your sister. He and Doc MacDonald celebrated New Year's maybe too much, but at least they had supper over at our place before we closed. They asked us to join them here, but Doc went home just a few minutes ago, saying he'd better get himself to bed."

Dad said, "Yup. Doc petered out. He and I had a great time, though. Doc was on a jag about all the good times him and Jess used to have, hunting and getting soused on their hunting trips together. And about the time he shot himself in the foot hunting ducks with Jess." Dad laughed and slapped the table, then tossed down what was left in his glass of whiskey.

I said, "I think we should go home now, Dad."

Archie Carmichael added, "Yeah, Noah. You better mind your boy and get yourself home." So after Dad praised the Carmichaels for a good supper and good friendship and told them again that I was the best, dearest son a man ever had, I got him into his overcoat and we left Mel's Bar.

It was a very cold night, so I made Dad pull down his earflaps and put on the mittens he had in his coat pockets. Dad couldn't walk without staggering, so I held his arm as we headed down the sidewalk, me hoping we'd not meet anyone we knew. I turned the corner at J. C. Penney's to lessen the chances of meeting someone. Dad put his arm around my shoulder, and told me I shouldn't be too ashamed of him, because he and Doc MacDonald had agreed they both deserved to celebrate the New Year. We stumbled along all the way home, Dad calling me his dear buddy boy and saying he knew Mom would sure be put out with him. "But you know she thinks the world of old Doc, so she shouldn't blame me too much for celebrating with him, do you think?"

I told Dad Mom had fixed roast pork especially for him and was really disappointed when he didn't come home for supper.

Mom helped me get Dad into bed just off the kitchen in my bedroom. I took my pajamas and slept on the couch in the dining room, remembering when Peggy Baney slept there. About two a.m. I heard Dad moan as he stumbled to the bathroom. He stayed in there longer than I expected, and I heard him moan more before he went back to bed. About five a.m. Dad woke me again, moaning loud enough to wake Mom in the bedroom off the living room. I went with Mom to see what was paining Dad. He moaned, "Can't get my bladder to drain, and it's killing me." Drinking warm water didn't make him pee, either, and seven a.m. when his face was all scrunched up in pain as he continued to moan, Mom went to the telephone. She called Doc MacDonald and told him, "Doctor, you'd better get over here and look after the man you got drunk with. I think his prostate has swollen tight around his bladder."

Doc looked beat when he arrived, but he catheterized Dad to give him some bladder relief. He went to our phone and made an appointment for Dad next day at Mayo Clinic. "He'll likely have to get a prostate operation. I'll drive him to Churchs Ferry to catch the Empire Builder to Minneapolis. Then he can take a bus to Rochester. Might as well get it done at the best place."

Dad had his prostate operation at St. Mary's Hospital in Rochester, Minnesota, phoning to tell us he'd be there a few more days before coming home. I drove to Devils Lake to meet him when he got off the Greyhound bus. On the way home he had a story to tell me. "Had to change buses in that big Minneapolis bus depot. St. Mary's gave me some methylene blue pills to ward off infection, and when I was pissing in the trough at the bus depot, the guy standing next to me said, 'My God, man, what's the matter with you, pissing green?' I told him, 'Got gangrene of the balls.' He hurried up and dashed away." Dad laughed hard, and I joined him, impressed at my dad's wit.

On April 12, 1945, when President Roosevelt died, our school had a day of mourning. Marge, as editor, asked if I'd write a memorial editorial for the school paper. But while I was trying to write something appropriate, Marge brought me what Ray Haugen had written and given to her. It was a moving statement of gratitude and honor, saying with real emotion what I'd been trying to say. So Ray's piece became the editorial for that Cub Reporter issue.

The junior class was always sponsor of the Junior-Senior Prom, which was organized, prepared, and promoted as a public dance to make money for the class to spend on its senior skip day. We had an election for prom manager and chose Bud Garber. We chose a cruise ship theme for decorating the Memorial Building gym. The class gave Bud lots of help, and he did a great job leading us to produce the best prom in years, with high attendance and good profit. Bud and I asked two girls from Churchs Ferry as our dates. They were both pretty, so we felt good about showing them off, but they barely knew us, and seemed uncomfortable at the event. I wondered why I hadn't asked some Cando girl to be my date, but couldn't find an answer to that question.

Summer of '45, we high school kids began driving to any town where a dance was being held, now that gas rationing had ended with the war in Europe over. Working at Torson's, I was able to buy more than the one pack of cigarettes the store rationed to its customers. I'd take several packs to a dance, trading a pack for a drink or two of someone's booze. It seemed a good trade with the Rosscup brothers from Rolla when we'd meet for a dance at Bisbee. Both Rosscups played on Rolla's basketball team, and I made friends with Beef Rosscup especially. Curly-haired Beef had booze and enthusiastic reports of his most recent sex events. One of his sex partners was his biology teacher, one was a nurse who roomed at the Rosscup home, and one was the mother of a girl Beef dated. Beef liked to sing catchy, nasty folk songs. The song called "One-Eyed Rider" was my favorite.

Often I'd go to dances with Bud Garber in his sister's '38 Olds. We'd drive down Main Street, and if we saw any high school girls, we'd ask if they wanted to go to the dance where we were headed. We didn't take them as dates, but we'd dance with them, be sure they were with some guy we could trust if they went out to a car to neck, and if they chose to take some other offer for a ride home. I liked the arrangement, because it made me realize I didn't have to be in love with the girl I was with.

One journey I made to a dance that summer was scary. Kenney Gilchrist and Ralph Schaeffer asked me to join them in riding to Bisbee with Peter Black. Peter had graduated high school when Olive did, but still had found no direction for his life. After the dance, Peter gave two girls from Egeland a ride to their home. He got out of the car when the girls did, but came back shortly, swearing about the sisters who apparently didn't give Peter what he wanted from them.

Peter had been drinking too much, and on the way from Egeland to Cando began driving at more than seventy miles an hour on the gravel road. We three passengers tried to get him to slow down, but he wouldn't. Beside him in the front seat, I turned off the ignition, grabbed the keys, and made sure the car stayed on the road as it coasted to a stop. We told Peter we wouldn't ride any farther with him, and I gave him back the keys.

The three of us began the six-or-so-mile walk to Cando, and about three miles from town we saw Peter's car, on its side in the ditch. Peter was not in the car and not anywhere near the car, so far as we could see. We walked on to town, and I told Kenny and Ralph I'd call the sheriff to tell what had happened.

I told my very worried mother why I was returning so late and rushed off to work at Torson's. There I told Joe Torson what had happened and he said it wasn't too early to report to the sheriff. A couple of hours later the sheriff stopped in at the grocery to tell me that the uninjured Peter had come walking out of the tall grain field where the car was in the ditch. He woke up when he heard the sound of the sheriff's siren coming to the scene of the accident. I vowed never to ride to a dance again with someone I couldn't trust to bring me home safely.

Wartime made people sort of patch together important personal events. When my cousin Vesper married her longtime beau, Bill Amundson Jr., on leave but still in the Navy, she had to settle for people available to be in her wedding party. Vesper's parents and her sister Veora were out in California where they had moved for war jobs. Her two oldest brothers were missionaries in Central America, and her brother Jimmy was overseas with the Seabees. But Bill's parents were still in Cando, and the couple wanted their wedding in the Assembly of God church they'd grown up in. I was asked to be an usher, and Vesper asked Dad, as her uncle, to give her away. Bill himself was the wedding's soloist, singing "I Love You Truly" in his dress blues as Vesper came up the aisle in her white gown.

My high point of the 1945 summer was going in late July to the Lake Agassiz Regional Scout Camp for a canoe trip in the Minnesota

Boundary Waters. I took the train to Minneapolis and changed trains for Duluth. There I got on a chartered bus that took me and other scouts to Ely. We gathered in a hall before going on to the base camp near Winton. I was put in a group with three scouts from Minnesota, two from South Dakota, and one from Iowa. Our guide was Jim Parks, an Eagle Scout from Rapid City, South Dakota, who, though only seventeen, had made the canoe trip already three times. Besides, he owned an island with a cabin that he was buying from his uncle who built the cabin.

Making this canoe trip seemed like the most exciting thing I'd ever done. We were given initial instruction about being safe in a canoe and about making portages. After supper we learned how to read a Boundary Waters map and how to pack all our belongings in a large Duluth backpack. Our departure next day was in rain, with a strong wind blowing across the lake. My partner in the canoe was Jack, who guided fishermen on Lake Minnewaska near Glenwood, Minnesota. Jack and I got swamped on the first lake, letting our canoe get sideways to the waves that were churned up by the wind. We had help from others in our party to right the canoe and continue on to the first portage. A fire at the portage helped Jack and me get partially dry.

On that first portage I found carrying two big Duluth packs was quite a load. Jack carried the canoe on the first portage, but we later took turns with the canoe and the two Duluth packs. Our trip plan was to cross over two Minnesota lakes before going into Canada's Quetico National Park, then cross three big lakes before coming to our guide's cabin. Ours was a lively, happy group, after the rain stopped. That first night, we set up our tents on the rocky bluff of an island, but even a rock-hard bed gave me a good night's sleep. The second day we had entertainment from the two scouts from Sioux Falls, South Dakota, singing parts of Handel's "Messiah." Our guide, Jim Parks, followed their singing with some jazz on his trumpet.

The island Jim owned was about half a mile long and a quarter mile wide. The log cabin his uncle had built was a big, two-room cabin with a wood floor in the sleeping room that held eight bunks, and a floor of tiny pebbles in the bigger, open room that included a kitchen and had a big stone fireplace. Jim told us his uncle had built the sleeping room in the summer, and had cut the trees for the big room and had peeled the bark off the logs and set them to cure in the autumn sun. With the help of good physics and banked snow, he had lifted the roof beams into place. It was a good cabin that we used for our base and for four days we canoed to three lakes nearby, catching fish to supplement our dried food. When the Sioux Falls scouts killed a porcupine, we had a wild-tasting stew.

The scouts I was with gave me a mix of feelings. I liked them all, but envied them, too, because I knew they had all accomplished so much and I couldn't help but feel I was inferior in their presence. The two Life Scouts from Sioux Falls played in band and orchestra as well as being choristers in their high school. My canoe partner Jack, almost a Life Scout, was a hired fishing guide in summer, and played football, basketball, and baseball for Glenwood High School's team. Life Scout Ollie, the other guy from Glenwood, could draw like an artist and helped manage his parents' resort and dance pavilion. The Eagle Scout from Minneapolis had his own furniture repair and refinishing business while still in high school. The Life Scout from Iowa was already a partner with his dad on a dairy farm and he himself owned purebred Holsteins that brought him more than a hundred dollars a month in sales of milk and cream. He was also a basketball player who expected after high school to play for Iowa State. Of course I admired our guide Jim. How many seventeen-year-olds owned an island in Quetico National Park?

My trip home turned out to be an adventure, too, but confusing. I took a bus from Duluth to Fargo, but arrived there too late to make a connection with a bus to Devils Lake. I went to a small hotel across the street from the bus depot, checked in, and went up to my room, knowing I'd share a bathroom down the hall. In a few minutes I answered a knock at my door to see the man I had seen removing cash from the hotel's check-in desk. He handed me a large peach, saying, "I thought you might like a bit of fruit. And I heard you ask the desk clerk where there was a public swimming beach. I'll be driving right by the beach on my way to ride my horse, and I'd be happy to drop you there." I accepted the ride to and from the beach on the Red River, and was told by the man that he owned the hotel.

While I was reading before going to bed, there was again a knock at my door. The hotel owner said, "You don't have to use the bath on this floor. I have a nice shower in my apartment upstairs. Why don't you come up with me, and we'll have some dessert after your bath." I went with him, and while I was in the shower behind the glass door, I saw he was watching me. After my shower he told me I had a beautiful body. He poured me a Coke and set out some grapes and cookies at his table, and he put in my hands a book of photos about Bali, mainly photos of nude girls and women. He also showed me his own photos of his cabin on a Minnesota lake and said he'd be happy to have me join him there for a week. I explained that I had a job to get to in Cando, and that my Boy Scout canoe trip was all the time off I'd have. I went back to my room, not worldly wise enough to realize that a practiced seducer had approached me, but was discreet enough not to embarrass both of us with any physical encounter.

At our Troop 82 meeting on August 7, one day after the U.S. dropped an atomic bomb on Hiroshima, Bill Schwartz was mightily upset. He told the rest of us that he and his dad had switched their radio to Canadian Broadcasting after the news from Bismarck ended, and they had learned much more about the horror resulting from the bombing. Bill described to us the terrifying news about the great number of deaths and about the suffering that would occur to those who hadn't been killed. I hadn't followed the war in the Pacific very much after V-E Day, but with Bill's report, I became as emotionally concerned as I had been in ninth grade, when I was reading the five books about fascism and Nazi Germany.

The surrender of Germany on V-E Day didn't have as much impact on Cando kids as V-J Day did. When Japan surrendered on August 14, a car loaded with my pals pulled up to the front of Torson's store, and Betty Belzer and John MacDonald came in to ask me if I'd join them in celebration. Bob Torson told me, "Sure. We'll see you tomorrow morning." All crammed together, we drove around in Belzer's Chrysler. Phyllis kept honking the horn and Betty passed around beers that she had talked their dad out of. Everyone began kissing everyone else, but I didn't join in. I didn't feel the desire to kiss anyone, and I hadn't yet learned that you can kiss friends without feeling any desire.

It was an early harvest season that year. One day Joe Eggl, buying groceries at Torson's, asked me in front of Bob if I could drive his grain truck while he combined his fields. John Schaeffer took my place as he had before, and Torson's let me help out Joe Eggl. Joe had married Miss Bergren, the former sixth grade teacher who was a good accordionist, and had joined the Eggl dance band. They had a three-year-old son who was still nursing. One day I saw the little guy pick up a stone and threaten his mother if she didn't give him the breast before she served lunch to Joe and me.

I was proud to drive Joe's grain truck to the elevator from his combine, and enjoyed the feeling of doing a man's job, as I'd pull into line to deposit the grain and take Joe the receipt for his grain. After about six days, Joe completed his harvest, and I went back to work at Torson's Grocery.

So much had happened in my junior year of high school, but I still felt anxious and discontented. I felt I was missing the intimacy of a sweetheart. I didn't feel as if I even had a very close friend. Sometimes I felt my closest friend was my dad, because Dad had told me so much about his life, which seemed so rich and full. I felt that so many of my own days seemed like sleepwalking, and I wanted to feel wide awake. Some nights, before I'd fall asleep, I'd start to remember those days when I was six, traveling from our farm life in Cando to live first in Little Rock and then near Mill Creek. Or I'd remember my grade-school years in Cando, so thick with emotions and joyous play outdoors. I'd fall asleep remembering how contented I was with the way I felt about myself in those years. The memories were such a contrast to the way I felt when I turned from sixteen to seventeen. Deep inside, I longed to be better than I was, but I wasn't at all sure I knew how to be better or what that would be.

CHAPTER 19

Will I ever feel sure about *Who I Think I Am*?

As the veterans came back to Cando, I tried to get to know them. Envious of their far-reaching experiences, I took every opportunity to talk with them. One was Mary Converse's brother Duane. He had been an army lieutenant leading a company in China where he had lost an eye. He told me about being as endangered from our ally the Chinese, as from our enemy the Japanese. The problem, he told me, came from Generalissimo Chiang Kai-shek, who was supposed to be a hero and friend of the U.S. During inspections, Duane found out that munitions and vehicles the U.S. gave Chiang had been sold to the Japanese.

When Bill Howard took a temporary job at Torson's Grocery, he told me about moving across France and into Germany as a soldier, and about his experiences with civilians along the way, making me acquainted with the wartime life that went beyond killing and avoiding getting killed.

I also had a great talk with Jack Schwartz, who had flown many bombing missions over Germany. Jack told me of his own inner conflict, feeling bad about killing innocent people during those bombing missions, yet feeling good about repaying Germany for its horrendous treatment of innocent Jews. Jack had just been hired by Associated Press to cover the upcoming Italian elections, which the world would be watching to see if Italy would become communist-governed.

My talks with veterans made me feel that they had found meaning for their lives. I longed for meaning in my own life.

The end of the war brought some interesting changes to Cando High School. Our new principal was a woman, Miss Oslund, who had been a physics professor at the University of Minnesota, but had moved back to her father's farm between Cando and Leeds because her father's health was bad. Besides physics, Miss Oslund taught algebra and higher algebra, and in all her interactions with students showed good humor and understanding of teens' behavior that seemed unusual for a principal.

Two other new teachers also came from a farm near Leeds. The Arneson sisters had both been in the service. The older sister, who had been in the Women's Army Corps, taught English, but didn't seem very happy about it. Each day she would back into the classroom and close its door, turn to the class, push out her ample chest, and sound a "Harumph." The only writing assignment I recall her giving us was to memorize all three verses of the National Anthem. When we were to hand in our writing, done during classtime, I turned in a pre-written page I pulled out of my notebook instead of the one I had scribbled on during class. I knew I had cheated, but didn't feel guilty because I thought the assignment was silly. The other Miss Arneson, who had been in the WAVE, taught social studies with enthusiasm and a great sense of humor. Sometimes she told us anecdotes of her wartime experiences, including being entertained by Bob Hope.

The new biology teacher was also our high school's first counselor. Don Hammer had been a counselor in a prisoner of war camp in western North Dakota. Though I wasn't in his biology class, he asked me to demonstrate a dissection of a guinea pig for the class. He was always friendly, and told me an anecdote about one prisoner of war who cried when he learned that his hometown, Dresden, had been practically obliterated by U.S. bombs. Don Hammer had all of us seniors take the Kuder Career Preference Test, and told me I showed more desire to be either a teacher or a journalist than a physician. That test finding bothered me very much, because I still kept becoming a doctor as my ambition.

The new phys ed teacher and coach arrived too late for us to have a football season, but put together a pretty good basketball team. He let me travel with the team to write about the games for the *Record-Herald*, although he often chewed me out about what I wrote, telling me my reports of games didn't need to include my opinions about who was the best player of the game.

Two things about my being editor of the *Cub Reporter*, in addition to my pride in seeing the paper all the way through its printing process, made me feel good. One was that I found a student in each grade, seven through eleven, to be a reporter who submitted a column each month about class news. The other was an editorial I wrote that reprimanded our school board for not hiring a band and vocal-music teacher. I pointed out that other schools in our region had been able to find music teachers, so the board's excuse that no music teachers were available didn't hold water.

I knew that if I'd had real courage, I'd have written an editorial about behavior of high school boys. Several of them seemed to delight in being bullies. An example was the cruelty displayed one day by one of the basketball players who announced he was taking up a collection to buy a pair of panties for a girl he said was not wearing any. He proclaimed in study hall that he'd seen what was missing as he walked behind her up the stairs. I felt guilty and cowardly for not writing such an editorial because I was afraid of the reaction and response of other kids to an editorial that condemned what a sports hero had said.

One appreciated advantage of editing the school paper was receiving other school papers in exchange. The paper I most admired was *The Southerner* from South High School in Minneapolis. It made me wish I were going to that school, because it seemed to have opportunities for every conceivable interest of South High's students. And the paper seemed to me a model of what a school paper should be. The great amount of time I spent on the *Cub Reporter* should have made me recognize that it was taking time away from my study of physics. I should have worked hard enough in physics to earn an A, if I sincerely wanted to become a doctor some day.

We didn't reopen the teen center in our senior year, because once the war was over and gas was no longer rationed we could drive to public dances all over the region—even as far away as Rugby, fifty-two miles. Usually, someone in the car that took us to a dance had a bottle of booze, which seemed easy to acquire through some war vet friend. Girls as well as boys would often get drunk on our trips to dance halls. Good dance bands, such as Wit Thoma's, would play at these small-town dances that were always crowded. When a bunch of Cando kids would arrive at a dance where Wit Thoma was playing, he'd stop the number being played and switch to "Skirts," which for some reason he'd chosen as the song to honor Cando kids.

One thing I did that to me sort of morally made up for my drinking when going to dances was having good serious talks with a couple of good men. One of these good men was Don McKechnie, who had been

English teacher and principal at Cando High, but had taken the job as superintendent of nearby Egeland Schools, while still living in Cando. Don had replaced Dick Pearson, who was at the University of North Dakota, as the bassist with me in Methodist choir. Sometimes he'd give me a ride home from choir practice, and we'd talk about books we were reading, or other serious stuff.

The other good man I often talked with was the new minister at Church of the Brethren, who lived in an upstairs apartment nearby. Ernest Walker was a very serious young minister in his first parish. The church wasn't paying him a livable salary, so he often had peanuts and milk for supper. Mom knew about that and invited him to dinner at our home at least once a month, and Aunt Delia had him join her for dinner at her farm. Ernest Walker liked to talk seriously about music and books, as well as about moral behavior. During Christmas vacation, Reverend Walker drove me with Olive and her fiancé, Walt Lab, to Grand Forks one bitterly cold night to hear Paul Robeson in concert. A church elder had sold the car to the minister on monthly payments that took the major part of his salary. The car's heater had quit working, so the four of us nearly froze on our trip to and from Grand Forks, but we loved Paul Robeson's concert.

Olive and Walt had Reverend Walker officiate at their January wedding, but chose to be married in the Congregational church, because it was such a pretty church. I was best man for their wedding. Walt's little brother Ralph and Ralph Schaeffer were ushers. Ralph Schaeffer was also their wedding photographer. They chose Winnipeg, Manitoba, for their honeymoon, going to even colder Canada to challenge their ardor of love. After their honeymoon, they moved to Culbertson, where Walt would work in a grocery until going next fall to Montana State University in Bozeman.

In late February, I got a letter that was addressed to the editors of every school paper whose teams were to play in the district basketball tourney at Rugby. The letter invited school editors to help publish a daily tournament newspaper. At the first meeting in Rugby, I saw that Miss Selfridge, who had been the librarian at Cando High whom I'd much appreciated, was advisor of the Rugby High paper and was overseeing publication of the tournament paper. She introduced me to Harlan Hannis, editor of Rugby High's paper, and Harlan and I worked together with enthusiasm. I reported the two first-round games and wrote an editorial that commended Rugby's taking on the challenge of a tournament paper. Working on the paper was for me compensation for the Cando Cubs' losing to Rugby in the tourney.

A bunch of us decided to take in the state basketball tournament for Class B schools in Minot. About five of us rode to the tourney with Bud Garber, and Bud and I shared a room in one of Minot's hotels. Several kids in Bud's car came stocked with booze and one sophomore got high on the way to Minot and stayed drunk all three days of the tournament. Most of us had no favorite team, but attended all the games anyhow. It soon became apparent that Mayville was the team to beat. One day, Dad came to our room at the hotel, admitting his concern that we kids might be misbehaving. Dad showed his fondness for me with his usual affection, and after he left, Bud said, "You're lucky. You know for sure your dad loves you." I'd never wondered about being loved by both of my parents, but Bud made me guess that maybe some kids did.

I came to the tourney with two wishes. One was to see Melby Miller and his dad, who was now superintendent of Minot schools. The other wish was to meet Beverly Baney, a cousin of Peggy Baney, who had told me her cousin was a little beauty. I called the superintendent's office and Paul Miller said he'd be happy to give me a tour of Minot High. I'd learned through exchange of school papers that Beverly Baney was on the Minot High's school paper staff, so I took a sealed envelope addressed to Beverly and gave it to the teacher who was advisor to the school paper. Kenny Gilchrist said he'd like to take the tour of the high school, too, so Kenny and I met Superintendent Miller at his office, and he gave us an excellent tour. Included was a visit to Melby's differential calculus class, a subject available only to a select group of students. I had a short visit with Melby after class, when he told me he was applying to Massachusetts Institute of Technology for the coming year. Superintendent Miller told us Melby was in a pre-collegiate class that was taking college-level inorganic chemistry, French, and a combination history and literature course that required an essay each week about the reading assigned the class. I felt so envious of the advantages Melby was getting at Minot High.

Beverly Baney was good enough to leave a phone message at the hotel for me, saying we should meet that night at the students' dance being held for kids attending the tournament. Man! I felt like I was in love as soon as I met Beverly. I must have felt a great need to love someone, and Beverly seemed to have all the qualities I most admired in a girl. She had dark blond hair and sparkly blue eyes. She conversed with me more easily than any girl I knew, and was obviously very bright. She danced easily with me, too, but with a smile, told me no dancing cheek to cheek. I talked her into promising to answer my letter if I wrote first.

In April, I took the step of bringing a war hero to our high school. Bill Considine had once been one of my *Saturday Evening Post* customers, and had just returned home from the South Pacific. Bill had left with the headquarters company of the National Guard as a lieutenant, and had been promoted to Lieutenant Colonel during his active duty, leading a platoon of the 164th Infantry in taking back islands from the Japanese. I got permission from Principal Oslund to ask Lieutenant Colonel Considine to address students, and Considine said he'd be happy to give a talk. In his talk, he skipped over the fighting for the islands and talked mostly about his visit to Hiroshima and Nagasaki to see the damage from atomic bombs. He told us students those weapons must never be used in war again, describing the horrid consequences of the U.S. dropping atomic bombs. It seemed the Lieutenant Colonel wanted to relieve our anxieties, too, by saying that the Japanese were medically treating those who survived, and that the two cities were being rebuilt.

Changes, even in Cando, seemed to come quickly after the war. Cando's reputation for producing superior certified seed potatoes was confirmed when a new partnership of growers moved to town. One of the partners was rumored to be a known homosexual, but to the town's credit, he seemed to be well accepted. He was friendly and generous to a number of high school kids, buying them hero jackets and lending them his car for special events.

Kenny Gilchrist had asked a pretty girl from Rugby to be his date for the prom, and Vic Johnston loaned Kenny his car for the event. Kenny asked me to come along and drive on the trip back to Rugby so that he could make moves on his date, a girl of Russian heritage. It was easy for me to help out my friend, because I hadn't made a date for the prom. Kenny drove Johnston's car back to Cando, complaining that his Rugby date hadn't responded to his passion in the way that he had hoped.

We seniors looked forward eagerly to our skip day in May, because our profits from the prom when we were juniors afforded us a good trip. At our class meeting we compared the attractions of Bismarck and Winnipeg, and decided on Winnipeg as our destination. Superintendent Stensland and his wife would be our chaperones, along with Mr. and Mrs. Ora Burkhart, who had no kids our age, but generously volunteered for the trip. We planned our skip day carefully to give us Friday off from school and to continue through the weekend. We arranged for six cars from six families to transport us. Doc MacDonald loaned a covered trailer to carry luggage that wouldn't fit in car trunks. Neal McLean drove his dad's car and pulled the MacDonald trailer. I rode in Neal's car, along with John MacDonald, Mike Westmiller, and Joe Welch.

We rented primitive cabins in a Winnipeg park not far from downtown, and planned to prepare our own breakfasts and suppers. When we were settled into the park, Superintendent Stensland suggested that I should go to buy the perishable groceries we hadn't brought with us. Bud Garber said I could drive his car to the grocery, and Cecile Nelson said she'd go with me.

When Cecile and I were buying groceries she said, "I bet people think we're a young married couple." We filled the grocery cart with three dozen oranges, four dozen eggs, four loaves of bread, eight quarts of milk, and five dozen wieners and buns, so I said, "If people think we're a married couple, they must think we have a lot of kids." As we went through the checkout, Cecile said, "The kids should have enough milk tonight." We got some quizzical looks from others checking out, and when we put the groceries in the car trunk, we felt good about our silly comments to amuse other customers.

Leaving the parking lot, we saw two young men with six-packs of beer and a bag of groceries waiting at the bus stop. Cecile called out, "Want a ride?" We took on two passengers.

They were University of Manitoba students whose apartment was located a dozen or so blocks away. They said, "Come up and have a beer with us for good neighbors' sakes." So Cecile and I had a beer before rushing back to our classmates in the park. After supper Superintendent Stensland reviewed with us the plans we'd recorded about who would be going in which groups to various locations. We went to our cabins early to catch sleep for a big Saturday next day.

On Saturday, I was in a group with two cars. We went first to the

Hudson Bay store downtown. Some guys bought graduation suits there because suits were still scarce at home following the war. I bought a light jacket and some fancy linens for Mom and for Olive. From Hudson Bay store we toured the Provincial Parliament building, a structure that made government buildings I'd seen in the U.S. look rather plain. Our next stop was at radio studios of the Canadian Broadcasting System that we all listened to often. After our guided tour, we were audience while a studio band played a couple of American pop songs. We had lunch in a café nearby, and I went into an adjacent music store and bought a record of Oscar Levant playing Gershwin's *Rhapsody in Blue*. I also bought the piano score for Grieg's Piano Concerto in A Minor. It was a piece I dearly loved, but I had no idea who should be given the pages of music. I almost forgot my promise to myself to buy Dad a good leather billfold, so I bought one in a nearby men's store. To end our visits, one carload of us went to the old French community of St. Boniface, and the other carload went to Lake Winnipeg.

Back at the park at our cabins, we learned that the senior class from Roseau, Minnesota, was also there for skip day. Jo Ann Peterson had been in our class when her dad was manager of Cando's J. C. Penney's. We knew the family had moved to Roseau, and some of the girls in our class brought Jo Ann and her friend Linn over to our site. Some of us had already decided to go to the Winnipeg Auditorium to dance to a popular Canadian dance band. Joe Welch asked Jo Ann to go with him, and Mike Westmiller asked Linn. Linn mentioned that their friend Bonnie wanted to go to the dance, too, so I said I'd like to take Bonnie, if she'd go with me. Jo Ann and Linn took us three guys over to the Roseau cabins, and when I met the very pretty Bonnie, she said she'd be glad to go to the dance with me.

Talk about luck! Once dancing, Bonnie immediately pushed up close to me, and seemed as attracted to me as I was to her. After several sets of dancing Bonnie said she didn't see Linn or Jo Ann anywhere, so we went out to Bud Garber's car, the Olds we had all stacked into with Bud and his date, Olive Palmer. The missing couples were necking in Bud's car, and said they'd come back into the dance a little later. Bonnie and I headed back to the dance floor, stopping twice to embrace and kiss. I hadn't been kissed like that since Peggy Baney paid a visit to my bed one night when I was in ninth grade. I could scarcely believe this pretty Bonnie was showing she really liked me. When the other couples returned, Bonnie said, "We don't have to trade partners. I just want to dance with you."

After the dance, when we returned to the cabin park, Bud left his car in front of our cabin while he and Olive Palmer drove away with Neil McLean and Betty Belzer in Neil's car to get something to eat. Betty and John MacDonald had a spat before the trip began, so Neil finally had the chance to be with Betty, which is what he said he'd always wanted. The Roseau girls went to check in at their cabins, but said they'd come back to us as soon as they could. In a short while they were back, and Joe and Jo Ann claimed the back seat of Bud's Olds. Mike and Linn led the way into our cabin, and the four of us lay down on the narrow beds across from each other. In a short while, Mike said, "Kennedy. You got any rubbers?" Of course I didn't, and when I said no, Mike and Linn both said, "Damn." Bonnie and I had been pressed as close together as we could get, kissing continually. Bonnie said, "We can't go all the way, then," and I let her know I agreed.

There was a soft knock on our door, and I heard the voice of Superintendent Stensland say, "All here?"

I went to the door, opened it a crack and whispered, "We're all here, but Mike and Joe and John and Neil are all asleep." The superintendent left, apparently believing me. Back to kissing and pressing against the girl who seemed so much to like it, my lower groin was feeling extreme pain.

Joe's coming into the cabin brought me relief. He said, "We sure lucked out. When I saw Stensland coming, Jo Ann and I dropped down to the floor of Bud's car and he didn't even look inside. But Jo Ann says it's time for the girls to go back to their cabin." We all said reluctant but sweet goodnights.

Sunday morning Neil took a carload of us to the Anglican cathedral to see what an Anglican church service would be. I thought the service was as beautiful as the cathedral itself. Betty said, "It's almost the Catholic service, but without Latin."

When we returned to the park the three girls from Roseau were sitting on the picnic table outside our cabin. Bonnie climbed onto my lap, kissed me, and said, "I have missed you so much." I knew Bonnie's affection for me surprised the girls in my class who saw it, because girls in Cando had never indicated any affection for me. Bonnie and I kissed goodbye, knowing we'd not likely ever see each other again.

Our skip-day schedule was to depart for home after lunch Sunday. On the way, the trailer holding luggage broke from its hitch, and smashing into the road, broke its tongue shaft. We were lucky to have a rope in Neil's trunk, and used it to tie the trailer to the bumper as we drove to the next town. There we found a filling station open with a mechanic who said he'd fix the shaft and trailer hitch right away. After an hour or so, we continued on towards home, but went somewhat out of our way to Grand Forks because Neil said he had to stop and give his sister Marge the money his dad was giving her for college expenses. We five guys had a fun visit with Cando girls in the Theta house, and began the drive on to Cando when it was already dark. We stopped at an all-night café in Devils Lake, and while we were eating, all decided to sleep in the next day rather than get up for school without any rest. When we returned to school Tuesday, we used the accident with the trailer as our excuse for missing school Monday.

I couldn't put my time with Bonnie out of my mind easily, and it made me feel I wanted more adventure in my life. One night when I was riding with a bunch of the guys in Bud's Olds, passing around a pint of whiskey, I thought, Here I am, talking about how much fun it'll be next year with the same gang of guys at the U, drinking together and joining older Cando friends there. It made me feel trapped in a little world I already knew too well and was tired of. I knew I needed to change where I'd be during the next period of my life. So I said, "Know what? I'm going to the recruiting station at Devils Lake tomorrow to join the Navy." All the guys laughed, and said, "Yeah, Kennedy, you do that." I knew they thought I felt as they did, that no one would want to break away from the hometown friendships they prized so much.

It wasn't easy the next day to convince Dad to drive me to the recruiting station and sign my enlistment papers. Dad said, "You know there's never been a Kennedy in our line in any part of the military. You know we've always been against killing, even in war." I explained that I'd read that the Navy was in need of hospital corpsmen, and that Navy corpsmen never carried weapons. Dad said, "Yeah, but you'd still be supporting the killing of others, wouldn't you?"

Almost always, Dad had let me go ahead with what I really wanted to do, so we drove that afternoon to the recruiter at Devils Lake. I took the test given me and the recruiter scored it right away. He said, "Highest score by any recruit this month." He assured me I could be enlisted as a Hospital Corpsman, Second Class instead of as an Apprentice Seaman. He said after boot camp I'd be sent to hospital corps school and then begin work as a corpsman, most likely in a Navy hospital. Dad sighed, but signed my enlistment papers with me. I was told to report to the Grand Forks recruiting station on June 10, which would be twelve days after graduation.

I was full of energy and began preparing for my departure right away. Mom emptied a trunk for me to store all the belongings I wanted to keep.

Our graduation week began with baccalaureate service at the Methodist church with the new Lutheran minister preaching the sermon. After the service, riding around with some of my classmates, I was glad to see I wasn't the only one who resented the Lutheran pastor's sermon. Cecile Nelson, a good Lutheran, was particularly miffed. "He doesn't even know us. He just came to town and already he's calling all of us a bunch of young wicked sinners."

Almost ready to leave high school, 1946

But on Tuesday night, before Wednesday evening's class commencement, I had to feel the Lutheran pastor was maybe right. Neil and Mike said they wanted to celebrate my joining the Navy, and Neil had a fifth of whiskey bought for him by an older friend. We began drinking the fifth on the outside back porch of the McLean apartment, cutting our drinks with water, which, because of the minerals in Cando's tap water, turned into what we called "black whiskey." Before long, all three of us were high, and we finished the fifth. Neil said we should all walk out to Belzers' house at the edge of town where he could see the girl he loved. I didn't know why he wanted Mike and me to come along, but he did. When we got right to the edge of town, we met John MacDonald coming back from the Belzer farm home.

Neil asked John if Betty was home, and John said, "I don't think you need to know."

Mike had been talking for more than a year that he was aching for a fight with Doc, the nickname John carried, and he said, "Don't get smart-ass, Doc. Just tell us if Betty's at home."

John came back with, "I wouldn't tell you anything, Mike." That was the challenge and Mike strode to John and popped him in the face. The fight grew fierce with both guys down on the freshly graveled road, locked in head holds on each other. John was able to drag Mike's face along the gravel, tearing open Mike's skin, but then Mike was atop John, pummeling his face with rights and lefts.

I grabbed Mike by the shoulder saying, "Enough, Mike. Get off him."

Mike got off, saying, "You like Doc so much you want to take me on, too, Kennedy?"

Before I could answer, a car driving by stopped. Barber Al Noraker, with his wife, got out, and Al said, "What's going on here? My God, John, you need some first aid. Get in the car. I'll take you to my shop and fix you up." Al looked at me with what seemed a rebuke. "You other boys better get yourselves home."

We headed back toward Mike's house with Mike trying to dig out the fine gravel from his cheek and cussing out Doc all the way. Neil and I dropped Mike off and headed on towards Main Street, where we said, "See ya," and went on to our separate homes.

The day of rehearsal for commencement next day, neither John, Mike, nor Neil were in school, but as is the case in small towns, people seemed to know already about Mike and John's fight. Mike and I were scheduled to sing a trio number with Clyde Stebbleton in the commencement program, and had been practicing it with Mrs. Harris, who would accompany us at piano. I phoned Mike at home. He told me he wasn't going to commencement, so Clyde and I practiced the number with Mrs. Harris on the city auditorium stage. Mrs. Harris said it would sound better if I'd sing Mike's second tenor part rather than the bass, which I'd practiced before. The song's title was "This is My Creed," and ironically the words were a declaration of respect and help for our fellow men. Maybe it was better that Clyde and I sang it without Mike that night at commencement. Either out of sympathy or guilt, I don't know which, Neil stayed away from commencement, too.

Graduation class, Cando High School, 1946

But John was at commencement wearing a black eye and bruised face. He passed out invitations to everyone in class for a post-commencement reception. Doc MacDonald and John's quite new stepmother gave everyone a splendid buffet and a cordial greeting. Aunt Dee had told me I could drive her V-8 to John's party after I drove her and Mom and Olive home. At John's home, Roy Pile told me that Gerry Sand and Cecile Nelson wanted to go to Devils Lake and take in a nightclub before going home, and asked if I'd drive us all there. So without asking Aunt Dee's permission, I drove her car to Devils Lake, only to find the nightclub wouldn't let us in because we were minors. So I drove back to Cando by way of Roy's farm home, and after dropping off Gerry and Cecile, I drove home, too.

The next day, Doris Johnson asked Olive if she'd be her bridesmaid for her wedding in Minot to a Montana rancher. Doris told Olive she didn't want her folks at the wedding, and asked if I could drive her and Olive to Minot. Aunt Dee was again generous with her V-8, so Olive and I drove Doris to Minot to meet her husband-to-be, Kenny Sage. I

was happy to go to Minot to have a chance to see Beverly Baney again, because she and I had exchanged letters once since the state basketball tournament.

I suggested to Doris and Kenny that my former scoutmaster, Amel Whitwer, as minister of Minot's big Congregational church, might officiate at their wedding. When we called Reverend Whitwer, he made an appointment for us to meet him at the parsonage the evening we arrived in Minot, and he arranged a time for the wedding of Doris and Kenny.

Beverly Baney had said by phone that she'd agree to see me, and when I picked her up at home she suggested we take a walk in one of Minot's city parks. I told her about joining the Navy to become a hospital corpsman, hoping that would help lead me towards becoming a doctor. Beverly asked me what kind of specialty I wanted as a doctor, and I said I thought I'd like to be a psychiatrist. Beverly said, "Oh, you're so full of feeling for people. If you were a psychiatrist you'd probably get depressed, working with people who have such emotional problems." I thought Beverly was wonderful, telling me the kind of person she thought I was and caring enough about me to suggest I avoid a painful career. We said goodbye, agreeing to write each other while I was in the Navy and Beverly was at Minot State Teachers College. Beverly let me give her a kiss when we parted, and though it was nothing like the kisses of Bonnie from Rosseau, I prized it.

Back home I phoned Aunt Ella Mae, whom I hadn't seen since she'd moved to Thief River Falls, Minnesota. Aunt Ella urged me to take the train to visit her before I went to the Grand Forks recruiting office. So on Friday Dad and Mom drove me to Egeland where I caught the Soo Line train to Thief River Falls. I found Aunt Ella's big home, an apartment house she'd bought so her renters would help pay off her mortgage. Aunt Ella was happy for my visit and gave me a travel kit as graduation present. She drove me over to visit her nephew, a broadcaster at the local radio station, and a private pilot. George told me he had to fly to Grand Forks the next Sunday, and said he'd be happy to take me as passenger.

After George flew the take-off, he said I could take over the controls. I flew the plane all the way to Grand Forks airport, where George took it in for landing. I thanked George and caught a bus downtown to stay all night in the Dakota Hotel, excited about going to the recruiting station next morning.

Next day there were about twenty of us that the recruiting officer put on a bus for Minneapolis where we would take our physicals and get sworn in. We arrived at the Federal Building and began taking the physical exam right away. That was my first experience standing in line naked with a bunch of other guys as we were herded through our physicals.

Next day, we stood in ranks as we took an oath of loyalty and were sworn into the Navy. Right after, we boarded a train for Great Lakes Naval Training Station for boot camp. I was eager to be a boot and then go to hospital corps school. I thought, now I can quit being a boy and start to become a man. The train trip to the Naval Training Station north of Chicago gave me more than three hours to remember my years growing up. The closer we came to our destination, the more eager I felt about what might happen after my boyhood.

EPILOGUE

In recalling my boyhood, I have tried to show how experiences in my family and in the mostly small-town communities where we lived shaped my search for identity. I think the closeness of the physical and social environments where I grew up helped me know and judge in essence the traditions and values I found around me. I believe the closeness was a good fit for boyhood growth.

Two years in the Navy Hospital Corps brought me into a more urbane, complex daily life and gave me direct contact with medical practice. When I entered pre-med at the University of North Dakota, I felt sure I wanted to be a doctor. But my fondness for performing had been kindled through singing in Navy choirs, and my whim to perform fit well with the expansive world I found in liberal arts courses. I was cast in plays, I fell in love with Joyce, and I decided that arts and humanities should be my life study.

Joyce and I were married in 1950 and moved to Madison and the University of Wisconsin. There the liberal arts made my world expand further. We both were English majors, Joyce a graduate student, and we both worked part-time to supplement my GI Bill support. I earned my BA in January 1952. Because we were pregnant, I felt teaching high school and directing plays would be more practical than going to grad school. But I needed a teaching certificate, so we moved to Mankato, Minnesota, where I worked as a disc jockey fifty-two hours a week while taking a full course at Mankato State University. Within a year I had a BS degree and a teaching certificate.

Teaching English and directing theater and speech activities a half-year in Delavan and two years in Forest Lake convinced me that Minnesota public schools were a good field to work. Two daughters, fifteen months apart, convinced me that one's own children are marvelous teachers. A summer to study theater in Seattle, Washington, gave our family more space to explore before moving to teach in Albert Lea High School.

Ten years in Albert Lea brought us extraordinary friends and a span of religion in the Episcopal church with an intellectually stimulating rector. Eager students, a creative principal, and a scholarly English-teacher colleague made teaching challenging as well as fun. A John Hay Fellowship grant to Columbia University came my way, and after a summer with my sister's family in Montana, New York City became our home for a year.

My humanities fellowship at Columbia was glorious, and my professors, all scholars of renown in philosophy, drama, history, and anthropology, helped me better understand life and learning. Attending thirty-two plays and the museums in Brooklyn and Manhattan brought meaning, too, as did living on the Atlantic shore in Belle Harbor and commuting daily by subway.

Now I was more than ever convinced that study in the arts and humanities brought the world clearer meaning. When I returned to teach in Albert Lea, I was ready to join colleagues Orville Gilmore and Nick Cords to set into place the nation's first high school sequence in humanities—American studies for grade eleven, European studies for grade twelve. Students of that humanities course have testified that humanities opened them to the world with a life-changing perspective.

Feeling compelled to greater study through a fellowship in American Studies and as a grad student summers at the University of Minnesota moved me towards a doctorate. But birth of son John, and the deaths of my parents, plus becoming a homeowner, made that move slower. Joyce wished to teach again, and Bloomington Schools wanted humanities in its high schools, so we became suburbanites. For me, leaving the superb qualities of a first-class high school was hard, but suburban kids were a mind-opening challenge, too.

I continued to take courses in American Studies part time until five different course preparations at Lincoln H.S. and directing plays and speech activities made pursuing a doctorate fade from my priorities. When I was asked to replace the secondary school English curriculum coordinator for her year of sabbatical, I took the job because I knew teaching practices needed improvement.

Working for an excellent curriculum director and devoting myself to instructional practices made me something of an activist in education change. I became director of special projects for Bloomington

Schools and helped creative teachers get funding for their exemplary ideas.

Joyce had returned to the university to be certified to teach elementary students. Her teaching in Bloomington schools was exemplary in using arts to help students learn in every subject. Her work with teaching to fit multiple intelligences brought her fuller recognition, and she was appointed director of gifted education.

Through attending arts events and museums in the Twin Cities, I had become personally acquainted with practicing artists, and after five years in Bloomington Schools I was hired by Minneapolis Schools to write a funding proposal and direct a program to give students instruction where the arts are created, housed, and performed, and to place artists in schools to co-instruct with teachers. The program took the name Urban Arts, and within three years, partially funded by the U.S. Department of Education, Urban Arts became known nationally.

My contacts with artists and arts venues gave me direct experience with the struggles and achievements in a flourishing community of artists. Students in Urban Arts proved that direct association with the arts as they are being created gave them a life-changing experience. Evaluation of the program made it the only purely arts program to be validated as a national model. After being program director for seven years, I moved to the University of Minnesota Teacher Center, and with grants from the U.S. Education Department, worked with schools in twenty states to adopt basic practices of Urban Arts.

It was a time when schools across the country were eager for internal change and improvement, a time before public education became a political kick ball in the pretense of bringing schools "up to standard" through compulsory testing. So long as we had governors and legislators who were forward-thinking, Minnesota schools continued to do well. When computers became a tool for learning, I went back to Bloomington to head its state-funded technology demonstration site for three years.

My last challenge to give students better learning came when I was appointed program associate for theater and media arts with the Minnesota Center for Arts Education, now known as the Perpich Center. We spent two years planning and preparing to open a state high school for the arts, and after working with the center for seven years, I retired, and Joyce retired from Bloomington Schools.

I've tried to show how my learning kept growing as I moved into environs that expanded it. Many close friends in those environs, the remarkable life of my sister, and the personalities of our offspring have been neglected in this epilogue, but they have been essential to my life-growth and learning. I'm almost seventy-eight, now, and the fifty years since I ended boyhood have been memorable, too.